SALVAGING COMMUNITY

Salvaging Community

How American Cities Rebuild Closed Military Bases

Michael Touchton
Amanda J. Ashley

Cornell University Press
Ithaca and London

First published 2019 by Cornell University Press

Library of Congress Cataloging-in-Publication Data
Names: Touchton, Michael, 1979– author. | Ashley, Amanda J., author.
Title: Salvaging community : how American cities rebuild closed military bases / Michael Touchton, Amanda J. Ashley.
Description: Ithaca [New York] : Cornell University Press, 2019. | Includes bibliographical references and index.
Identifiers: LCCN 2019002332 (print) | LCCN 2019004116 (ebook) | ISBN 9781501739774 (pdf) | ISBN 9781501739781 (epub/mobi) | ISBN 9781501700064 | ISBN 9781501700064 (pbk.)
Subjects: LCSH: Military base conversion—United States. | Military base conversion—California—Case studies. | Community development—California—Case studies.
Classification: LCC HC110.D4 (ebook) | LCC HC110.D4 T67 2019 (print) | DDC 307.1/4160973—dc23
LC record available at https://lccn.loc.gov/2019002332

The authors created maps 1–4 using ArcGIS.

To our families
Michael Touchton would especially like to thank
Mom, Dad, and Paul
Amanda Ashley would like to thank Mom, Dad, and Seth

CONTENTS

Preface and Acknowledgments

This book emerged from the identification of an ongoing problem surrounding defense conversion and a general lack of knowledge on the topic. We also recognized the need for interdisciplinary, mixed-methods collaboration early in our research: the problems we saw were too big; crossed too many boundaries, both literal and metaphoric; and were too complex for either of us to engage on our own. Political science and urban planning both offered incomplete answers to many of our early questions, as did both quantitative and qualitative methods as means to answer the complicated questions and data that arose from former defense communities. Moreover, we saw the need for a book that engaged policy makers and practitioners, not just academics. This recognition led us to a fruitful, mixed-methods collaboration that extends far beyond political science and urban planning. It also took extensive time and resources: we began this project in our second years on the tenure track at Boise State University. We were interested in interdisciplinary collaboration and were fortunate enough to work at institutions that support that kind of research.

We saw great value in drawing on each other's expertise across disciplines and spent five years expanding our knowledge across disciplines. This let us address questions about defense conversion that simply combining our distinct methodological backgrounds would not have. Many questions remain, but this book represents one of the most comprehensive efforts to date to grapple with a challenging, comprehensive subject. However, it is still just the first step toward helping communities convert closed bases, a complex challenge that Americans will face for a long time. We look forward to continuing our work in this area.

We could not have written this book without considerable help from many people. First, we thank the many people we interviewed in San Diego; the Monterey area; Alameda, California; Holy Loch, Scotland; Soesterberg, Netherlands; and Frankfurt, Germany. Everyone was very generous with their time and provided critical information surrounding defense conversion in their communities. Their insights informed our work in significant ways and made us both question and strengthen our research assumptions. We especially thank Alan Ziter, of Liberty Station, San Diego; Michael Houlemard, of the Fort Ord Redevelopment Authority; and Jennifer Ott, of the city of Alameda for extensive assistance during our fieldwork in each area. We also thank the United States Navy for its assistance and contribution to data collection in Washington, DC. We received institutional support from a variety of sources. First, Boise State University's Public Policy Research Center, directed by Eric Lindquist, generously supported our research. Similarly, Boise State University's School of Public Service, including Dean Corey Cook and Associate Dean Andrew Giacomazzi, provided research funds in support of our work at several different stages of the research process. Lori Hausegger was also a strong proponent of our interdisciplinary collaboration and championed our work to many audiences. The University of Miami's Department of Political Science and College of Arts and Sciences also provided generous support for our work in the field and throughout the publishing process. Susan Clarke of the University of Colorado provided considerable encouragement and advice throughout the project, as did Eugenie Birch at the University of Pennsylvania, who also saw the value in connecting urban politics with urban redevelopment. Editors and anonymous peer reviewers at *Urban Affairs Review* and *Journal of the American Planning Association* offered valuable suggestions and commentary. We also thank panelists at the Urban Affairs Association, International Planning History, and American Collegiate School of Planning conferences for their helpful feedback on conference papers that helped form our initial ideas for this book. We thank several research assistants who helped with various aspects of the project. Most notably, Aaron Mondada at Boise State University and Richard Hankins at the University of Miami provided excellent research support during the research and writing process. It is important for us to recognize Michael McGandy, senior editor at Cornell University Press, and the CUP staff for their valuable insights and tremendous assistance in translating our research into this book. Michael McGandy's editorial guidance was essential for striking a balance between pure academic scholarship and accessible public scholarship so that our work could speak to broader audiences. Napoleon said that an army marches on its stomach, which was certainly true for us in this project. Burger Belly, in Boise, Idaho, provided the best fuel for our march, and for that we are grateful. We are also grateful to Monica Hubbard of Boise State for her support during research trips to Boise. Finally, we thank our families for bearing with us while we worked on this project. Seth and William Ashley and Jim and Marian Johnson deserve special recognition in this area.

Salvaging Community

INTRODUCTION

The Base Closure Crisis

In 1991 a *USA Today* headline proclaimed, "Base-closing battle under way; Fort Ord's future is bleak." Marina, California, Mayor Edith Johnson added: "It's like we've been hit by a Scud missile. Only we have no Patriots left to defend ourselves" (Goodavage 1991). Similar statements accompanied unwelcome closure announcements for more than 350 U.S. military installations between 1989 and 2005, including 122 military bases that operated as mini-cities within larger metropolitan regions. The strategic decision of the United States Department of Defense (DoD) to mothball many of its bases following the end of the Cold War left communities stunned, alarmed, and uncertain about how to respond to the impending disaster. Pragmatic communities openly questioned whether recovery from a base closure was even possible—or simply a naive dream.

The DoD currently owns, operates, and manages 4,262 military bases and defense installations in the continental United States and another 737 bases in 130 countries across the globe (U.S. DoD 2010). The DoD spends an estimated 24 percent ($270 billion) of the discretionary funds in the U.S. national budget to build, support, and maintain its military base infrastructure and support its personnel in the Army, Navy, Air Force, and Marine Corps (U.S. DoD 2016a; U.S. Office of Management and Budget 2016). Defense investment, including building and maintaining military bases, has altered the economic geography of the United States and shapes the fates of cities and regions (Markusen et al. 1991; Kirby 1992; O'Mara 2015). Shifting military priorities diverted these investment flows following the end of the Cold War and an international drawdown of forces. Maintaining vast installations throughout the country was politically popular because of the jobs and revenue the military spread throughout communities, but it was no longer a strategic priority because of the diminished military threat.

Early winners and beneficiaries of public and private defense investment from World War I, World War II, and the Cold War faced uncertainty after the Cold War ended. The end of this era spurred a desire for new, mobile force structures and new weapons systems, and calls for reduced defense spending and the elimination of aging domestic bases. To protect elected officials from base closure controversies and repercussions, the federal government created the Base Realignment and Closure Commission as the primary public policy mechanism for closing bases that the military deemed extraneous. The DoD began closing bases in 1989 in favor of new, mobile security programs as well as to accommodate ongoing federal demands for efficient spending. The five rounds of closures that followed created quasi–ghost towns throughout the country and the rest of the world. As Michael Houlemard, executive director of the Fort Ord Reuse Authority, put it, "BRAC is set up to benefit [the] federal government, not structured to help local communities. It is to help them get out of a problem. They do it through a command-and-control process, but at a national level, we don't know how communities work. There is a cultural difference here: communities are not command and control" (Houlemard 2013).

Military base conversion is a significant challenge facing many U.S. communities. The sum of the arrangements made through the DoD's Base Realignment and Closure (BRAC) process has culminated in one of largest transfer of federal infrastructure, buildings, and land to municipalities in recent U.S. history. The stakes surrounding defense conversion are high and vary depending on the stakeholder, whether an environmentalist, a university president, a county planning and zoning commissioner, a master developer, or a small-town mayor. There is no single, ideal outcome for all interested parties; the notion of "public interest" for defense conversion is routinely debated and contested, with no consensus in sight.

This book provides a foundation that practitioners working in former military communities can use to improve redevelopment performance and salvage failing communities. It addresses several central questions: How does military base redevelopment work? What communities have been successful and under what conditions? How can communities use these lessons to convert their own former defense sites? This book helps former defense communities convert closed bases and recover their economic, political, and social vitality by uncovering and aligning national data with a comparative case study of three base closures in California: San Diego's Naval Training Center (NTC, now Liberty Station), Monterey's Fort Ord Army Base, and Alameda's Naval Air Station (NAS, now Alameda Point).

Converting America's Closed Military Bases

Converting former defense sites is central to the United States' general security and economic health as well as to specific communities' survival. At the national level, the federal government seeks fiscal solvency and a defense budget devoted to security, not continued maintenance of aging, inefficient bases. Bases that the DoD deems unnecessary carry large opportunity costs: every dollar spent maintaining these bases is one that cannot be spent on defense systems, personnel designed to increase national security, or other federal programs designed to deliver services and improve standards of living.

The federal government created the BRAC process in 1988 to provide a neutral or politically protected commission to make tough choices about which bases to close. The BRAC process requires the president to appoint nine commissioners to decide what military installations to close or shrink based on a set of complex, opaque factors (Sorenson 1998; Freedman and Ransdell 2005; U.S. DoD 2005). Since its creation, the BRAC process generated five rounds of closures in 1988, 1991, 1993, 1995, and 2005, ultimately resulting in the downsizing of 350 military installations in the

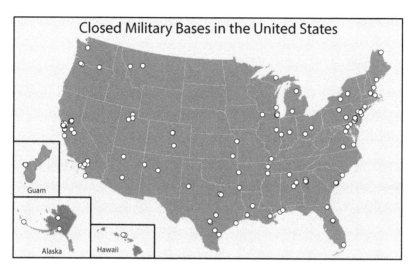

Map 1. U.S. bases closed under BRAC since 1988

United States (U.S. DoD 2005).[1] As of 2018, the Pentagon has formally requested additional rounds of base closures, but these rounds have yet to be scheduled (U.S. DoD 2015; Scarborough 2012). The rate of domestic base closures may not reach the post–Cold War peak of the early BRAC rounds, but more U.S. bases will undoubtedly face scrutiny. It is not a question of *if* bases will close but *when* and how the federal government will support communities that are going through or will go through this process. Map 1 shows the U.S. bases that have closed since 1988.

Once the BRAC process finishes, the difficult, multi-decade process of redevelopment begins. At the most basic level, the federal government first conveys its properties to municipalities to prepare them for redevelopment in formalized, negotiated agreements. Specifically, the federal government makes deals with municipalities, states, quasi-public redevelopment authorities, and private developers to transfer management and/or ownership of land and property for eventual redevelopment and/or conservation (Gilmore 2005; U.S. Environmental Protection Agency 2006). These highly complicated negotiations often progress by fits and starts and take decades to complete because of a variety of factors, including arguments over who gets what among local, state, and federal stakeholders; the extent and cost of environmental remediation; policy shifts surrounding the conveyance process under different presidential administrations; and market conditions that alter the attractiveness of redevelopment.

The complexity and expense of redevelopment negotiations often require local governments to partner with public, private, and nonprofit sectors from around the country to share in risks and rewards. Partners in these collaborations include the federal government, state government agencies, state university systems, community development associations, redevelopment authorities, private foundations, chambers of commerce, and a host of private firms. Together, and often in conflict, they plan new college campuses, science and technology enclaves, office parks, neighborhoods, and airports as part of their new master-planned community strategies. However, the plans often face significant challenges caused by market climate, project timing and readiness, conflict over ideal outcomes, intergovernmental regulations, and community acceptance of development trade-offs.

Hundreds of former defense communities engage the closure process relatively blind and alone because of scant evidence on redevelopment performance. The Presidio's conversion is perhaps the best-known illustration of military redevelopment in the United States because of its location and history. However, it is a singular example, and its use as a model overlooks the unique planning culture and deep resources of San Francisco and the Bay Area. Any "best-practices" plans stemming from the Presidio's experience may still be useful but cannot be the only information or guidance that other communities use.[2]

The federal government has also generated numerous redevelopment reports through the Office of Economic Adjustment and Government Accountability Office to provide local communities and other federal agencies with guidance on closure processes. Other agencies, such as Housing and Urban Development (HUD), are tangentially involved in defense conversion through special-issue areas, such as providing housing for the homeless on local bases. Again, this information is useful when trying to improve the federal response, but these reports skim the surface and cannot serve as broad redevelopment templates. Similarly, no existing academic research identifies systematic factors driving redevelopment choices or successful outcomes. Existing studies of military base redevelopment rarely provide comprehensive evaluations of all redevelopment processes *over the life of their plans* (Hill et al. 1991; Bagaeen 2006; Stern 2006;

Urban Land Institute 2009). Instead, researchers emphasize base closures' immediate impact on regional economies, the problems associated with environmental remediation, questions of equity surrounding development decision making, and/or the supremacy of federal considerations over local decision making (Hultquist and Petras 2012; Hooker and Knetter 2001). Or these scholars perform case studies that focus on a single conceptual theme at one point in the redevelopment processes (Lynch 1970; Hill et al. 1991; Hess 2001; Hansen 2004; Bagaeen 2006; Davis et al. 2007; Curtis 2011; Kosla 2010; Stanley 2002). These studies provide ample, valuable information about the redevelopment process from a few high-profile cases, but they tell an incomplete story.

Our Theoretical Approach

This book provides a comprehensive account of defense conversion using a theoretical framework emphasizing governance. Governance refers to *the processes by which public policy decisions are made and implemented.* It is the result of the evolving and adapting interactions, relationships, and networks among government, public, private, and civil-society actors and the institutional structures that frame these relationships. The dynamic collaborations and conflicts between stakeholders determine who gets what, when, and how (United Nations Development Programme 2014).

Strong governance is essential for defense conversion. Military redevelopment challenges are complex and require extensive resources and heightened regulatory interaction. Additionally, these project build-outs and rehabilitation take decades to complete in a climate of fluctuating market forces and political uncertainty. Strong governance creates the foundation for weathering these challenges and capitalizing on redevelopment opportunities.

Strong governance makes it more likely that communities will be able to navigate the conversion process in a way that culminates in broad community benefits. In contrast, communities with weak governance never convert bases or else cede the economic benefits of defense conversion to concentrated, private interests. The question of who governs the process of military redevelopment is pertinent because it offers insight into the question of who wins and who loses in redevelopment coalitions. Here, this book shows that the presence of broader sets of official redevelopment partners across the public, private, and nonprofit landscape tends to result in more public-goods–oriented land-use outcomes. Governance is not an outcome but a set of processes that leads to a variety of outcomes surrounding place that are not limited to pure economic benefits through defense conversion. These include creating economic opportunities for the poor, creating mixed-income communities, building affordable housing, and addressing racial inequality.

The book focuses specifically on the emerging concept of collaborative governance to explain defense conversion. Collaborative governance entails "a governing arrangement where one or more public agencies directly engage non-state stakeholders in a collective decision-making process that is formal, consensus-oriented, and deliberative, and that aims to make or implement public policy or manage public programs or assets" (Ansell and Gash 2008, 543). Collaborative governance also traditionally encompasses fluid and evolving partnerships across public, private, and nonprofit sectors.

In the case of military redevelopment, local governments and authorities partner with governments at regional, state, and federal levels as well as with private firms and nonprofit groups. Collaborative governance cannot always overcome the many challenges of defense conversion, but it offers the potential to improve outcomes and greatly increases the probability of completing projects, restoring the environment, replacing revenue, and providing benefits across the community. The size of the governing coalition and how it is situated in the local context also determine the extent of collaborative governance and whether it generates positive results, negative results, or fluctuating outcomes over time. The pursuit of collaborative governance is not a utopian ideal or a perfect fix, but strong collaboration over time increases the odds of achieving the best possible arrangement for redevelopment, considering the circumstances.

Collaborative governance is also a way to approach the serious questions of equity and equitable development that conversion faces: Do communities value open space over mixed-income housing? Historic preservation over housing for the homeless? Residential over commercial development? Environmental justice over quick conversion and job creation? These questions of equity are not mutually exclusive, of course, but they showcase many of the challenges of governing defense conversion in pursuit of broad community benefits. This book argues that collaborative governance allows for a broad set of beneficiaries in defense conversion, which is more likely to serve public interests than projects that benefit only narrow groups of stakeholders.[3]

Our Research Approach

This book's interdisciplinary, mixed-methods approach leverages theories from political science, urban planning, public policy, geography, and economics to explain what works in defense conversion and to identify ways for communities to use that information. This approach allows for a description and explanation of *how* military redevelopment occurs at the micro and macro levels, *where* it takes place, *who* benefits from redevelopment, *why* it takes certain forms and scale, and *what* this knowledge means for policy makers and practitioners.

This book draws on a unique data set containing redevelopment inputs, processes, and outcomes for former military communities. The data set includes information on every closed base over the duration of each redevelopment project, such as each community's redevelopment projects and important outcomes associated with redevelopment.[4] For instance, the data set includes information on the extent to which defense conversion contributes directly to the return of jobs and revenue following base closures. Expanded data on conversion outcomes then incorporate the types of projects that communities achieve through conversion and the extent to which these projects generate benefits for a broad swath of community stakeholders. Land-use categories such as residential, commercial, industrial, institutional (schools, museums, public agency offices), and recreational provide a general framework of conversion development choices. These categories do not speak to individual design solutions or other context-specific land constraints. Yet they do allow us to identify general trends in the kinds of projects that tend to appear on former bases and draw some inferences about project beneficiaries.

The database also includes information on redevelopment inputs and processes to help explain variation in conversion outcomes. Redevelopment governance, market conditions, community resources, and conversion costs are all potentially relevant for defense conversion, helping to determine whether it contributes to a community's economic recovery and, if so, who it benefits. This includes information on the characteristics of the primary developers, such as their status as public or private entities and their position at the local, state, or federal levels. The database also includes the funding sources for redevelopment, the projects' completion date and cost, the relative wealth of the community (as measured by per capita gross local product), and the former military function of the site. Other elements of the former base might also influence conversion choices, such as the region, geography, the size and function of the former military base, and the year that it closed. Data on these areas come from public records from the DoD, the Census Bureau, other federal agencies, community redevelopment master plans, publicly available documentation of redevelopment outcomes on city, state, and local government websites, and extensive e-mail and phone inquiries to supplement public records.

This book leverages extensive source material to paint a dynamic, quantitative picture of redevelopment on 122 former bases beginning with the first, post–Cold War BRAC round in 1988. No other data set of this breadth or depth currently exists for military base redevelopment. The database will give policy makers and planners the benefit of information covering all closed military bases. This will also supplement extensive material from existing case studies and offer many other scholars the opportunity to explore defense conversion across the United States.

Quantitative analysis illuminates national redevelopment trends, which reflect the average U.S. experience surrounding redevelopment inputs, processes, and outcomes. This analysis incorporates data from all closed bases, but it cannot explain military redevelopment performance on any individual base. Information on national redevelopment trends thus represents a significant step forward for scholars and practitioners, but it is incomplete without thorough investigations of military redevelopment in individual communities. This is because the quantitative data reveal only general relationships surrounding redevelopment rather than the causal mechanisms driving redevelopment performance. Supplementing the quantitative analysis with case studies then uncovers the causal processes driving defense conversion. Process tracing provides information about the context, processes, and mechanisms that contribute to distinctive leverage over causal inference, which the quantitative view from

30,000 feet does not provide (Collier et al. 2004). Additionally, interviews with key redevelopment actors capture knowledge before those involved in defense conversion retire or move on to other positions. This material is time-sensitive in terms of institutional and individual memory, and complements the analysis of national trends in defense conversion.

Comparative Case-Study Analysis

The statistical analysis and literature review suggest causal mechanisms driving defense conversion outcomes. However, case studies of the redevelopment process on individual bases demonstrate the extent to which these causal mechanisms drive redevelopment *in practice*. Thus, statistical models inform our case studies, which address the precise questions of how and why redevelopment works. The breadth and depth of this approach also advance beyond quantifiable facts surrounding redevelopment and address salient questions surrounding to what end redevelopment occurs and to whom redevelopment benefits accrue.

A nested-analysis approach involves selecting cases from the national analysis that the statistical model predicts well; thus, the case studies fall within the "predicted line" of the model, along a continuum of low to high redevelopment performance in terms of project completion, economic recovery, and community benefits from defense conversion (Lieberman 2005). This strategy yields a selection of three most-similar sites: San Diego's Naval Training Center (NTC); Fort Ord, near Monterey, California; and the Naval Air Station Alameda (NAS), near Oakland, California. The three cases all represent wealthy areas, enviable locations, strong real estate markets, diverse economies, and active civic communities as well as ambitious plans to convert their former military bases.[5]

Case studies of the three California bases provide additional leverage for military redevelopment in California, which is important in its own right; California lost twenty-seven large facilities under BRAC, which is more than three times as many as any other state.[6] Redeveloping closed bases also connects to the larger context of planning and administration surrounding critical water, conservation, and land-use issues in the state. Therefore, California has incentives to focus extensive resources and oversight on military redevelopment. California's redevelopment experience is equally important from a national standpoint because this state acts as a policy pioneer: many other states adopt similar regulations after observing outcomes in California. For instance, California's Proposition 13 limited property tax increases in 1978. By 2015, more than half of the remaining forty-nine states had adopted similarly restrictive legislation (Institute for Taxation and Economic Policy 2015). In this sense, information gleaned from case studies in California potentially applies to more former defense communities than information collected from any other state. Evaluating redevelopment performance on three California bases thus complements national statistical analysis to produce a set of lessons and recommendations for all communities.

The research design takes advantage of similarities across the three bases to isolate and evaluate factors that might influence redevelopment outcomes. Each case represents dramatically different outcomes: nearly complete conversion and reuse in San Diego, partial conversion of Fort Ord, and a stalled, barely initiated conversion process at Alameda. NAS Alameda falls approximately one standard deviation below the mean level of redevelopment performance, Fort Ord is near the mean level, and NTC San Diego is approximately one standard deviation above the mean performance level. The way that each community governed defense conversation also varies considerably. In contrast, other explanatory factors that are relevant for redevelopment outcomes in national models are relatively constant across the case studies. Then qualitative process tracing helps to explain the causal mechanisms in national statistical trends that are also evident at these three sites (Lieberman 2005; Mahoney 2010). Process tracing provides information about the context, process, and mechanisms that contribute to distinctive leverage over causal inference (Collier et al. 2004). In this sense an understanding of the ways in which communities redevelop closed bases hinges on their configuration of assets and political, economic, legal, and social environments, and complements the statistical models to provide a thorough explanation of military redevelopment.

The case selection strategy does not follow the same logic as statistical sampling, in that these cases are not definitively representative of the national redevelopment experience. There are far too many variables in play surrounding redevelopment processes and local contexts to select individual cases that are representative of the national redevelopment experience. Instead, case selection follows a logic of replication (Yin 2013). Conventional wisdom would predict similar redevelopment outcomes in the three California cases because of desirable coastal locations, high land values, and similar overarching regulatory environments. Yet wide variation in redevelopment performance is evident on these bases because of differences that quantitative models point to at the national level. Thus, examining these cases follows the replication logic common in case-study practice (Yin 2013) and provides cumulative evidence of general patterns, even though the three California cases lie on the national margins in land values and have unique regulatory environments (George and Bennett 2005).

The three California cases represent what one would expect to be the easiest former military sites to redevelop. Visiting these former defense communities to collect information on base conversion was not a hardship: NTC San Diego, Fort Ord, and Alameda are all in beautiful, high-value areas. Many former Navy bases are in very attractive settings as well: "The Navy has lots of high-value coastal property," said Bryant Monroe, program director for downsizing, DoD Office of Economic Adjustment (2014). Some bases from the other services are also in desirable locations. Casual observers can therefore be excused for thinking that these bases, and many like them, should be relatively easy to redevelop. Instead, wide variation in outcomes appears across similar cases, which allows for an examination of why redeveloping closed bases is so difficult, even in high-value areas.

The analysis does not lead to a step-by-step formula for developing every closed base; rather, the evidence in this book constitutes a theoretical and thematic portrait about how communities reimagine and remake closed bases. This research is designed to help former defense communities across the country convert closed bases and recover their economic, political, and social vitality. As such, we are not suggesting that a community which loses a base in rural Texas is in the same situation as a former defense community in urban, coastal California. In contrast, the book presents macro-level analysis of national trends coupled with micro-assessment of California cases to explain the unique challenges in redeveloping former military sites and to reconceive urban redevelopment in general. The analysis thus provides a point of departure for all former military communities around the country; quantitative analysis identifies national redevelopment trends that the California cases situate in practice. Yet not every California experience applies directly to other closed bases across the country. Coastal communities redeveloping California's bases benefit from stronger market conditions, which should improve conversion outcomes, on average. However, California communities also operate in a low-revenue context because of state regulations, which makes conversion harder than in many other states, on average. California also recently dissolved its redevelopment authorities that had served as clearinghouses for all conversion-related decisions and processes. Other states have retained local redevelopment authorities, which is likely to improve conversion efficiency and performance. These distinctive elements of defense conversion in California motivate us to also include material in each chapter about what to generally expect on closed bases outside of California.

The Cases

The results of broad statistical analysis motivate an examination of national trends in the specific contexts of military base redevelopment in San Diego (formerly the Naval Training Center, now Liberty Station), Monterey (formerly Fort Ord, now California State University, Monterey Bay; Fort Ord National Monument; and a variety of other projects), and Alameda (formerly Naval Air Station Alameda, which now has a variety of residential and temporary uses as it awaits conversion). NTC San Diego exceeded expectations for rapid conversion and achieved outcomes for broad groups of beneficiaries that were superior to those of Fort Ord and NAS Alameda. NTC San Diego is now almost fully converted, with mixed residential, commercial, educational, recreational, nonprofit, and corporate uses. As Whitney Roux, program director for the NTC Foundation, describes, "The Navy and military are a huge part of our culture. This is our heritage . . . Coronado, North Island, etc. Preserving our heritage is so important. We, through this process, helped NTC become theirs again. This was critical. A place for San Diegans" (2014). Fort Ord represents an intermediate level of defense conversion. California State University, Monterey Bay (CSUMB), was founded on the former base and now uses it as its main campus. Fort Ord also has some commercial uses, a Veterans' Administration hospital, and the large Fort Ord National Monument. However, hundreds of dilapidated, contaminated structures and extensive unexploded ordnance limit potential for conversion and reuse on the former base: "Stuff was built when requirements were different—contamination, building code, uses, etc. Lead based paint, TCE, asbestos, leaking PCBs, etc. And, those are the easy ones. Munitions issues. Radiation. 300 sub-surface detention vessels. Unlined landfill. Huge environmental-contamination issues" (Houlemard 2013). NAS Alameda has made the least progress of the three bases. It spent fifteen years with only temporary, leased uses available because of a high federal conveyance fee for the land and difficulty in brokering a redevelopment deal acceptable to residents, developers, and the Navy. Converting NAS Alameda has been a very slow process: the community advanced with its redevelopment plan only in 2012 despite closing in 1997. As Jennifer Ott, director of base reuse for Alameda and chief operating officer of Alameda Point, reminds us, "The federal government doesn't have the same community planning element. They can do whatever they want. This is a 20–25-year process" (Ott 2013).

Each parcel on each base has its own story, with distinct, specific redevelopment challenges. It is an uncanny feeling to leave Monterey Dunes State Park on Fort Ord and to be told that you cannot step out of the car a few miles away for fear of triggering unexploded ordnance. Moreover, just ten minutes later one can walk on the beautiful CSUMB campus, a very successful aspect of Fort Ord's conversion. Similarly, historic architecture on the former NTC San Diego or NAS Alameda might catch your eye. However, closer inspection reveals many of these buildings to be empty and in disrepair. Thus, there are even stark differences in conversion outcomes from parcel to parcel on individual bases in addition to the broad conversion differences across bases.

These differences in defense conversion outcomes highlight the great importance of military redevelopment for individual communities. San Diego's redevelopment experience is far from optimal, but residents and a wide variety of stakeholders now benefit from the former base, perhaps more so than when the base was operational. Fort Ord's conversion has been partial and difficult, but the former base now provides educational, health care, commercial, and recreational benefits to local and regional stakeholders. Alameda has made the best of the long-delayed conversion of its Naval Air Station. However, Alameda's costs in site maintenance and opportunity costs in lost revenue and benefits for community stakeholders are enormous. The stakes were just as high for Fort Ord, which managed a partial conversion, and San Diego, which achieved a nearly full conversion. This begs the question of what explains the variation across these cases, which chapter 3 describes in greater detail.

Naval Training Center San Diego

The U.S. Navy commissioned the Naval Training Center San Diego (NTC) in 1923 in San Diego's Point Loma waterfront community. The site is located on San Diego Bay, west of the airport and a few miles north of downtown. Now marketed as Liberty Station, the 361-acre project includes 52 buildings listed on the National Register of Historic Places and is district focused, including a retail and commercial district, a promenade focused on nonprofit activities, an educational district, a residential district, a hotel district, an office district, a 46-acre park, and 125 acres of open space along a boat channel. San Diego converted the former NTC quickly and for the benefit of broad groups of stakeholders. Governance challenges were still present in the NTC's conversion, but the conversion outcomes go further to convert and integrate the base into local economic, political, social, and cultural networks than are found at most other former bases around the country.

Converting the San Diego NTC benefits a private-sector master developer, to be sure, but also provides large community benefits relative to other former bases. Tens of thousands of visitors, thousands of students, and hundreds of residents now live, work, learn, play, and shop on the former base. These outcomes, including a unique, nonprofit arts district, schools, housing, restaurants, parks, and grocery stores, reflect the "making of place" in many senses (Imbroscio 2012). Achieving these types of multi-stakeholder benefits through defense conversion is elusive for most former military communities. Conversion of the San Diego NTC thus represents a relative success story.

Redevelopment of San Diego's NTC reflects the ways the city partnered with a master developer to address many of the governance challenges surrounding defense conversion. The master developer, the Corky McMillin Company, clearly profits most from the conversion. However, the partnership spared the city and the public the redevelopment cost and many of its associated risks. San Diego did not receive the same national accolades as San Francisco for converting the Presidio, but San Diego also converted its base much faster and with broader benefits than almost all of the other bases in the dataset: "This is a mini-city with something for everyone; new homeowners all got a bike" (Garey 2013).

A relative lack of environmental contamination also improved outcomes on San Diego's former NTC. Converting buildings and opening parts of the base to recreational use still required more than ten million dollars of environmental remediation and are not complete as of 2017. However, San Diego's remediation cost is low compared to the tens and hundreds of millions of dollars in estimated remediation costs on many other bases. San Diego's road to defense conversion was contested and sometimes bumpy, yet a strong redevelopment partnership and favorable redevelopment conditions ultimately led to rapid conversion with relatively wide stakeholder benefits.

Fort Ord

The Army commissioned Fort Ord in 1917. The base is the largest of the three cases from a physical standpoint and spans forty-four square miles on the Monterey coast. However, only a portion of Fort Ord is marked for redevelopment: several large parcels are allocated for conservation and recreation, and others constitute former firing ranges and training grounds awaiting environmental remediation before they can be reused in any capacity.[7] Fort Ord surpassed expectations to achieve conversion outcomes that place it near median national levels for economic rebound and the benefits that conversion offers community members. Expensive and extensive environmental restoration prevents conversion on other former bases, but strong regional governance and conversion leadership have created a new campus in the California State University system (CSUMB), a VA hospital, a commercial shopping center, and the Fort Ord National Monument.

Thousands of students now benefit from converted facilities on the former base, and hundreds of residents also benefit from new medical facilities and recreational opportunities at the national monument. Fort Ord still has a long way to go for conversion, but its regional redevelopment authority effectively navigated many difficult redevelopment challenges to benefit a variety of stakeholders with contrasting interests. The redevelopment process has also been appropriately incremental to avoid the extremely high costs that would have accompanied an attempt to fully convert the base at once. Such an attempt might have bankrupted the redevelopment authority and delayed stakeholder benefits for decades longer than necessary.

Regional governance best explains defense conversion outcomes on Fort Ord. It lies within many overlapping political jurisdictions, considerably more so than for other closed bases. Financing, transportation, environmental restoration, and infrastructure remediation represent a small sample of the many conversion issues that affect the entire region. The state of California created the Fort Ord Reuse Authority (FORA) with federal support to formally incorporate dozens of governmental, nonprofit, and private-sector stakeholders into the redevelopment process and to provide a venue for them to pursue their own interests across the region. Resolutions for conflicts among these stakeholders are difficult to achieve without a regional governance perspective: "One of the key things that we did is we formed a separate legal entity called the Fort Ord Redevelopment Agency. We reverse engineered—we got the legal stuff done first. We made the board members represent the seven mayors . . . they would be engaged in shaping the decisions . . . they would always feel they had the meaningful participatory voice," said Barry Munitz, former chancellor of the California State University system (2013). FORA also has the essential decision-making authority to engage stakeholders vertically up and down scale and horizontally across space and sector (Kirkpatrick and Smith 2011; Jonas and Ward 2007; Cox 2010). FORA curtailed and mitigated political battles, governed redevelopment processes, and incorporated different authorities' interests into policy decisions in a way that many former defense communities could not.

Fort Ord's redevelopment narrative is also more closely associated with leadership at the federal level than on other former defense sites. Specifically, Leon Panetta and his federal connections deserve credit for many of the successful aspects of Fort Ord's conversion, including the creation of CSUMB. Panetta represented Monterey County and the Fort Ord Army Base in the U.S. Congress (and chaired the Joint Budget Committee) in the 1980s. Panetta took immediate action following BRAC's announcement of plans to close the immense base: he led efforts to organize more than a hundred community leaders and to brainstorm redevelopment alternatives that supported local themes of education, environmental conservation, and economic recovery by "doing no damage to what [they] do well" (Houlemard 2013). This leadership was critical to Fort Ord's early redevelopment successes.

The high level of environmental contamination on the site contributes to Fort Ord's conversion outcomes as well. Unexploded ordnance is spread across the former base, which also contains more than a thousand structures that must be disassembled to abate lead and asbestos contamination. Driving around the base presents challenges even today: many roads remain closed to the public because so much unexploded ordnance close to roads makes it dangerous to even set foot outside of the car. FORA spearheaded negotiations with federal representatives to identify contaminated areas and set decades-long remediation efforts in motion. Management of relations with the federal government was essential to transferring uncontaminated areas for a national monument and wildlife refuge as well as planning for incremental remediation. The result is conversion that leaves a lot to be desired, but it shows how strong regional governance can improve outcomes and make the best out of very difficult redevelopment situations.

NAS Alameda

The U.S. Navy commissioned the Naval Air Station Alameda (NAS) in 1940. Now known as Alameda Point, the site sits on a prime location across the bay from downtown San Francisco. The base spans 1,600 acres (2.5 square miles) near the commercial Port of Oakland and carries a proposed redevelopment price tag of $2 billion. Part of the 1993 BRAC round, the base closed in 1997 and was later declared both a Superfund site and a National Historic District. Alameda Point's redevelopment authority followed a template that planning experts championed, but it met with little redevelopment success. The redevelopment authority established a master plan, selected a master developer, and negotiated with appropriate parties. However, Alameda Point has fallen prey to changing federal defense policy about land exchange and valuation, federal and state development constraints, rampant market speculation, and local opposition surrounding project trade-offs. The city of Alameda has thus struggled to redevelop the site and officially purchased it from the Navy only in 2013. However,

Alameda has enjoyed some minor redevelopment successes in areas where the Navy allowed Alameda Point to lease property: several artisanal producers of beer, wine, and spirits as well as a variety of nonprofit organizations temporarily lease buildings on the bay to capitalize on existing warehouse spaces and excellent views. Additionally, other industries in need of large warehouse space and/or access to the water lease warehouses on the former military site.

Alameda's temporary uses provide some community benefits, but its lack of progress toward permanent conversion resulted in millions of dollars of direct maintenance costs, which temporary commercial activity only partially covers in taxes and fees. Temporary uses create a fun, eclectic community on the site in the form of distilleries, wine-tasting bodegas, art galleries, tech start-ups, shipbuilders and racing teams, and regular weekend events. These uses build community, too, because nearby residents, visitors, and workers all enjoy spending time on the former base. However, temporary uses can undermine permanent redevelopment opportunities: "We shot ourselves in the foot and did a lot of interim leasing. It's a huge benefit to us, but we're hesitant to do long-term leases. No one is going to spend money without a long-term lease, and so the buildings deteriorate. We don't do a lot for tenants like give them tenant improvement allowances. It was our own policy decision. We didn't want to shoot master developers in the foot as well" (Ott, 2013). Temporary uses are always under threat of ending, so they can never go all the way to create the community that people would like to see on the base.

More importantly, the very slow initiation of the conversion process resulted in enormous opportunity costs. The mixed-use Alameda Point development could have generated very large community benefits in terms of residential, retail, and recreational use. Furthermore, residential and commercial development on the former NAS site could have potentially generated hundreds of millions of dollars in commerce, sales, and property tax revenue. This revenue could potentially have improved services for all Alameda residents and mitigated some of the impact of denser residential development—for instance, through new transportation infrastructure. Conversion of NAS Alameda may still generate these benefits, but twenty years later than might have been possible under other circumstances.

Thus, conversion delays represent a missed opportunity for an entire generation of Alameda residents.

The inability to convey Navy land to the city represents the most significant challenge for redeveloping the former NAS. Two different presidential administrations' shifting priorities undermined Alameda's conversion processes and outcomes. Alameda missed the Clinton Administration's window to convey former defense sites at no cost and instead found itself negotiating over a $108 million federal asking price. The high conveyance price made it nearly impossible for master developers to break ground on several different conversion plans and pitted redevelopment proponents in the city and master developers against Alameda residents. Rejected ballot measures, broken partnerships, and lawsuits all reflect difficulty in navigating shifting federal priorities in pursuit of conversion. The city ultimately completed a deal for no-fee land conveyance in June 2013, thirteen years after Fort Ord and NTC San Diego were conveyed.

Our case studies delve into the intricacies of the development process, spanning deal making, policy regulation, partnership structure, and constraints. The layered, microanalytic approach thus adds context to the national database and refines its theoretical and practical contributions at the macro-level. In turn, these approaches offer a thorough explanation of how communities convert bases given their configurations of assets and political, economic, legal, and social environments. Ultimately, a deeper, broader understanding of defense conversion will aid communities around the country as they face similar challenges.

The Plan for the Book

Each chapter in the book develops a rich ecology of military redevelopment inputs, processes, and outcomes. The first two chapters present broad, long-term views of national trends in military redevelopment based on historical analysis and statistical models of redevelopment outcomes. Historical redevelopment trends help to develop hypotheses that can be tested against the national database, which chapter 2 presents. The results of the quantitative analysis showcase national trends that serve as a point of departure to assess precisely how conversion unfolds in each of the three California cases.

The next four chapters are organized thematically to evaluate key issues that communities face in converting former bases and to provide policy recommendations for other communities converting similar sites. This structure better situates the contributions within development and redevelopment practice as well as the national trends identified in chapter 2. Additionally, this structure shows how each thematic area impacts specific communities in different ways. Then each of these chapters develops these arguments through evidence from Naval Training Center San Diego, Fort Ord, and Naval Air Station Alameda. The chapters thus highlight thematic trends while also explaining why communities respond differently within each area. The chapters end with take-home messages and recommendations for communities around the country.

Converting former bases with equity in mind provides an opportunity to salvage and rebuild community. Residents' quality of life and the viability of the city-region depend not only on rebounding jobs and revenue but also in ensuring that redevelopment promotes community benefits. This represents a herculean task for many former defense communities because of the disruption that base closures represent. Yet these events represent a common threat to residents' livelihoods across a former base's regional footprint. These residents are still relatively immobile and place-based even in the context of globalization. Capital and goods are mobile, but a strong connection to place does foster some opportunities to band together to respond to economic, political, and social disruption caused by base closures, natural disasters, or deindustrialization.

Collective action hurdles stemming from a lack of resources, experience, and organizational capacity are high in former defense communities, but outcomes are not predetermined. Instead, the depth and breadth of community benefits stemming from defense conversion vary greatly across the U.S. landscape. Communities *can* re-form over the course of defense conversion in pursuit of common redevelopment goals. Moreover, some former defense communities do convert closed bases while providing broad community benefits. These laudable outcomes are not common: most former defense communities do not achieve equitable defense conversion. Nevertheless, transparent decision making and accountable, democratic governance of redevelopment planning, financing, and implementation go far to promote a broad distribution of redevelopment benefits and improve outcomes in this area. At a minimum, good governance improves outcomes compared to other city regions that govern redevelopment poorly or for the few. Public participation and collaborative governance arrangements renew the prospects for collective action across the many territorial scales of defense conversion. Rebuilding community reenergizes civil society, strengthens city-regional governance, and increases competitiveness in attracting investment and residents to the city-region (DeFilippis and Saegert 2013).

1

BRAC and Federal Public Policy

Defense Conversion from 1945 to 2016

Military base closures have occurred throughout U.S. history. The expansion and contraction of defense investment and its impact on regional economies are well-documented (Markusen et al. 1991; Sorenson 1998). The argument that military base infrastructure, including bases, should expand and contract as needed to respond to global threats is an old one. However, it has been difficult to close bases even during relatively peaceful eras because of continuous political opposition in Congress and from defense communities that rely on a defense-driven economy. This politically charged environment explains the necessity of the BRAC process as well as its evolution. The DoD has managed to shutter more than 350 installations in five recent BRAC rounds (1988, 1991, 1993, 1995, and 2005) despite considerable opposition. Hundreds of other surplus facilities have closed in the past, and many more will close in the future.[1]

The policy framework for closing bases evolves over time, and the resources and assistance available for conversion take different forms in different eras. The BRAC legislation has evolved in ways that both promote and impede defense conversion in conveyance, environmental restoration, and governmental collaboration. In turn, these evolving policies and processes have important implications for defense conversion and reuse. The result is conversion processes and outcomes that make redevelopment with community benefits difficult to achieve.

It is important to note that federal base closure policies do not exist in a vacuum. Long-term changes in defense community economics, politics, and demographics occur alongside evolving federal policies. Some bases that were on city margins when the bases opened are now in the midst of an expanded urban footprint. Other communities were rapidly growing when the bases opened but were in decline before the bases closed. All to say that federal policies are clearly not the only historically influential factors for converting former bases. However, communities have little agency over broad economic or demographic trends. This is one reason why collaborative governance of redevelopment processes that intersect federal policy is so important. Communities have considerable agency in how they face long-term challenges, particularly with regard to governance structures.

Pre-BRAC Closures

The Cold War and the Korean War catalyzed the expansion of U.S. military installations in the 1950s (Sorenson 1998; Markusen 1992). The lull between active conflicts in Korea and Vietnam once again fostered a desire to close bases and redistribute spending to missile-based nuclear defense strategies, intelligence, and other noninfrastructure expenditures. The Eisenhower and Kennedy administrations shuttered 574 U.S. bases around the world between 1960 and 1964 (U.S. DoD 2016a). The DoD closed an additional 700 of its 7,000 facilities in 1965, as the Vietnam war placed pressure on the Pentagon to shift military budgets away from domestic base maintenance and toward combat operations.

The Pentagon successfully closed surplus bases with the support of the White House prior to 1966. Congress considered military matters to be the Pentagon's purview and did not oppose domestic base closures in the late 1940s and early 1960s. The power to close bases unilaterally created political disincentives for members of Congress to oppose the Pentagon and the White House. For instance, the president could punish political opponents in Congress by taking spending away from the representative's district or the senator's state through base closures. The threat of such punishment allowed the White House and the Pentagon to extract legislative concessions from congressional delegations in a way that disadvantaged Congress and undermined its constitutional "power of the purse" (*Congressional Quarterly* 1965).

Congress recognized the political and economic benefits of keeping bases open in members' districts and used lobbying and legislation to claim authority over the base closure process in the mid-1960s (*Congressional Quarterly* 1965). Most importantly, Congress passed the Military Construction Authorization Bill in 1966 to slow the process and give representatives and lobbyists more time to strategize ways to retain defense spending in each congressional district (*Congressional Quarterly* 1965). The 1966 bill ultimately served as a compromise between the executive and legislative branches and temporarily resolved the political fight over base closures. The bill allowed the Pentagon and the White House to retain some authority to close bases but also gave Congress oversight of large waves of closures, including any bases with numerous employees. Congress exercised this authority over the process following the Vietnam War and prevented Pentagon plans to close 160 domestic bases. Specifically, Congress delayed base closures until 1976, when it passed legislation requiring environmental-impact statements, prohibiting studies to evaluate the impact of potential closures, and preventing any spending on base closures (U.S. GAO 1997; Mayer 1999). No base with more than 300 employees closed over the long stretch between 1976 and 1988 as a result of this bill.

The Pentagon and the Reagan administration attempted to close more bases throughout the late 1980s as defense spending priorities shifted and the Cold War waned. By 1988, the number of U.S. troops had indeed fallen dramatically from peak levels in the Vietnam War because the Pentagon still possessed authority over force numbers (Defense Manpower Data Center 2016). However, Congress was invested in maintaining economic and political rents from keeping bases open and would not vote for their closure, despite the end of the Cold War and the Pentagon's persistent requests (Beaulier et al. 2011). The number of military bases and spending on their maintenance therefore barely budged between 1976 and 1988, a situation that supported congressional reelection efforts but also included billions of dollars in annual spending that the Department of Defense believed to be detrimental to its mission (Poppert and Herzog Jr. 2003; U.S. GAO 2002a; U.S. DoD 1998; U.S. GAO 2002b).

Calls to close bases reached a pinnacle at the end of the Cold War, when the cycle of peace and military drawdowns began anew. The military argued that it could not modernize its weaponry or effectively pursue its global role in a post–Cold War environment while also maintaining its domestic infrastructure (Sorenson 1998; *Congressional Quarterly* 1987; Shaw 2004). Many members of Congress agreed that closing bases should be a priority (Armey and Goldwater 1987). But Congress could not agree on which bases should close and, more importantly, in whose districts. Political battles ended in stalemates because representatives from defense communities could form blocs to keep bases open despite general agreement to close them, cut defense budgets, and reallocate funds to post–Cold War defense and civilian priorities. Closing bases had become a political nightmare. This contentiousness paved the way for BRAC's emergence.

A Brief History of BRAC

Congress created the BRAC process in 1988 to close bases that the Department of Defense deemed unnecessary to its mission while avoiding political battles and insulating members of Congress from blame for any closures in their districts (Mayer 1999; Sorenson 1998; Dell 1998). The legislation promotes these goals by creating an appointed commission and empowering commissioners to make base closure recommendations based on DoD proposals (Congressional Record 17762 1988; Pub. L. 100–526; 10 U.S.C. 2687). The process first requires the DoD to submit a list of excess facilities that could be closed or realigned without harming the military's combat readiness. BRAC legislation necessitates that the secretary of defense develop an inventory of existing infrastructure and a force structure plan to inform the selection of bases for closure. Then the DoD uses specific criteria surrounding the likely impact of closures on military strategy and finances as well as the local environment and employment to select bases for its list. The process occurs as follows: the secretary of defense forwards his or her recommendations for realignments and closures to the BRAC Commission, an independent nine-member panel that the president appoints. This panel hears testimony from stakeholders in communities with bases on the list and visits the communities in question. The commission then provides the president with its recommendations. The president then reviews and approves the list for submission to Congress, which has only two options at this stage: fully approve or fully disapprove of the list. The list is then finalized after a congressional decision, and the closure process advances. The list is automatically approved if Congress neither approves nor rejects the list within the forty-five-day window that the BRAC legislation stipulates.

The 1988 BRAC bill represented a compromise between the executive and legislative branches by giving Congress the power to veto the complete list of closure recommendations by majority vote. The Senate gained the power to hold hearings and confirm or reject the nine panelists on the BRAC Commission. Additionally, the legislation stipulated that no more than half of the commission's staff could be employed by the military in the previous year to prevent the Pentagon from automatically having undue influence over the commission. This delegation of power to a commission thus fostered the diversion of military spending from domestic base infrastructure to new weapons systems, personnel, or bases overseas, while allowing representatives to vote against closures in their district and dodge political blame. The legislation gave concessions to the Pentagon as well: it increased the prospects of cost savings and provided a path to base closures by avoiding an imbalance of power in favor of Congress in the process. The legislation also mandated that the DoD pay only for partial environmental remediation before conveyance, unlike the full remediation that many in Congress had requested.

New legislation in 1990 and 2001 authorized additional closure rounds in 1991, 1993, 1995, and 2005 based on commission recommendations. The most recent 2005 BRAC commission authorized the closure of dozens of facilities and made two central recommendations: a 2015 round of closures and future closure rounds at eight-year intervals. Yet additional BRAC rounds have not materialized because of strong congressional opposition. Concern for economic damage to communities during the Great Recession, the prospects for subsequent loss of political support, and questionable cost savings from the later closure rounds all drove congressional and White House reluctance to authorize new base closures. In 2012 the House Armed Services Committee voted down the possibility of new closure rounds, and the Obama administration reversed its previous position supporting closure. President Obama put the prospect of authorizing new closures in a presidential election year simply: "You know, I don't think now is the time for BRAC" (Obama 2012).

The Pentagon and the White House have called persistently for base closures since 2012. The DoD has even set aside several billion dollars per year for pre-closure planning in annual defense authorization bills (U.S. DoD 2016c). Yet Congress remains opposed to closing domestic installations with more than 300 employees. In fact, the National Defense Authorization Act of 2014 expressly forbids additional BRAC rounds until the Pentagon performs a complete review of overseas bases and reports to Congress on the need to maintain these sites. The clear implication of this legislation is that the DoD should find cost savings in overseas base closures before shuttering domestic bases to protect Congress from politically damaging choices.

Congressional opposition has not deterred the Pentagon from consistently requesting other BRAC rounds, including requests to close both domestic and overseas bases. Secretaries of Defense Panetta, Hagel, and Carter (2011–2016) have all made formal requests to close bases, with Congress refusing to authorize additional rounds in each instance (U.S. DoD 2010, 2015, 2016c). Exasperated, the DoD threatened to close bases unilaterally in 2016 and began budgeting for personnel reductions and base closures beginning in 2019, even without congressional approval (U.S. DoD 2016c). The legal authority to close bases has not been tested, but the military has oversight regarding troop levels and maintenance budgets in most cases. Military services could therefore empty bases of most personnel and simply not budget for maintenance on active but unwanted bases. The result could be dozens of de facto closures around the country and subsequent decreases in local revenue.

The Evolving BRAC Process

The BRAC process for closing bases has evolved since its inception in 1988. Most importantly, the Pentagon gained authorization for future closures by responding to increasing pressure to justify redevelopment delays and community impacts. The most important policy shift in the early BRAC rounds occurred in 1993, when the Pentagon created programs to streamline the conveyance and environmental-restoration processes and to provide community assistance for planning and implementing defense conversion. Prior to 1993, defense communities lacked adequate information and expertise to prepare for transitions to fewer jobs, decreased revenue, and curtailed service provision. Once planned, conversion was delayed for years as cumbersome military processes slowed environmental-impact assessments and environmental restoration. The 1993 shift in favor of community support for conversion marks one of the earliest realizations that former defense sites require decades-long environmental-remediation efforts that limit the attractiveness of investments in conversion, often necessitate private-sector redevelopment partners, and require complex governance arrangements to achieve.

The fluctuating rules surrounding property conveyance also hindered land transfers. The Pentagon was bound by law to convey property suitable for private commercial, industrial, or residential redevelopment only at fair market value. Bureaucratic delays exacerbated the glacial pace of fee-based conveyances (U.S. DoD 1999; U.S. GAO 2002a; U.S. GAO 2002b; U.S. DoD 1998). As the Clinton administration plan to improve post-BRAC redevelopment noted in 1993, "Disposal of the land, buildings and movable property on military bases has been slow, bureaucratic and penny-pinching. Many businesses wanting to locate on a newly closed base have been unable to get an interim lease because of Pentagon red tape. And disputes over fair market value of military property have resulted in the worst of both worlds: land and buildings that could support commercial activity and create jobs sit idle, while the DoD continues to pay to maintain property it doesn't need" (Clinton 1993a). The DoD acknowledged the unexpectedly slow nature of land conveyance in several reports during this era and requested legislative support to revise the BRAC land-transfer process (U.S. DoD 1998; U.S. GAO 1998).

The Clinton administration and Congress recognized the need for reform and developed new legislation to close bases while supporting local governance and economic redevelopment. The 1994 Base Closure Communities Assistance Act tasked the DoD's Office of Economic Adjustment (OEA) with overseeing the transfer of military assets suitable for conversion to local authorities. The OEA was created in 1961 to support communities facing base closures, expansions, or economic disruptions because of military activities. The 1994 BRAC legislation expanded a variety of community support programs but, more importantly, required former defense communities to form a local redevelopment authority (LRA)[2] to access federal assistance and resources in defense conversion. LRAs create and implement redevelopment plans based on discussions among all stakeholders that the closure affects. Then the DoD and other community groups jointly make future decisions surrounding conversion based on the reuse plan. This legislation demonstrates federal recognition of the need for local governance arrangements in former defense communities, many of which were adrift following base closures and had difficulty addressing complex challenges without a single, local governing authority explicitly authorized to do so.

The Base Closures Community Assistance Act (CAA) included several key elements beyond empowering the OEA, including the possibility of property conveyance at low or no cost to a local redevelopment authority if the resulting land reuse created jobs and promoted economic development. The legislation also streamlined environmental assessment and restoration, and placed transition coordinators with knowledge of federal requirements, regulations, and funding opportunities on every base. As well, it gave the DoD freedom to encourage temporary uses on former bases to create short-term jobs while communities awaited final land transfers (U.S. DoD 1998). In a separate legislative move, the 1994 Base Closure Community Redevelopment and Homeless Act (CRHA) added additional land-use regulations and required the LRA to work with HUD and local advocacy groups to secure appropriate property for homeless residents' use, which spread community benefits through conversion.

At the federal level, environmental restoration, property transfers, and redevelopment support improved under the 1994 framework. By 1997, base closure cleanup teams and EPA collaborators had initiated environmental-restoration processes at all bases where it had not begun for bases closed in the 1993 BRAC round. Similarly, the DoD conveyed land through 51 economic development conveyances at low or no cost through 1999. These transfers generated a large share of the 50,000 civilian jobs created on former bases (U.S. DoD 2006; U.S. GAO 2002; U.S. GAO 1998). The 1994 legislation also harnessed resources from a variety of federal agencies to support defense conversion and redevelopment. For example, the Office of Economic Adjustment, the Department of Labor, the Economic Development Administration, and the Federal Aviation Administration contributed more than $2 billion toward defense efforts between 1993 and 1997 to convert bases in a variety of areas. The Office of Economic Adjustment's planning grants resulted in an almost two-thirds decrease in the time that communities took to develop a reuse plan: from 57 months for bases closed in 1988, 1991, and 1993 to 21 months for those closed in 1995 (U.S. GAO 1998).

BRAC reforms were rolled back during the latter part of the Clinton administration and during the Bush administration. Most importantly, amendments to the Base Closure Act in 1999 restricted no-fee or below-market-value economic development conveyances in order to extract maximum federal revenue from defense conversion, especially on former bases in areas with high real-estate values. This shift underscores the reality that former defense communities remained at the mercy of federal policies in many respects. Fee-based conveyance requirements halted redevelopment plans on dozens of former sites and slowed land transfers to a crawl for many others. The high fees required for conveyance then forced communities to take on private-sector partners and revise or even abandon their reuse plans. For instance, communities where property had high perceived market values had to raise considerable sums or reach agreements with private-sector partners to pay DoD conveyance fees. In turn, these partners emphasized profits over jobs or community benefits and therefore pushed communities toward new projects with concentrated, private benefits. In many cases, communities created new reuse plans to pay federal fees but found themselves in redevelopment limbo when they could not raise funds to match increasing property values (Alameda Point 2013; U.S. DoD 2010).

In 2001 Congress authorized a new round of closures for 2005 and reformed the closure process again. The 2005 BRAC Commission gained the authority to add bases to the DoD's closure list and did so in July of 2005. The communities where bases closed after 2005 also benefited from some additional support from the federal government, even as the fee-based conveyance requirement remained in place. For instance, the DoD reached a memorandum of understanding (MOU) with the EPA to support environmental restoration on former bases (U.S. EPA 2008). This memorandum allowed the military to contract with the EPA to complete environmental restoration, bringing far more resources and expertise to environmental-cleanup processes: a key area where local governance underperforms. Congress eventually passed the National Defense Authorization Act in 2010 to ensure no-cost conveyances to local redevelopment authorities when redevelopment projects emphasize job creation. This policy reversal removed one of the largest barriers to defense conversion, although the dismal economic climate of the Great Recession made redevelopment slow to emerge following the reform effort. The no-cost conveyance and a growing economy reinvigorated several large-scale conversion projects in former defense communities by 2016, especially in communities with strong market conditions, such as Alameda, California.

Several additional programs now prioritize BRAC-affected communities in resource transfers from the federal government to state and local governments. Federal transfers from Community Development Block Grants (HUD), Community Service Grants (HHS), Economic Development Administration projects (Commerce), and Rural Development Administration projects (Agriculture) totaled $26 billion in 2015 (U.S. Office of Management and Budget 2015). The exact percentage of these grants that go to BRAC-affected communities is unknown, but these programs all include language prioritizing former defense communities in grant allocation. For example, HUD works with former defense communities as they comply with 2005 legislation mandating housing for the homeless on former bases: "Homeless vets and newly unemployed people are all over former bases. The 2005 legislation acknowledged this issue and required a homeless plan before property could be conveyed. These communities are not equipped to deal with a large increase in the homeless population and need extra help. We provide funding to expand existing services for the homeless—off base when possible," said Linda Charest, BRAC coordinator, Department of Housing and Urban Development (2014).

These types of programs reflect U.S. history in general as well as former bases' specific history. For example, many programs are designed to redress grievances from earlier eras, such as the challenges of providing veterans with mental health care following the Vietnam and Gulf War conflicts, or the way many federal development transfers now operate through community development block grants. There is an obvious path-dependent aspect of redevelopment challenges on former bases as well as the options at national, state, and local governments' disposal to address those challenges.

The Federal Role in Defense Conversion

The federal government wields considerable authority over defense conversion, and its policies drive much of the redevelopment process. It is critical for city-regional governance to engage and incorporate federal authorities at many turns. Almost every individual interviewed for the book highlighted the need for a productive working relationship with military representatives as well as those from other federal agencies: "We have good relationships with the Navy. Having a positive working relationship is key. It is in all of our best interests to get along—we could make their lives miserable, but we would lose in the end" (Ott 2013). The extent to which governance structures can accommodate diverse federal actors, challenges, and opportunities has made historical differences between rapid conversion and stalled redevelopment processes.

The national military goal of streamlining the DoD takes priority over local communities. The federal government is the primary decision-making authority in determining which bases stay open and which close through the BRAC program. These decisions are rarely overturned and occur through a top-down selection process. The BRAC process is designed to be politically neutral and to protect politicians from having to make unpopular decisions to close bases in their districts (Sorenson 1998; Reifsnyder and Holman 2005). But the base closure decision-making process is opaque and limited from the local perspective. This is not surprising in the sense that the BRAC closure process is a system for solving a federal problem rather than incentivizing, subsidizing, or catalyzing local economic development. The Pentagon now weighs urban redevelopment challenges and opportunities facing targeted communities in making recommendations for future closures and advising former defense communities in the present: "Flexibility has to remain the prime directive. The tools for disposing of real estate have to be tailored to local communities' needs," said Patrick O'Brien, director of the DoD Office of Economic Adjustment (2014). Also, according to Steven Iselin, deputy assistant secretary for the

Navy's Energy, Installations, and the Environment department, "We try to encourage early transfers of the cleaner sites because we think this pushes communities to stick with their plans" (2014). Military branches may have more community interests in mind now than in earlier base closure rounds. However, the base closure and redevelopment process still fundamentally progresses under federal authority, not local or state.

The federal executive branch also has great influence over local aspects of the redevelopment process such as the speed of redevelopment, the type of projects selected, and the way that projects are phased. The military service branch operating each base makes decisions and coordinates with local authorities throughout the closure and conversion process. The DoD's OEA plays an integral role in improving governance, conveying military land to communities, and converting it for reuse. The Pentagon created the office in 1961 to assist communities as they adapt to base closures, expansions, and conflicts between local military operations and economic development. The Clinton administration expanded the OEA and mobilized it under BRAC (Reifsnyder and Holman 2005). OEA representatives work with defense communities to organize, plan, and implement redevelopment projects in areas where bases are slated to close. Providing communities with information for how base closures and redevelopment projects progress is the first area where the OEA collaborates with defense communities. The OEA then provides technical assistance for creating a local redevelopment authority to coordinate land transfers, restoration, and redevelopment. The OEA also leads each former defense community's economic adjustment committee. This committee serves as a clearinghouse for resources from twenty-two federal agencies that distribute resources to communities suffering from base closures (U.S. OEA 2015). The committee then works with the LRA and representatives from these other agencies to distribute federal resources throughout the community.

The DoD sets the course of economic development conveyance (EDC) through its Office of Economic Adjustment, and its objectives for land transfer can vary widely: sometimes the goal is to unload outdated DoD infrastructure quickly, but at other times the White House has stalled land transfers to generate greater revenue from the transaction. The DoD also sets the general terms of the conveyance agreement. These terms are central to projects' fates. For example, the OEA requires a master plan as part of the EDC process; however, shifting market trends can make these plans irrelevant and make it impossible to meet many communities' redevelopment needs: "The reuse requirements change when the community/local redevelopment authority changes their plans for redevelopment. In terms of environmental remediation, this requires a new set of environmental-impact reviews and a new strategy for cleaning up land" (Iselin 2014). The result is unanticipated cost overruns as communities regularly revise their plans to match market demands: a key lesson from the Urban Renewal program's naive "build it, and they will come" mantra. The glacial pace of the federal EDC process further exacerbates mismatches between planning requirements and local market realities. Executive-branch–level decisions on base value and transfer goals are thus important factors in the speed, type, and phasing of the redevelopment process for all sites. These critical federal policies often represent the difference between project success and failure. For example, the OEA coordinates a wide variety of programs designed to assist former defense communities, but a lack of understanding of barriers to conveyance and conversion challenges plagued its early efforts under the BRAC program: "The rapid first rounds of closures went too fast, and no one knew what was going on in the earlier communities by the time the next bases were closed. The military got a new disposal authority in the mid-1990s. There still aren't a lot of win-win situations. Now they focus on adaptive use rather than radical transformation of land use" (O'Brien 2014).

The complexity and scale of converting closed defense sites require local redevelopment authorities to collaborate and negotiate with federal agencies on such complex topics as environmental contamination, historic preservation, and wildlife conservation, among many others. For example, the Environmental Protection Agency (EPA) is directly and thoroughly involved in redeveloping contaminated sites that demand expensive, long-term, brown-field remediation from weapons storage on one part of the base along with more pedestrian types of contamination from asbestos on another part. Table 1 provides an expanded view of the changes in planning authority and redevelopment performance across BRAC rounds.

These bases, then, have certainly shrunk in size, scope, and their share of maintenance resources, but it is highly misleading to claim they have all closed. The LRA and local governments must therefore continue to

TABLE 1. Planning authority and redevelopment performance across BRAC rounds

BRAC round	Redevelopment governance	Environmental-remediation needs	Conveyance status	Redevelopment outcomes and costs
1988	Community partnership with master developer	Relatively light contamination	No-fee conveyances with all land transferred are common.	Pursuit of mixed-use redevelopment. Greater completion rates than in later rounds. Broader community benefits.
1991	Local redevelopment authority, public-private partnerships	Contamination is high, and much of it is unknown.	No-fee conveyances are common, but conveyance slows as extent of contamination becomes clear.	Partial, mixed-use redevelopment stalled because of environmental-remediation needs. Narrower community benefits.
1993	Local redevelopment authority, public-private partnerships, and master developer	Contamination is high, and much of it is unknown.	Fee-based conveyances are common.	Partial, mixed-use redevelopment stalled because of environmental-remediation needs. Narrower community benefits.
1995	Local redevelopment authority, public-private partnerships, and master developer	Contamination is high, and much of it is unknown.	Fee-based conveyances are common.	Partial, mixed-use redevelopment stalled because of environmental-remediation needs. Narrower community benefits.
2005	Local redevelopment authority required	Contamination is high, but DoD and communities are better-informed.	No-fee conveyances are common, but conveyance slows as extent of contamination becomes clear.	Return to pursuit of mixed-use redevelopment with broad community benefits. Most projects remain incomplete.

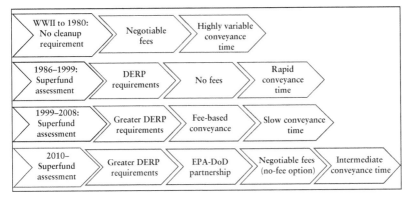

Figure 1. Environmental-remediation and conveyance process on former military bases under BRAC

work with rump federal military authorities to govern the community for decades after most of a base is closed and transferred (see figure 1).

Land as Asset or Liability?

The multi-decade nature of large-scale redevelopment puts communities at great risk of falling victim to shifts in federal priorities and general base conversion philosophies. The Clinton administration did not charge communities fees for taking possession of former military sites for most of the 1990s. No-cost conveyances promoted land transfers and lowered redevelopment costs beginning in 1994. President Clinton signed new legislation in 1999 that made no-cost EDCs easier to approve when conversion projects included a job-creating component. However, this legislation also made it easier for the Bush administration to levy fees for conveyance when redevelopment plans on parcels did not include permanent job creation. The Clinton and Bush administrations pursued this policy modification because some communities, such as San Francisco, received valuable former military sites, such as the Presidio. San Francisco paid nothing for the Presidio but converted it to a recreational, residential, and commercial asset worth tens of millions of dollars. The Bush administration considered the Presidio to be a taxpayer-funded subsidy to an already-affluent part of the country and an expensive lesson in budgeting; the federal government could have charged many millions of dollars to transfer the base and used the proceeds elsewhere (Benton-Short 1998; Bill 2014).

The Bush administration saw value in many military properties and began charging communities conveyance fees indexed to market conditions and perceived land values on the former bases. This policy shift slowed the transfer process considerably because cities had not planned for federal fees and did not have the resources to raise millions of dollars before getting approvals for land distribution. Base conversion is very expensive in the best of economic circumstances. The added government treatment of bases as space with exchange value, rather than places where citizens live (use value), was very damaging to redevelopment prospects. The fees stymied redevelopment efforts around the country because, unlike many normal real estate assets, land on former bases often requires extensive environmental remediation before it can be used for residential, recreational, educational, or retail purposes. These environmental costs occur in addition to the other costs necessary to integrate physically central but economically, politically, socially, and culturally isolated former bases. Most closed bases are thus conveyed as community liabilities, not assets. The costs of remediation are high enough in many cases to prevent profitable redevelopment on their own, much less with extra fees incorporated into the redevelopment costs. Such costs would need to be offset by even larger profits to convince private developers or taxpayers to fund projects on the former sites. Communities in the era of fee-based conveyance then often face difficulty governing decision-making processes that focus on the choice between redevelopment with relative benefits for concentrated, private interests or no redevelopment at all.

The Obama administration distanced itself from the Bush administration's stance on fee-based conveyance and treated fees as negotiable rather than mandatory. The Obama administration lobbied Congress to support an easier conveyance process, which culminated in the 2010 National Defense Authorization Act. This legislation reduced or eliminated fees associated with conveyance as the administration worked to shut bases from the 2005 BRAC round and before, convey land, and build support for another BRAC round. Despite these efforts, it became clear that the cost savings expected from the 2005 round did not materialize, both because there were fewer obvious targets for closure remaining by 2005 and because the costs of environmental remediation were much higher than expected for these bases (Hutchison and O'Hanlon 2013). Even without conveyance fees, it became clear that many former military assets should be treated as liabilities.

Governing Environmental Restoration?

Former military sites are frequently contaminated from an environmental perspective. Contamination is common in water, soil, and buildings on former bases because of their previous military use. These uses and hazards range from the mundane, such as lead and asbestos in former barracks, to the exotic, such as radioactive soil from nuclear weapons manufacturing. Weapons storage, fuel depots, training ranges, and landfills frequently contaminate water and soil on former bases. Unexploded ordnance is also widely distributed on some sites. Environmental hazards must be removed and sites restored prior to conveyance, conversion, and reuse. But governing the remediation effort by identifying, removing, and restoring former military sites is complex and costly, and it requires decades of dedicated efforts. Governing environmental-remediation efforts requires intensive collaborative connections with the federal government because communities are at such a relative disadvantage in terms of resources and expertise. For example, many communities are not aware that the DoD and EPA are not required to clean up certain prevalent pollutants on former bases, such as fuel spills, lead, and asbestos. It is thus critical that communities have structures in place to work with government agencies to understand their rights and responsibilities in environmental remediation.

Base remediation and restoration first occurred under the Comprehensive Environmental Response, Compensation, and Liability Act of 1980 (CERCLA), also known as the Superfund program (42 U.S.C. § 103). Congress amended and reauthorized the Superfund program in 1986 and established the Defense Environmental Restoration Program (DERP) to accompany it. DERP is designed for the "identification, investigation, research and development, and cleanup of contamination from hazardous substances, pollutants, and contaminants" (10 U.S.C. § 2701; U.S. DoD 2016a). DERP mandates the restoration of all sites under DoD jurisdiction, including active facilities and formerly used defense sites (FUDS).[3]

DERP also governs site restoration for BRAC sites, which occurs with the assistance of the EPA. The EPA not only oversees Superfund cleanup but also provides communities with technical assistance to identify other contaminants on the base and to pursue redevelopment in general through redevelopment and remediation primers (U.S. EPA 2015). The DoD also contracts with other federal agencies, state agencies, and nonprofits to provide restoration services and manage restoration processes.

DERP requires the DoD to create a technical review committee, consisting of public officials at the state and local levels, to discuss restoration proposals. The DoD then drafts a management-action plan for each site and submits annual restoration reports to Congress. Following 2001, DERP also requires the DoD to keep and maintain a comprehensive list of contaminated sites with hazardous waste or unexploded ordnance throughout its installations inventory (10 U.S.C. § 2701; 10 U.S.C. § 2687; 10 U.S.C. § 2710). Then the DoD performs an environmental-impact analysis and issues environmental-impact statements regarding property disposal and conversion on BRAC sites. DERP actions for BRAC sites fall into three general categories: environmental restoration, munitions removal, and building demolition and debris removal. By law, unexploded ordnance takes restoration priority over other hazards on active and former military installations. But the DoD also prioritizes restoration across its installations based on risk to the public outlined in management-action plans (10 U.S.C. § 2710).

The DoD inventory includes more than 30,000 contaminated sites across active FUDS and BRAC sites (see map 2).

The DoD spends approximately $200 million per year on BRAC restoration activities as of 2015, but has spent over $30 billion on restoration across its portfolio of current and former installations since 1984, more than $10 billion of this for BRAC sites (U.S. OEA 2015; U.S. DoD 2016b). Legislation in 2000 and a 2008 memorandum of understanding with the EPA provide the framework for recent restoration efforts (U.S. EPA 2008; 10 U.S.C. § 2701). The EPA forms a BRAC cleanup team for each site and appoints a remedial project manager. The manager and the team of toxicologists, hydrologists, community relations officials, and risk-management experts identify and remove hazards, restore the site, and inform local officials and the public of environmental-restoration

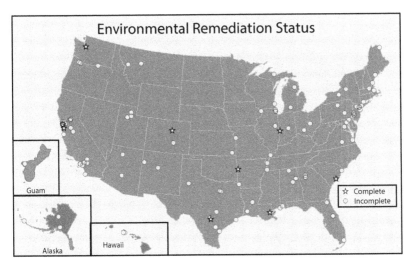

Map 2. Environmental-remediation status of all bases closed since 1988 under BRAC

plans and activities. The goal of these programs is achieved when land can be transferred to nonmilitary ownership.

The federal government stipulates considerable support for *some* environmental restoration on BRAC sites. However, defense conversion depends on identifying hazards and understanding just how much environmental restoration the federal government *does not* fund. Superfund legislation does not encompass lead, asbestos, or fuel spills, all of which are present in significant quantities on many former bases and make it extremely difficult to redevelop or preserve large portions of those bases. Neither CERCLA or DERP mandates funding to support lead or asbestos mitigation or soil and water restoration caused by fuel spills (U.S. EPA 2015). The omission of these common hazards from environmental-restoration legislation means that state and local governments, private-sector partners, and nonprofit collaborators must fund remaining, non-Superfund restoration efforts prior to reuse. For many bases, the cost of remediating these sites easily exceeds DoD and EPA contributions by tens of millions of dollars. Moreover, there is frequently no funding at all to clean up these types of pollutants. Local redevelopment authorities and governments thus face significant funding challenges at the earliest possible stages of the conversion planning process. Connecting future land use to site conditions and restoration timetables is complex and often difficult, but it is also essential for converting bases in a way that benefits communities and maintains local governments' fiscal health.

Environmental justice is often overlooked as a critical aspect of redevelopment. This omission is particularly important for military redevelopment because former military sites are almost always polluted. A drive to redevelop quickly can also place marginalized populations at risk of long-term harm from environmental degradation that is not remediated. Moreover, redevelopment dynamics on some bases result in the most affluent in the community receiving the best parcels on the site and the least affluent receiving nothing because no remaining parcels are environmentally suitable for redevelopment. Defense conversion, then, raises challenges not just for environmental remediation but for environmental justice as well.

Trade-Offs in Base Closures and Redevelopment

Closing bases benefits the military directly because base funding can be reallocated to weapons systems. This reallocation may increase the military's fighting capabilities, which in turn benefits the country by theoretically making it more secure.[4] However, the parallel trend in base closures is that redevelopment costs fall hard on former military communities. These communities tend to be ill-equipped to face the governance, economic, and social challenges associated with base closures and redevelopment. Closures then result in diffuse security benefits and very concentrated community losses. Moreover, the regional distribution of BRAC closures concentrates individual community losses. The U.S. government created many new bases in the West and the South from the beginning of the twentieth century through World War II. These bases closed at disproportionately high rates under BRAC; 69 percent of bases in the data set closed in the South and West between 1988 and 2005. These closures challenged communities around the country but hit the South particularly hard because many southern states' economies were already struggling at the time. Much of the region remained dependent on agriculture during this time frame, which preceded the recent shift of manufacturing to the South. The South was thus a region with a low likelihood of generating new service-sector employment comparable to what military bases had previously provided communities.

Beyond the military, weak governance of defense conversion often provides private-sector developers with outsized financial benefits. Military redevelopment thus tends to favor the socialization of costs and the privatization of benefits from the conversion of public assets. This is when redevelopment advances, which does not always happen because of the literally toxic assets that former military sites represent. The high cost of environmental remediation does not excuse the privatization of public resources, but achieving redevelopment without private beneficiaries is relatively rare.

The cost transfer for base maintenance and conversion from the Department of Defense to other federal and state agencies is a third trade-off in base closures and redevelopment. The EPA, HUD, the Department of Labor, and the Department of Commerce all play roles in defense conversion. However, these and other federal agencies have smaller budgets and fewer resources than the Department of Defense. Their roles in defense conversion represent unfunded mandates that strain budgets, in many respects. Such mandates, if met, still carry opportunity costs for other areas where the agencies are active and where finite resources can no longer be devoted. The rest of the country that these agencies serve then bears some of the costs of base closures as well because funds and programs that would have otherwise gone elsewhere now go to military redevelopment.

Prioritizing Community Outcomes

Federal legislation requires programs to assist local homeless populations during defense conversion. Veterans represent up to one-quarter of the total homeless population around the country and one-third of the homeless male population (National Coalition for the Homeless 2009). Many advocates for homeless veterans lobbied Congress and the Pentagon to consider veterans' plight as they close and convert bases. The result was the Base Closure Community Redevelopment and Homeless Assistance Act of 1994, which redresses grievances of corporate welfare going to property developers for defense conversion while veterans remain homeless in the community. The 1994 law (Pub.L. 103–421) exempts BRAC installations from the McKinney Act (42 U.S.C. 11411–11412), which requires the agency controlling surplus federal property to work with HUD to make the property available to state and local governments as well as nonprofit groups that assist homeless people in the community. Instead, the 1994 bill replaces the HUD-driven process and now requires homeless advocacy groups' inclusion in conversion planning. Incorporating these groups into the conversion process requires strong, collaborative governance, which is not common in defense conversion; by 2016, housing for homeless and low-income residents appeared on only 24 percent of former bases closed under BRAC. Providing housing for the homeless is often a hard sell for former defense communities, as evident by the general reluctance to comply with the federal requirements: "No one involved in redevelopment wants the homeless around. We want to encourage mixed-use redevelopment, but we don't want to scare off developers. We also have a mission to support the homeless, and communities don't seem to understand how many new homeless residents they'll have after the bases close," said Linda Charest, BRAC coordinator for the Department of Housing and Urban Development (2014).

Other federal agencies, such as the EPA (discussed above), Department of Commerce, and Department of Health and Human Services, also assist former defense communities to convert their bases. For example, the Department of Commerce's Economic Development Administration offers redevelopment grants and technical assistance to former defense communities. However, former defense communities are frequently unaware of the federal opportunities to assist conversion because their governance models do not incorporate experts across multiple sectors and multiple levels of government: "They lose so much short-term revenue in all but the biggest cities that they don't have the employees they need to ask for help. We provide technical assistance when possible, but it's usually the larger cities like SF [San Francisco] or SD [San Diego] that can apply for the grants. They get them first because they asked first and have better proposals, and so sometimes there's not much left for the smaller towns" (Melinda Matson, senior staff, Department of Commerce Economic Development Administration, 2014).

The National Historic Preservation Act (1966) also provides social benefits on former bases. The act mandates that all federal agencies, including the DoD, review surplus federal property for historical significance and apply for national designation. Preserving memory on former bases provides social benefits to veterans who served on the bases and to long-term community residents. The DoD recognizes this and often requires national historic designations as part of the deal to convey land to communities. Converting closed bases with preservation in mind also speaks to the preservation challenges of large-scale redevelopment endeavors. Bases have many preservation identities because their public nature gives them military, architectural, and cultural significance. Mixed-use megaprojects on former bases encompass several different preservation dimensions and engender multifaceted conflicts because of their size, their connection to the broader community, and their development opportunities. Compliance with federal historic preservation requirements is a difficult task because preservation is an ongoing process as well as an outcome and requires careful attention, funding, and oversight (Ashley and Touchton 2016). This process requires moving beyond historic designation to maintaining and negotiating different preservation claims that have yet to arise as well as overcoming future challenges. Ultimately, communities' governance structures must provide for conflict resolution surrounding multiple stakeholders' preservation interests while also complying with federal and state requirements. This is difficult and uncommon, but essential for achieving conversion with broad community benefits.

American Bases on Foreign Soil

The BRAC process extends globally and alters American allies' economic geography as bases close. The U.S. military maintains a presence in more than 160 countries around the world. Overseas military sites support forward operations in theaters with an active U.S. military presence. For example, hospital facilities in Germany are located relatively close to conflicts in Iraq and Afghanistan so that injured U.S. troops can be flown to Germany and operated on quickly. The U.S. military presence in a host country may also be essential for mitigating regional threats to that country. Furthermore, a U.S. military presence is often designed to stimulate military cooperation with the host country and to improve the country's military capabilities. To that end, the U.S. military and the host country's military share many bases.

American bases overseas use a variety of ownership and leasing arrangements. Host countries, such as South Korea, lease land or space on their own bases to the U.S. military at very low costs. In some cases the United States occupied bases and other military facilities as part of other countries' surrender, as with Japan and Germany's capitulation at the end of World War II. Bases are leased rent-free to the U.S. in most cases, with the bases returned "as is" at such time when the U.S. military might no longer deem them necessary. Elsewhere, the U.S. government covers leasing fees for bases, often on portions of host countries' existing bases.

Overseas bases are attractive for closure because shutting these bases down does not impact U.S. communities. Congressional opposition to foreign base closures because of constituents' concerns is thus considerably diminished relative to domestic closures. Moreover, closing foreign bases may be less expensive than domestic closure alternatives because the U.S. government rarely pays for overseas conversion costs. This is reflected in Senate Resolution 132 (Congressional Record 2014), which expresses the Senate's position that requested base realignment and closure rounds in 2015 and 2017 are neither affordable nor feasible because of high environmental-remediation and conversion costs. But the overseas base closure process is different from the domestic process because BRAC Commission approval is largely unnecessary to close overseas bases. Senate and House Committees on Foreign Affairs are still incorporated into the overseas closure process to evaluate closures' impact on regional security environments and allies' concerns around the world. However, this involvement suggests that decisions surrounding which bases to close or shrink are therefore based on military considerations rather than socioeconomic concerns.

U.S. Code 2687a governs overseas base closures, realignments, and basing master plans. It stipulates that the secretary of defense submit an annual report on base closure and realignment actions as part of the United States' global defense posture. The Senate's Committee on Foreign Relations and the House Committee on Foreign Affairs receive this report, which includes information on how overseas realignments or closures affect security commitments in international treaties and host countries' regional security environments. Additionally, these reports include a discussion of efforts to gain compensation from the host countries for any improvements made on leased bases that would revert to the host country following the U.S. military's departure. The members of congressional committees monitoring overseas closures then have thirty days to object to agreements surrounding property transfers or other improvements on the base before the military is free to move forward with the closure plan.

The process for selecting international facilities for closure contains elements of the domestic process and is based on legal codes governing closures and the secretary of defense. Many of the concerns surrounding the closures are similar, too, with host countries lobbying the Pentagon through the State Department and other U.S. government contacts to keep the bases open to protect jobs and local revenue. In announcing a set of 201 closures, Defense Secretary Hagel made a point of noting the inevitable job losses that will result for the countries currently hosting U.S. bases: "I know that this will result in a reduction of our local host nations' workforces at some locations, [but] I value the tremendous support they provided us for decades" (U.S. DoD 2015). Of course, the U.S. government's concern is not retaining or creating jobs overseas, and the local impact of overseas base closures is of little consequence for the Pentagon.

The U.S. armed forces depend much less on local considerations surrounding base closures in foreign countries relative to domestic closures. However, one of the biggest differences between closing international and domestic bases is the strategic importance of simply having U.S. troops in harm's way. Stationing American personnel in the path of potential invaders reassures host countries, such as South Korea, Japan, or those in Eastern Europe, that an attack on their territory would engender a U.S. military response that would honor mutual defense treaties. That is because such an attack—from North Korea, for example—would likely result in the loss of American lives and the resulting political resolve to stand with U.S. allies against foreign aggressors. Concern for an empty bargain motivates U.S. allies to request reassurances of a commitment to mutual defense when bases close. The United States is sensitive to this concern. The DoD has recently created reassurance packages to reposition at least some U.S. personnel within host countries, extend regional training exercises, deepen military ties with former host countries, upgrade existing facilities, and increase self-defense capabilities in foreign countries when U.S. bases close. The Obama administration's 2015 European

Reassurance Initiative funded these efforts to the tune of $985 million following the announcement of fifteen American base closures in Europe (U.S. DoD 2015).

American communities' costs associated with base closures and redevelopment prompted Congress to press for additional overseas base closures before domestic bases would be considered in another BRAC round. Specifically, the National Defense Authorization Act for Fiscal Year 2014 precludes future BRAC rounds:

> No future Base Realignment and Closure round for military installations within the United States, its commonwealths, territories, and possessions for realignment or closure shall be authorized until, at the very earliest, the DoD has completed and submitted to Congress a formal review of the overseas military facility structure, which incorporates overseas basing consolidations, an assessment of the need for bases to support overseas contingency operations, and the DoD's Strategic Choices and Management Review. (Pub. L. 113–66)

The U.S. military finds it easier to close overseas bases relative to its domestic inventory and has closed or realigned more than a thousand overseas installations following the end of the Cold War, with more than two hundred closing in Germany alone. U.S. bases overseas subsidize communities in the same way as domestic bases: overseas bases support extensive local economies through employment and demand for goods and services (Paloyo et al. 2010; Hooker and Knetter 2001; Andersson et al. 2007). Employment and sales then generate tax revenue for communities so that they may provide residents with infrastructure and services. U.S. military sites in foreign countries usually sit on land that belongs to the host country's national government. Almost all land formerly used for U.S. military purposes therefore reverts either directly to the host country's national government or to the host country's armed forces, in the common case of "co-bases."

Broad differences in the distribution of land between former military sites in the United States and former U.S. bases around the world leads to broad differences in redevelopment opportunities. For example, local considerations are much less likely to shape redevelopment on former U.S. bases abroad than on former bases in the United States. Instead, national governments in host countries determine how to convert the former base for reuse, if they even plan to convert it in the first place. Local governments and citizens may be included in the resulting redevelopment process, but there is usually no legal requirement that they be included because the land belongs to the national government.

Local communities in host countries may lack influence surrounding defense conversion after the U.S. military leaves. Neither these communities nor national host governments tend to receive conversion assistance from the United States, which raises the prospects of unfunded conversion mandates in host countries. However, local communities are also insulated from the costs of conversion because the national government tends to fund redevelopment on its own land unless it sells or transfers the land to a local government, as with Germany's conversion of the Army's Abrams Complex. Thus, there are broad trade-offs in terms of the differences between defense conversion in the United States relative to other countries where the U.S. military operates bases. Greater local control in the domestic context also comes with greater local funding responsibility: an enormous challenge on large, contaminated, isolated sites. In contrast, funding support from the national governments in Europe and East Asia often comes with less decision-making authority for local communities.

National trends paint a dire picture of hamstrung, under-resourced communities that struggle to convert their closed bases, especially in ways that produce broad community benefits. Strong governance is possible but uncommon in defense conversion. However, the historical analysis produces plausible, testable hypotheses for why communities' redevelopment performance falls at different points along a spectrum of redevelopment outcomes. For instance, a lack of redevelopment governance across multiple levels of government and across multiple sectors undermines redevelopment processes and limits conversion. Similarly, the challenge of governing environmental remediation hinders redevelopment.

The historical view showcases different outcomes along this spectrum, but its focus on anecdotal evaluations results in a great deal of knowledge surrounding a few very positive outcomes along with several largely negative redevelopment processes. It does not provide a systematic way to determine what the communities with positive outcomes did well or the communities with negative outcomes did not that includes all of the bases. The anecdotal, historical focus thus risks omitting dozens of cases in the middle—without spectacularly strong or weak redevelopment outcomes—that are potentially more representative than the better-known cases. Policy recommendations and, ultimately, community redevelopment performance suffer without information from a broader, representative group of cases. Chapter 2 takes a large step to resolve this issue by testing hypotheses for redevelopment performance against a national database of all military bases closed under the BRAC program since 1988.

2

NATIONAL TRENDS IN MILITARY REDEVELOPMENT

Challenges of Governance, Financing, and Environmental Remediation

The DoD has transferred hundreds of installations and millions of acres of land under BRAC legislation. Converting and reusing closed installations is critically important for former defense communities' economic, political, and social health. Communities exhibit wide variation in conversion outcomes on former bases. Some communities have converted bases, renewed their tax base, and even surpassed employment figures from when bases were open. Some forms of conversion have extended redevelopment benefits to broad groups of citizens in the city-region. In contrast, other communities have failed to make even marginal steps towards conversion in the twenty-five years since the shutdowns began. Many others have converted bases but have concentrated redevelopment benefits in the hands of narrow, private interests. It is important for scholars, public officials, and advocacy groups to understand the wide variation in redevelopment outcomes to improve conversion performance across the country.

A unique database on redevelopment inputs, processes, and outcomes on all U.S. bases closed under the BRAC program is the source material for statistical models that explain national redevelopment patterns.[1] Several general trends emerge from the analysis that can help structure communities' redevelopment plans. For example, collaborative governance improves fiscal health, improves environmental health, and spreads conversion outcomes across broad groups of stakeholders. Strong governance contributes greatly to redevelopment performance, but local economic conditions and the extent of environmental remediation necessary for conversion are also critically important for redevelopment outcomes.

Local conditions are destiny: local economic health and the types of assets on former bases drive redevelopment outcomes in a way that governance can influence but not overcome or counteract entirely. Economic conditions and contamination on former defense sites are largely beyond communities' control. Strong governance does not change these underlying conditions, but strong governance can still lead to better outcomes than one might otherwise expect. Governance is an area over which communities have considerable agency, which provides a reason to be optimistic about defense conversion. These results thus provide a road map for precisely where agency in governance will matter, when, how much, and to what end.

A National Database on Military Redevelopment

Explaining variation in redevelopment outcomes is important for communities. Yet scholars have failed to capture the wide variety of conversion outcomes on former bases because the data to do so have not been available. Collecting data on redevelopment processes and outcomes on all bases closed under BRAC resolves this issue. Inputs to redevelopment include community wealth, base infrastructure, environmental hazards, market conditions, and other factors likely to influence the costs of redevelopment and the resources available to mitigate those costs. Redevelopment processes such as governance and partnership structures, funding sources and availability, and stakeholder participation can also help or impede redevelopment. The database also includes information on defense conversion outcomes such as employment, tax revenue, municipal bond ratings, environmental remediation, the projects appearing on the former base, and the stakeholders that these projects serve. No other existing database comprehensively covers political, economic, and social aspects of military redevelopment for the universe of cases over the entire redevelopment time frame.

A national database of military redevelopment thus offers a unique opportunity to evaluate redevelopment inputs, processes, and outcomes for all U.S. bases closed under the BRAC program. Analysis of these data identifies *average* redevelopment experiences in former defense communities that vary greatly in the extent to which they reflect redevelopment relationships in any *individual* community. Quantitative analysis serves as a point of departure for diverse former defense communities across the country; some common aspects of redevelopment appear on former bases across urban, suburban, and rural contexts in all U.S. regions. However, local context is critically important for explaining specific outcomes on specific former bases. Readers interested in those outcomes should thus consider how to apply the national trends we identify to local contexts rather than to conceive of these trends as fully determining outcomes in individual communities.

What Explains Redevelopment Performance?

Redeveloping closed bases is complex, and the history of redevelopment points to a variety of factors that might explain redevelopment performance. For example, where funding comes from and how influential funders are in the redevelopment process may explain performance. Former military communities pursuing ambitious projects may have difficulty achieving their goals of conversion for a broad group of beneficiaries while retaining purely local control. Single-use projects and other limited forms of conversion serve a comparatively narrow range of end users. But completing these projects may also be less costly, require narrower partnership structures, and require less funding support up and down the local, state, and federal ladder than projects that benefit broader groups of stakeholders. Narrower redevelopment ambitions may also therefore help local communities retain control over defense conversion.[2] The data set adds information on funding sources and many other factors that might explain redevelopment performance. The next section develops hypotheses surrounding each factor. These variables' technical specifications appear in the appendix.

Defense conversion may benefit from public-private and nonprofit partnerships where multiple stakeholders collaborate to create developments with diverse, mixed uses such as residences, commercial centers, schools, parks, and museums. A range of partnership structures among public entities (local, regional, state, federal), private-sector groups (real estate developers), and nonprofit institutions (educational institutions, community-based organizations, advocacy groups) govern 65 percent of the redevelopment projects in the data set. More complicated, ambitious redevelopment projects must serve varied stakeholders and overcome considerable regulatory challenges. They may therefore require multiple funding sources covering multiple aspects of redevelopment.[3]

Redeveloping closed bases is complex, and communities' learning curves are steep. For example, communities must work with governments or other entities with a claim to authority over the former base in many different areas. Funding for redevelopment authorities is essential if communities are to navigate the challenges of governance at different scales in pursuit of defense conversion. Better-funded local redevelopment authorities may hire stronger employees, and more of them, to help govern the redevelopment process.

Market conditions and communities' access to resources based on the relative productivity of the surrounding area may also influence redevelopment outcomes. Economic output is likely to be strongly correlated with access to resources and proxies for market conditions, which condition the types of redevelopment that communities can pursue and the resources that they can devote to project implementation and oversight.[4] The former military function of each closed base also limits potential conversion options as well. For instance, former Air Force bases or Naval air stations often have infrastructure conducive to frequent arrival and departure of aircraft, and former shipyards are conducive to shipbuilding. An airport is arguably easier to create from a former air base than is a residential redevelopment.[5]

The cost of environmental remediation creates significant barriers to redevelopment on many former bases. Most former bases suffer from environmental degradation, but the ones that produced, tested, or stored weapons are likely to suffer more environmental issues than those that did not have weapons production or storage facilities. BRAC rounds are not random in this sense in particular, and the BRAC process is historically specific. For instance, the types of installations the DoD tries to dispose of and their former functions differ from era to era. Furthermore, the military may have selected early base closures for their relatively strong redevelopment prospects, whereas "easy" redevelopment prospects had been exhausted by later rounds. It is possible that the bases which were selected to close are those that could rebound quickly, whereas those selected to remain open were in communities that would be devastated by base closures. These communities were therefore able to fight closure decisions successfully. In contrast, it is possible that communities with few resources were unable to defend themselves from the closures and did not rebound as frequently as wealthy communities. Those evaluating base closures should therefore draw inferences only on their impact on communities where bases closed, not relative to other communities without a military base or to defense communities whose bases remained open. Including a "BRAC round" variable assesses whether early closures are systematically different than those closed in the most recent round.[6]

The BRAC round in which bases close may also reflect time's influence on redevelopment success. Temporal redevelopment influences could include both the longer time frame over which communities with early base closures used to convert their bases and the relative success of those projects in terms of community perceptions. Different timing trends seen in other areas of redevelopment may apply to military base redevelopment as well. For example, policies creating local enterprise zones or federal empowerment zones and enterprise communities may target particularly troubled areas in early rounds but relatively more-productive areas later as the policy grows. The result is likely to be systematically different outcomes for early versus late participants in the program (Greenbaum 2004; Greenbaum and Bondonio 2004). The opposite could also be true: early redevelopment targets might have been selected for their redevelopment potential and thus attractiveness to public, private, and nonprofit funding entities. Applied to BRAC rounds, it is entirely possible that the DoD selected certain bases for early closure because of their high redevelopment potential. These bases then might have attracted relatively more private capital than less attractive bases closed in later rounds and thus required less public or nonprofit redevelopment assistance. The result could be improved outcomes for these early bases because of federal programs from specific areas or targeted selection for closures. The point here is that addressing the temporal aspects of redevelopment performance on closed bases insulates our results from challenges of omitted-variable and selection bias and provides another opportunity to test theoretical arguments surrounding what works in redevelopment.

The history of military redevelopment in the United States points to geographic influences on community performance at different scales. Communities in one part of the country, such as the West, may pursue systematically different land-use strategies in military base redevelopment than communities in another part, such as the Northeast. Geographically speaking, bases closed since 1988 are overwhelmingly situated in the West and the South (38% and 31%, respectively). This is partially accounted for by the distribution of U.S. military installations in general: the boom in military construction surrounding World War II and the Cold War primarily occurred in the West and the South because of available land and strategic necessity (Markusen et al. 1991). By 1988, there were more bases in these regions; therefore, it is not surprising that more bases recently closed in the West and South as a percentage of total base closures.

Beyond the region, whether the former base is physically located near an urban center may also explain redevelopment performance. For example, military redevelopment projects located closer to the urban core are systematically different from those situated farther away, in the same way one might expect general redevelopment near urban areas to be distinct from redevelopment in suburban or rural areas.[7] At the smallest scale, the relative physical size of the base may influence land-use choices in redevelopment. Land-use opportunities for a wide variety of redevelopment projects could increase with a larger parcel available for redevelopment or decrease because of the difficulty of integrating different uses across a larger physical space: infrastructure costs and the distance from services. Land-use outcomes may therefore be associated with the physical size of the parcel to be converted.[8]

Modeling Land Use in Military Redevelopment

This chapter presents statistical models of military redevelopment using several different techniques. Our data underlying these models are cross-sectional and allow us to evaluate outcomes by recording information using the most current measures of redevelopment inputs, processes, and outcomes possible.[9]

We use ordinary least squares to estimate continuous outcomes such as those surrounding jobs and revenue. Cross-sectional logit models supplement this technique for binary outcomes, such as whether environmental remediation is complete or whether low-income housing appears on the former base. Ordered logit models drive estimates of performance on the defense conversion index, which allows us to estimate the odds of communities receiving lower or higher scores. In general, regression analyses evaluate the likelihood of achieving specific levels of conversion and community benefits among a range of outcomes in the rebuilt environment. The likelihood differs depending on the outcome, but hypothesis tests encompass a wide variety of conversion outcomes given the relative presence of government support; the relative collaboration between the public, private, and nonprofit sector; the former military function of the site; the community's per capita GDP; the BRAC round when the base closed; the region where the site is located; the proximity to a metropolitan statistical area (MSA); and the physical size of the former base. Table 2 presents descriptive statistics of redevelopment indicators.

TABLE 2. Characteristics of redevelopment inputs, processes, and outcomes on closed bases, 1988–2015

Variable	Mean	Standard deviation
Jobs created (per capita)	0.08	0.09
Jobs replaced (percentage)	0.19	0.16
Revenue created (per capita, logged)	1.28	0.73
Revenue replaced (per capita, logged)	0.68	0.21
Percentage of land transferred	0.67	0.14
Environmental-remediation cost (per capita, logged)	3.25	0.62
Low-income housing	0.30	0.59
Defense conversion index	2.41	1.13
Physical size (square miles)	6.40	2.90
Location bordering an MSA	0.81	0.82
Funding across scale	2.19	0.56

(Continued)

TABLE 2. (Continued)

Variable	Mean	Standard deviation
Number of collaborative partners	4.72	2.88
Redevelopment agency funding (per capita)	5.31	2.80
Redevelopment staffing	11.20	6.30
Gross local product (per capita, logged)	0.42	0.16

Sources: LRA websites, Association of Defense Communities, U.S. Census Bureau.

Table 3 presents the results of analysis across nine central indicators of defense conversion and its beneficiaries. The results begin where many former defense communities also begin their redevelopment discussions, with how conversion can replace jobs lost when bases close. Replacing job losses following base closures is an important challenge for communities. Job creation should not be the only aspect or even the largest aspect of communities' redevelopment goals. However, replacing lost jobs is economically important in clear, direct ways. The data set therefore includes a measure of jobs created through the redevelopment process relative to jobs lost, based on a survey from the U.S. defense communities and other public documents from former defense communities.

A per capita measure of jobs created in the redevelopment process based on the size of the local population supplements the first dependent variable. It should be noted that jobs created rarely approach jobs lost for the bases in the data set. It should also be noted that job-creation numbers are prone to manipulation in several ways, including double counting and selective reporting (Davis et al. 2006; Dalton and Lewis 2011). Job-creation numbers have the advantage of availability for former defense communities, but they are difficult to assess: one cannot say how many jobs would have been created in the absence of base closures or in the absence of a base altogether. Job-creation data thus represent a first step toward quantitative evaluation of redevelopment performance that requires corroboration across a series of additional indicators. Nevertheless, job creation is an important dependent variable because policy makers and residents frequently associate it with economic opportunities and redevelopment success. High job creation is also associated with high levels of redevelopment performance in the analysis, but job-creation data has clear limitations, and jobs represent only one component of redevelopment performance.[10]

TABLE 3. Ordinary least squares model of job creation in U.S. defense conversion

Independent variables	Dependent variables	
	Per capita jobs created on former base, through 2013	Jobs created relative to jobs lost
Funding across scale	0.11 (0.15)	0.20 (0.17)
Number of public/private/ nonprofit collaborators	0.07 (0.06)	0.09 (0.09)
Funding for redevelopment authority (per capita, logged)	0.14 (0.10)	0.05 (0.05)
Former air base or shipyard	0.13** (0.04)	0.08* (0.03)
Environmental-remediation costs (per capita, logged)	−0.04* (0.02)	−0.12** (0.03)
Per capita gross local product (by county, logged)	0.05** (0.01)	0.08** (0.01)
Late BRAC round	−0.11 (0.14)	−0.06 (0.04)
MSA within county	0.03** (0.01)	0.05* (0.02)
Size of the base (square miles, logged)	−0.06 (0.05)	0.07 (0.05)
Constant	0.03** (0.01)	0.05 (0.05)
Number of bases	122	122
R^2	0.65	0.70

Notes: The first model uses Association of Defense Community data on the total jobs created on the former base through 2013. The second model uses local documents on job losses to create a ratio of job creation relative to job losses in former defense communities.

Standard errors in parentheses are robust. $*p < .05$; $**p < .01$.

Local economic productivity, environmental-remediation costs, and physical locations in metropolitan areas best explain job creation on former bases. Job creation stems from opportunities for investment: economically productive areas, sites with relatively few environmental hazards to raise redevelopment costs, and sites with proximity to markets increase the number of jobs on converted bases. These variables capture many aspects of local and regional economies that would make investment in former base communities attractive, such as the presence of industrial capacity, infrastructure, the costs of site preparation, and access to human capital.

Replacing lost jobs is important for communities, but descriptive statistics show that only a very small percentage of jobs lost through base closures ever return to the average community.

Beyond jobs, communities desperately need to replace lost revenue to maintain services for remaining residents, fund continued conversion efforts, and integrate converted bases into the community. A drive to replace lost revenue through redevelopment can also be an important aspect of attracting future residents. Jobs are difficult to replace, but replacing lost revenue may be easier for communities because revenue can come from many different sources. Measuring revenue can provide a broader view of how conversion can refill public coffers and provide the opportunity to retain or extend public services. Revenue generation may therefore be a precursor to extending the benefits of conversion to a broad population of stakeholders and thus represents a superior measure of redevelopment success than jobs alone.[11]

Municipal bond ratings over the course of the redevelopment process are also important for fiscal health because they reflect the risk associated with lending money to an affected city and the subsequent cost of borrowing money to finance redevelopment, capital improvement projects, and service delivery. Increased borrowing costs following base closures results in a larger percentage of city budgets going toward debt servicing and thus fewer opportunities for spending in other areas, such as services. Fewer services can limit residents' quality of life and make attracting new residents and creating a new revenue base difficult. Bond ratings are subject to local manipulation, much like job-creation numbers. For example, special authorities can issue debt that stays off municipal books and separate unserviced debt from the rest of a city's obligations. Thus, it is possible for heavily indebted communities that are not truly servicing their debt to maintain a strong municipal bond rating (Kirkpatrick and Smith 2011; Blount et al. 2014). Moreover, cities can issue bonds and service debts to the exclusion of services for residents. Cities would then maintain a high bond rating, which would not necessarily reflect the quality of local services or the quality of redevelopment governance.

There are data limitations inherent in bond ratings, yet they are one of the few indicators of fiscal health that are theoretically comparable across former defense communities in the data set. This measure therefore contributes to the constellation of redevelopment performance indicators in this chapter, but bond ratings alone are not the foundation for causal inferences from the analysis.[12] Table 4 presents the results of estimation explaining 2015 per capita revenue as a percentage of revenue from the year before bases closed and also lists a city's bond rating.

TABLE 4. Ordinary least squares model of local revenue in former military communities, through 2015

Independent variables	Dependent variables		
	Per capita revenue	2015 revenue as a percentage of pre-closure revenue	City bond rating
Funding across scale	0.38** (0.11)	0.12** (0.03)	0.24** (0.05)
Number of public/ private/nonprofit collaborators	0.04* (0.02)	0.03** (0.01)	0.06* (0.03)
Funding for redevelopment authority (per capita, logged)	0.10** (0.03)	0.05** (0.01)	0.08* (0.03)
Former air base or shipyard	0.12* (0.06)	0.15** (0.02)	0.03 (0.02)
Environmental-remediation costs (per capita, logged)	−0.19** (0.01)	−0.10** (0.02)	−0.23* (0.10)
Per capita gross local product (by county, logged)	0.24** (0.03)	0.15** (0.01)	0.31* (0.14)
Late BRAC round	0.10 (0.07)	0.14 (0.16)	−0.19 (0.11)
MSA within county	0.35** (0.10)	0.27** (0.08)	0.14* (0.06)
Size of the base (square miles, logged)	0.15 (0.12)	0.07 (0.05)	−0.10 (0.08)
Constant	0.72* (0.29)	0.30* (0.12)	0.34 (0.19)
Number of bases	122	122	122
R^2	0.73	0.65	0.53

Note: Standard errors in parentheses are robust. *p < .05; **p < .01.

Different aspects of redevelopment governance, funding, environmental remediation, and market conditions influence revenue and bond ratings. Importantly, many of the factors that are not statistically connected to job creation do have strong connections to these areas. In particular, measures of collaborative governance and how redevelopment arrangements are structured both explain city revenue and bond ratings in redevelopment. Negotiations surrounding base conveyance and redevelopment plans often showcase political bargaining and interaction across federal, state, and local levels of government. Whether federal, state, and local governments provide support in terms of direct capital that a government agency transfers to the local redevelopment authority is essential for understanding redevelopment performance. State and federal agency support may advance defense conversion by mitigating high redevelopment costs, the challenges of securing long-term funding, and the loss of local revenue following base closures. For instance, environmental rehabilitation is expensive, and nearly all bases feature at least some contaminated land. The resources of the DoD and other federal agencies, such as the EPA, are essential for local communities that place housing developments, commercial centers, and parks on their former bases. Furthermore, navigating the regulatory environment to reuse land and integrate it into the community requires federal and state expertise because many communities lack the experience and resources to devote to the effort after bases close and local government revenues fall.

Conversion for Whom?

Revenue generation and financial solvency provide communities with the opportunity to extend services to residents and to improve quality of life following base closures. Jobs and revenue tend to follow examples of broad defense conversion, such as San Francisco's Presidio or the Brooklyn Navy Yard, but converting former bases can easily take thirty years or more. In that sense, jobs and revenue generation represent redevelopment indicators that might appear in the data only after decades of redevelopment efforts. Furthermore, public officials are not always motivated to use replaced revenue from converted bases to increase residents' quality of life. The results of defense conversion deliver concentrated benefits to private firms in many cases and may leave residents no better off than if redevelopment had not occurred. Whether defense conversion benefits broad groups of community stakeholders rather than simply jobs, revenue, and bond ratings is just as important—maybe more so.

Military bases function as large communities with residential areas, commercial sites, and extensive public services such as education and health care. Recreational opportunities through parks and open spaces also contribute to residents' quality of life while bases are still open. Military communities on active bases are often isolated from the surrounding population, but converting and integrating the bases following closure can be critical for serving remaining residents. Evaluating environmental remediation, the presence of public housing, and the set of stakeholders that benefit from defense conversion through land use on the former base is important for communities and reflects equitable, sustainable defense conversion.

The percentage of the base that is transferred at a certain time is also a key indicator for how the redevelopment process is progressing because land must pass from the military to another entity before conversion can occur. Conveying land does not mean that it will be redeveloped in a way that represents the highest and best use of the former site or redeveloped at all. Yet transferred land does mean that conversion projects have advanced beyond the planning stage or will advance in the future.[13]

The percentage of the environmental cleanup that has been completed is another indicator of redevelopment efforts on former bases as well as whether defense conversion will be viable in the future. Environmental remediation must be completed prior to land conveyance for a given parcel, but cleanup on other portions of the former base may last decades after some parcels have been conveyed and converted.[14] Table 5 presents the results of analysis for environmental-remediation performance in defense conversion.

The types of redevelopment projects that appear on the bases and who uses these sites are also important. The data set records the projects that are physically present on each former military site, such as a private shipyard, a public park, a commercial shopping center, a nonprofit organization's headquarters, and private housing. Then we categorize these projects as one of the following land uses: residential, commercial, industrial, institutional, recreational, and airport. This approach fosters a general understanding of the ways that communities use former military land.

TABLE 5. Multinomial logit model of environmental-cleanup completion and land transferred in former military communities, through 2015

Independent variables	Dependent variables		
	Environmental cleanup complete	Odds ratio of cleanup completion	Percentage of land transferred
Funding across scale	0.29* (0.10)	1.31*	0.37** (0.09)
Number of public/ private/nonprofit collaborators	0.09* (0.04)	1.01*	0.06* (0.03)
Funding for redevelopment authority (per capita, logged)	0.14** (0.01)	1.08**	0.11* (0.04)
Former air base or shipyard	−0.22* (0.10)	0.83*	0.25 (0.18)
Environmental-remediation costs (per capita, logged)	−0.68** (0.09)	0.27*	−0.41** (0.01)
Per capita gross local product (by county, logged)	0.26** (0.01)	1.26**	0.14** (0.04)
Late BRAC round	0.21 (0.24)	1.13	−0.27 (0.20)
MSA within county	0.18 (0.22)	1.08	0.22 (0.16)
Size of the base (square miles, logged)	−0.18 (0.12)	0.87	−0.19 (0.14)
Constant	0.24 (0.20)		0.52* (0.12)
Number of bases	122	122	122
Pseudo R^2	0.68		0.60

Note: Standard errors in parentheses are robust. *p < .05; **p < .01.

This information also offers a valuable point of departure for evaluating smaller categories or project-specific endeavors such as parks or museums on former military sites. Simultaneously, evaluating land use highlights conversion trends for all former military bases, not just for a few specific sites that may not accurately represent the broader experience of military base redevelopment.

Information on land use following defense conversion leads us to construct an index of the breadth of beneficiaries that conversion serves. The index is scaled from 1 to 5, which reflects the breadth of land-use categories described above (residential, commercial, industrial, institutional, recreational, and airport).[15] A score of 1 describes narrow conversion, where only one type of land use appears on the former base. These types of projects may be very important to the city-region in terms of jobs and revenue, such as with a large industrial park. However, they do not serve a broad group of stakeholders directly and do not foster sustainable, equitable redevelopment (Imbroscio 2012; Williamson et al. 2002). Similarly, a score of 2 or 3 reflects complementary projects that can serve as the foundation for economic clustering. For example, an industrial park and a port facility foster market access for manufactured goods and additional commercial traffic for the port. These uses might be sensible from a reuse perspective because they attract jobs and revenue to the city-region. Nevertheless, they do not create the sense of place and community that a score of 4 or 5 reflects.

Former bases receiving scores of 4 and 5 resemble master-planned communities within an urban setting if sufficient funding, resources, and other opportunities to pursue these types of conversion are available. This is because defense conversion for these bases includes a mixture of residential, commercial, institutional, and industrial uses that serve a broad population, provide income for the region, and offer revenue for the city; in short, these types of conversion serve many functions following redevelopment that resemble those the bases served while operational. Former bases scoring fours and fives on our conversion index now have homes, stores, schools, hospitals, parks, and job opportunities; even industrial uses commonly appear in conjunction with a wide variety of other uses on physically large sites. However, many communities are well aware of their limited resources, expertise, and/or market conditions, and probably do not pursue extensive conversion in the first place because of the low chance of completion. Instead, many former defense communities pursue options with a lower price tag and a greater chance of completion. What communities may have tried and failed to accomplish in defense conversion across the entire spectrum of bases shuttered since 1988 is unknown. Yet the database does take stock of what appears on the former base in 2016 and who it benefits through our conversion index.[16] Table 6 explains variation in overall scores for equitable redevelopment in defense conversion.

TABLE 6. Ordered logit model of defense conversion scale in former military communities, through 2015

Independent variables	Dependent variable
	Defense conversion score
Funding across scale	0.53**
	(0.17)
Number of public/private/nonprofit collaborators	0.21**
	(0.04)
Funding for redevelopment authority (per capita, logged)	0.36**
	(0.07)
Former air base or shipyard	−1.20*
	(0.51)
Environmental-remediation costs (per capita, logged)	−0.56*
	(0.29)
Per capita gross local product (by county, logged)	0.33**
	(0.02)
Late BRAC round	−0.19
	(0.16)
MSA within county	0.48*
	(0.21)
Size of the base (square miles, logged)	0.29
	(0.25)
Constant	1.24
	(1.03)
Number of bases	122
Pseudo R^2	0.75

Note: Standard errors in parentheses are robust. *$p < .05$; **$p < .01$.

The relative presence of low-income housing on a base is another way to determine the extent to which defense conversion benefits a specific, vulnerable population. Explaining variation in low-income housing assesses the argument that conversion privileges real estate developers, well-positioned industrial or retail firms, and wealthy residents but leaves marginalized populations behind. Commercial developers often resist low-income housing on former bases because it lowers their profits, both from the sales or rental of the low-income units and the decreased value of market-price units. Residents in need of low-income housing also have relatively quiet political voices compared to commercial real estate developers and residents with higher incomes. Advocates for low-income housing therefore face a challenging path to using base conversion to expand city-regional options for low-income residents. Yet offering housing for all residents, not just those with high incomes, is part of equitable, sustainable redevelopment (Saegert et al. 2009; Fields 2015). The presence of low-income housing on a former base therefore serves as a proxy for whether defense conversion incorporates one of the former defense communities' most marginalized populations. Twenty-four percent of former bases feature at least some low-income housing as part of their conversion. Table 7 explains variation in low-income housing that appears on converted military bases.

TABLE 7. Multinomial logit model of low-income housing in former military communities, through 2015

Independent variables	Dependent variables	
	Low-income housing on former bases	Odds ratio for having low-income housing
Funding across scale	0.57** (0.04)	1.44**
Number of public/private/ nonprofit collaborators	0.06* (0.03)	1.01*
Funding for redevelopment authority (per capita, logged)	0.18** (0.02)	1.13**
Former air base or shipyard	−0.45** (0.11)	0.58**
Environmental-remediation costs (per capita, logged)	−0.32* (0.14)	0.74*
Per capita gross local product (by county, logged)	0.36** (0.01)	1.04**
Late BRAC round	−0.10 (0.15)	0.98
MSA within county	0.38** (0.09)	1.23**
Size of the base (square miles, logged)	0.26 (0.21)	1.11
Constant	0.31 (0.37)	
Number of bases	122	122
Pseudo R^2	0.55	

Note: Standard errors in parentheses are robust. *p < .05; **p < .01.

Explaining Defense Conversion with Community Benefits

Local revenue and fiscal health, environmental cleanup, and defense conversion for broad groups of stakeholders are elements of redevelopment
success that may be more important than job creation alone. Remaining
residents benefit greatly from redevelopment that extends community services and spreads access to benefits from defense conversion. Additionally, equitable redevelopment and long-term community health are much
more likely to stem from redevelopment with broad community benefits
than from narrow redevelopment that concentrates benefits in a few private hands. From this perspective, it is possible to replace jobs following
base closures without achieving broad community benefits through defense conversion. However, realizing some benefits from defense conversion is better than realizing none if conversion on former bases stagnates
and a former base drains community resources.

The bottom line in converting closed bases is that there is no perfect
solution bringing all benefits to all stakeholders. However, limited, concentrated redevelopment benefits are still inferior to outcomes that benefit broad groups. A full discussion of the results of quantitative analysis
explaining military redevelopment outcomes follows below. These results
open the doors for community agency in governance for achieving beneficial community outcomes through defense conversion. The models
demonstrate that the highest redevelopment performance occurs in the
presence of strong governance and underlying economic and environmental conditions. These areas each influence redevelopment performance in-
dependently of one another. However, they are stronger together when
governance serves as a vehicle to assess former defense sites, plan for
conversion, implement redevelopment projects, and navigate challenges
to sustain projects over time. Local economic conditions fuel the vehicle,
in large respect, and therefore provide some limits on the redevelopment
distance that communities can travel.

Local Conditions Fuel Redevelopment

Economic productivity is critical for explaining redevelopment outcomes.
Moving from mean local GDP per capita to one standard deviation above
the mean is associated with an estimated 28 percent increase in replacing

lost jobs, a 35 percent increase in replacing lost revenue, a 40 percent increase in having a AA bond rating or higher, an 18 percent increase in the likelihood of completing environmental cleanup, and a 21 percent increase in the percentage of land transferred. More economically productive communities are 17 percent more likely to have low-income housing on the former base and exhibit 22 percent greater defense conversion index scores than are less productive communities. Communities that are more economically productive are also attractive to investors because of existing infrastructure, access to human capital, and (often) stronger market conditions than in less productive areas. The result is that communities that are more productive have more resources to bring to bear on redeveloping closed bases and that investors will find these communities attractive. In turn, communities' abilities to clean up their former bases and prepare them for mixed-use redevelopment for a broad set of stakeholders is greater in economically productive communities. This finding is in keeping with expectations about redevelopment in general: communities with greater economic output likely have stronger market conditions and more resources than less productive communities (Pastor and Benner 2008). Furthermore, more productive communities may have greater access to planning resources, on average. These communities may therefore be better able to govern the redevelopment process in a way that completes plans and directs benefits toward a wide variety of stakeholders than those with fewer resources.

The results of analysis provide support for the possibility that less affluent communities may pursue less comprehensive defense conversion. Isolated projects may meet poorer areas' specific needs more often than the varied but less imperative needs of more affluent areas. For instance, a poorer community may seek a hospital or an airport before adding parks, housing, or even more jobs through commercial development on former bases. Furthermore, it may be easier to fund an isolated project addressing a direct community need in areas with a relatively small tax base that usually contracts following the loss of military jobs. In contrast, communities with stronger market conditions are not as likely to be so heavily dependent on the taxes that military families pay because of other, nonmilitary employers that remain in the area.

Next, the models demonstrate the influence of environmental-remediation costs on redevelopment outcomes. Moving from the mean cost of environmental remediation—already high at $88 million—to one standard deviation above the mean results in an estimated 23 percent fewer jobs, 27 percent less replacement revenue, an 81 percent decrease in the odds of having completed the cleanup, a 64 percent decrease in land transferred, and a 38 percent decrease in defense conversion for broad groups of stakeholders. The higher the cleanup costs on the former base, the less likely mixed-use redevelopment, or any redevelopment at all, will occur over the time frame of the study. This reflects environmental remediation as one of the largest barriers to redevelopment, from jobs, to revenue, to equitable conversion. The results surrounding environmental remediation are also consistent with Hansen (2004) and other redevelopment research on contamination (Fitzgerald and Leigh 2002; Bagaeen 2006; U.S. GAO 2007b): environmental hazards make residential, institutional (parks, schools, museums), and commercial redevelopment difficult to achieve because of high cleanup costs and the length of remediation. Instead of broad conversion, communities are likely to redevelop environmentally damaged sites as isolated industrial projects or airports because these land uses are relatively less sensitive to the hazards nearby than are other types of projects.

The former base community's location in an MSA also influences redevelopment outcomes. Location within an MSA increases replaced jobs by 16 percent, local revenue by 53 percent, and the odds of having AA bond ratings or better by 37 percent, on average. Location in an MSA increases the odds of low-income housing appearing on the former base by 23 percent and improves performance on the defense conversion index by 26 percent. These results reflect the metropolitan communities' resilience relative to more isolated communities.

Communities in an MSA are attractive for investors from the perspective of existing infrastructure, access to human capital, and (often) stronger market conditions than in rural areas. This reflects differences among urban, suburban, and rural development in general (Newburn and Berck 2006; Fulton et al. 2001; Theobald 2001; Cowan 2012). Yet urban redevelopment projects do not feature faster environmental cleanups or overall land transfers. This speaks to a paradox of centrality, where urban bases are physically central but are not necessarily any easier to integrate into the surrounding city-region than are nonurban bases. Per capita GDP is higher in urban areas than suburban or rural areas in the data set, and financing cleanup and conversion might be easier in urban areas. Nevertheless, former military parcels still carry serious challenges for urban communities: they do not represent a gift to the urban city-regions where strong market conditions might have convinced some observers that redevelopment would be easy.

Governance as Redevelopment Vehicle

Collaborative governance across federal, state, and local scales is associated with high levels of revenue, high bond ratings, better odds for completing environmental remediation, and conversion for broad sets of beneficiaries. Having federal and state government funding partners increases the estimated percentage of local revenue relative to pre-closure levels by 33 percent. It increases the likelihood of having a AA or greater bond rating by 15 percent, of having completed the environmental cleanup by 31 percent, and the percentage of land transferred by 27 percent. It also increases the odds of low-income housing appearing on a former base by 44 percent, and it raises scores on the conversion scale by 39 percent, on average. These results demonstrate the importance of governance at scale for several critical redevelopment outcomes. Funding and collaboration beyond the local level dramatically improve the odds of sustainable, equitable redevelopment projects on former bases.

The models show how multiple funding partners in the private and nonprofit sector are also associated with redevelopment outcomes. We estimate that municipal revenue increases by approximately 2 percent, on average, with each additional funding partner in the public, private, and nonprofit sectors. The likelihood of completing environmental remediation increases by 1 percent per funding partner, as does the probability of low-income housing appearing on the base. Scores on the defense conversion scale increase by 4 percent per partner, all else equal.

Funding the redevelopment authority to govern relationships between funding partners and regulatory authorities is also crucial for redevelopment success. Greater funding reflects greater capacity and expertise to navigate complex redevelopment governance across vertical and horizontal scales (local, regional, state, national-level partners/authorities) and across public, private, and nonprofit sectors. We estimate that moving from the mean level of redevelopment authority funding in the data set to one standard deviation above the mean is associated with a 15 percent increase in local revenue, a 31 percent greater chance of completing environmental cleanup, and a 28 percent increase in the percentage of land transferred. Funding the redevelopment authority at relatively high levels is associated with a 23 percent greater chance of having low-income housing and a 34 percent improvement in community scores on the defense conversion scale.[17]

The results above show that the complex, expensive nature of converting former bases in a way that benefits broad segments of society requires considerable expertise and funding from outside the community. This result is consistent with general development scholarship as well and provides justification for the attention many scholars now pay to the institutional geography of development and redevelopment (U.S. GAO 2010; Hansen 2004; Kosla 2010; Kirkpatrick and Smith 2011; Agnew 2016a; Cox 2013; Ward and Jonas 2004). Similarly, it is likely that communities with multiple, vocal stakeholders across different sectors generate different redevelopment plans with more stakeholders in mind than communities with just one powerful group in the first place, particularly because more dialogue is likely to occur around denser, mixed-use projects that are near population and employment centers. Strong governance thus harnesses available resources to achieve communities' redevelopment visions, although its presence alone is not associated with the strongest levels of redevelopment performance; we estimate that communities featuring strong economic conditions and low environmental-remediation costs are likelier to achieve strong redevelopment outcomes, on average.[18]

Several variables are not statistically connected to defense conversion outcomes in the data. Bases that closed in early BRAC rounds do no better, on average, at replacing lost revenue and achieving fiscal health, completing environmental cleanup, building low-income housing, and achieving equitable defense conversion than those that closed in the most recent (2005) round. This is somewhat surprising considering the shift in redevelopment trends across the country over the last twenty years and the possibility that bases selected for early closure rounds were chosen for ease of conversion (Greenbaum 2004; Greenbaum and Bondonio 2004). However, the lack of results in these areas suggests only that military base redevelopment is not influenced by national redevelopment trends as much as by other factors such as market conditions, the costs of environmental rehabilitation, and redevelopment governance. The same argument holds for the lack of connection between the size of a former base's physical footprint and the outcomes we observe on converted bases: large bases are not systematically different from small bases in this area, even though large bases have more room to host more redevelopment projects. Again, this is unexpected because land area is usually part of the traditional development process for site and project selection. The lack of statistical relationships in this area provide additional evidence that other factors such as market conditions, the costs of environmental rehabilitation, and redevelopment governance best explain defense conversion outcomes.

Interactive Effects

Job creation, revenue generation and fiscal health, and equitable, sustainable defense conversion represent related but distinctive measures of redevelopment performance. Jobs and revenue are correlated at 0.68, which reflects a strong, positive connection between the two. Jobs and the conversion scale are correlated at 0.41, a moderately positive connection. This suggests that the number of jobs replaced through conversion and the distribution of benefits from conversion are related but that communities can replace jobs without distributing benefits from conversion broadly. Similarly, communities can convert bases in a way that spreads benefits across many different stakeholders while creating only a few jobs. Table 8 presents the results of analysis for job replacement, revenue generation, and distinct beneficiaries of defense conversion.

Revenue generation is closely connected with the conversion scale, with a correlation of 0.64. In this sense, conversion with a diverse set of beneficiaries is associated with higher levels of revenue, and city-regions with greater revenue tend to achieve conversion for more-diverse stakeholders. We do not use dependent variables in one regression as independent variables in the others because of the multi-collinear nature of their relationship with the other independent variables. However, the moderate to high correlations across some dependent variables suggest that job creation and revenue generation both buttress equitable, sustainable defense

TABLE 8. Models of job replacement, local revenue, and beneficiaries of defense conversion in former military communities, 2015

Independent variables	Dependent variables		
	Job replacement	2015 revenue as a percent of pre-closure revenue	Beneficiaries of defense conversion
Beneficiaries of defense conversion	0.18** (0.04)	0.26** (0.01)	
Job replacement		0.04** (0.01)	0.38** (0.15)
Revenue generation	0.02* (0.01)		0.03** (0.01)
Number of bases	122	122	122
R^2	0.40	0.42	0.54

Note: Standard errors in parentheses are robust. *p < .05; **p < .01.

conversion, and vice versa. Bivariate regressions in Table 8 demonstrate that these outcomes are mutually constitutive in some senses. Job creation and revenue generation in the past (any given time$_{t-5}$ in the data) are strongly associated with the breadth of defense conversion in the present (time$_t$). Defense conversion scores at time$_{t-2}$ are also associated with 2015 jobs and revenue, but the magnitude of the relationship is not as great. Far from being mutually exclusive, the analysis provides evidence that jobs, revenue, and defense conversion for multiple stakeholders can begin a virtuous circle of community benefits as each area begets increases in the other over time.

Communities govern defense conversion, and collaborative governance structures play an extremely important role in redevelopment. However, governance alone will not replace jobs and revenue or maintain a city's bond rating at high levels. Instead, agency in governance offers opportunities to improve outcomes, on average. Communities with governance at scale and across the public/private/nonprofit divide enjoy superior redevelopment outcomes than those communities that do not govern defense conversion as comprehensively, all else equal. Former defense communities with strong economic conditions and low remediation costs may enjoy excellent redevelopment outcomes without strong governance; the odds of strong redevelopment performance are high under such circumstances. However, these communities *perform better still* with collaborative governance.

Economic and environmental conditions also influence defense conversion performance. This result is not surprising but may discourage communities because it is difficult or impossible to alter the amount of environmental remediation necessary to prepare a site for conversion, the level of economic productivity in a community, or a community's proximity to metropolitan areas. Yet communities have considerable agency in how they design, implement, and oversee defense conversion. Communities can thus potentially anticipate many of the challenges associated with defense conversion and exercise this agency to achieve more-equitable, sustainable outcomes, even though they cannot control their economic, environmental, or geographic circumstances. Who partners with the city and how these partnerships function are two additional areas where communities have some agency. The extent to which communities use this agency to build a redevelopment coalition goes far to explain how communities pursue redevelopment, the degree to which they convert former military bases, and who benefits from this conversion. Good governance can overcome poor market conditions and the costs of environmental remediation in terms of replacing revenue and converting former defense liabilities to assets that serve broad groups of stakeholders.

3

PLANNING FOR TRANSFORMATION

The Folly of Best Practices in Redevelopment

Base closures are community and regional planning crises. The three California cases show how these closures are also examples of how governance works, and doesn't, for ordinary cities in extraordinary regions. Ideally, public planning could reform fragmented communities and implement conversion strategies to extract the most community benefits from defense conversion. Communities would not only be able to replace base activity in this scenario but could also leverage the former base in ways that were previously impossible because of the constraints of military operations. The base conversion experience and the negotiation of community benefits around redevelopment reflect the unique planning culture of each former defense community as part of its collaborative governance structure.

No single pathway to conversion exists for former defense sites. Rather, each community and its embedded region embody their own historical narrative, cultural context, and economic circumstances. These fundamental conditions set the stage for defense conversion and determine the broad realm of redevelopment possibilities. Traditional explanations of conversion outcomes focus on economic markets and demographic shifts. However, conversion experiences also differ along the primary dimensions of collaborative governance, which greatly influence conveyance fortunes. Collaborative governance greatly influences the ability to navigate the regulatory context of defense conversion, which changes over time. Fortunately, former defense communities do have considerable agency in creating governance arrangements and thus the potential to improve conversion outcomes by focusing on this area. Collaborative governance is not a panacea, but such governance approaches improve conversion outcomes and boost communities' outcomes above where they might otherwise be relative to the state of the former base and local economic conditions. Weak governance does the opposite and lowers the redevelopment ceiling relative to where it otherwise might have been.

We caution against the impulse to pursue best-practices approaches to conversion. Such truncated but prevalent wisdom is misguided and naively assumes that conversion success can be copied from one specific place and time and pasted on another. As Dreier and colleagues (2004) convincingly note, *place matters*. Context building is key for defense conversion and reinforces the need for robust comparative case studies that showcase a spectrum of experiences. Different aspects of planning cultures and history in each of the three California cases contribute to many different conversion processes and help us both explain and question what quantitative analyses of national trends suggest. The remainder of the book therefore explores planning history and culture on each base rather than isolating this theme in a single chapter.

Connecting Planning and Governance

Conversations with stakeholders in former defense communities and analysis of public documents showcase important connections between planning and collaborative governance as well as missed opportunities to link the two areas. Disaggregating governance to the municipal-department level places a greater focus on planners' roles. Some researchers treat planning as increasingly political and encourage soft skills of negotiation and agenda setting to generate desirable outcomes. Others treat planners as ineffectual and incapable of shaping broader governing forces. In contrast, planners may be at the mercy of elected officials or entrenched bureaucratic systems and engage in an "esoteric activity of a professional elite" (Long 2010, 167). Both extremes show how scholars of urban development and redevelopment grapple with planning's potential for varied impacts on local, regional, and state governance. For example, planners exert greater influence over regional infrastructure problems, such as transportation, and lesser influence over localized problems outside of land use and development, such as hiring practices in education. Planning thus serves as both a willing and contested conduit for collaborative governance. Moreover, explaining defense conversion requires expanding the traditional concept of governance to include planning's critical role for laying a redevelopment foundation.

In reality, defense conversion is about creating places that become community assets. Place making emphasizes four primary goals: governance, economic rebound, environmental well-being, and equity (Imbroscio 2012). Governance greatly influences these goals because it determines who gets what, when, where, and how in defense conversion. But connecting governance to planning and defense conversion represents a significant departure from how most contemporary planners view and pursue place making. However, this expansive view of the role of governance in planning allows us to incorporate power dynamics in the city-region and better explain conversion and reuse outcomes on former military bases.

This chapter provides the case-centric framework and contextual background necessary for understanding subsequent chapters on governance, integration, and financing. In so doing, it highlights the complex planning processes resulting from a combination of federal, state, and local policy regulations as well as a diverse mix of internal and external actors. Planning processes include an evolving collection of public, private, and community stakeholders who negotiate conversion based on individual interests. These actors pursue a variety of outcomes through defense conversion planning. Some of these outcomes may be in the interest of constituent publics, but many are not, and not all actors share all goals. It is clear that planning does not represent an orchestrated, uniform act by monolithic and public agencies or a set of professional public-sector planners. Instead, planning defense conversion serves as an expansive arena for pursuing a variety of interests, some more conducive to redevelopment with community benefits than others. It is particularly important to note, then, that different constituencies pursue different ends in defense conversion.

Conversion Planning Challenges

The challenges of planning for defense conversion are immense. Converting bases is akin to reconstructing cities and integrating them with larger, surrounding cities as well as the broader region. Planning these efforts and governing the ensuing processes are not for the faint of heart: defense conversion is often a fifty-year effort fraught with economic constraints. A focus on common, basic planning considerations in this chapter provides a foundation for later discussions of governance, integration, and financing defense conversion that also connect to the planning process. Planning challenges surrounding defense conversion vary significantly from site to site, but governance structures, the state of conveyance, environmental remediation, and the relative completion of conversion plans represent comparable elements in each of the three cases. Base redevelopment presents serious planning challenges, but communities can select strategies to overcome these challenges. However, successful strategies reflect the unique characteristics of each community and region.

One of the most enduring critiques in planning theory is that comprehensive or rational planning is inconsequential because redevelopment plans are so rarely implemented. Many redevelopment administrators point to dozens of plans and the high hurdles associated with providing community benefits through traditional, long-range planning. Long-range plans end up as nothing more than cumbersome, inflexible, planning artifacts in most former defense communities. In contrast, critics of traditional planning practices highlight the imperative of incrementalism and pragmatic planning approaches to respond to market forces, changing political dynamics, and evolving sociocultural practices. Yet the pragmatic push to value adaptability and flexibility in planning theory may allow "the gap to close between being right and doing good" (Hoch 1984, 335). Malleable planning theory does not translate well to practice because of the uneven distribution of local and regional power. Incremental plans are vulnerable to interest-group capture and general dilution, even if they do result in higher completion rates because of their ability to respond to changing circumstances.

Base conversion experiences demonstrate both pros and cons of adaptable short-term planning strategies as well as more idealistic long-range planning. Long-range plans often represent broader community interests and are a reminder of collective ideals, but they rarely take market realities into account and are not often updated to reflect changing interests. Incremental planning is adaptive, flexible, and parallels regular bureaucratic decisions that account for changing market conditions; however, incremental planning also favors private interests and well-resourced individuals and organizations. A planning approach that unites adaptability with long-term goals offers a realistic but hopeful path toward defense conversion and reuse. Here, even the best of plans do not achieve full implementation because of the exceptionally long-term nature of the redevelopment process. Instead, plans act predominantly as guides rather than prescriptions and can protect communities against private-sector capture in implementation.

Base redevelopment magnifies communities' planning philosophies. The immense size of the mothballed bases, the complex governance network of competing interests, and the significant economic and environmental challenges of conversion all put planning under a local microscope. Many communities require thirty to fifty years to fully convert and redevelop their bases. Grand expectations confront the desire for quick successes, which snarls planning processes because of powerful political interests. For example, politicians' short-term electoral time horizons can make long-term political decisions difficult. The result can be stagnant conversion where planners create long-term redevelopment pathways that are too ossified to also encompass short-term political needs for quick successes. Thus, expectations for incrementalism and flexibility are essential for planning defense conversion. Yet disjointed incrementalism is also common in planning defense conversion, and a lack of transparency and accountability accompanies such practices. For example, many incremental conversion plans ignore or only indirectly touch on the challenges of negotiating different public interests. Because of loopholes and lack of specificity in development contracts, master-developer deals are prone to increment-creep away from public interests.

A balance between long-term and short-term planning philosophies is necessary for converting bases. Plans should be flexible and continually renegotiated because of many different economic, political, social, and environmental factors that influence outcomes. However, those renegotiations should also focus on end users and public beneficiaries over the long term to limit private-sector influence and potential capture. For example, the Fort Ord redevelopment plan changed based on renegotiations as more information became available and community preferences became clearer: "The community valued environmental protection as part of the California legacy. [Leon] Panetta was very good at sizing up what the public wanted and then achieving it. He was a big part of Monterey Bay Sanctuary. When I was on the Board of Supervisors, he initially didn't want a big sanctuary, but we beat him up, and he responded when people made it clear that they wanted it. That's my idea of a good representative," said Gary Patton, former executive director of LandWatch Monterey County (2013).

Negotiating Defense Conversion

Negotiation is a central element of any redevelopment process, and defense conversion requires highly complex and diverse deal making that is almost unintelligible to the layperson. Negotiation occurs around land-use mix, replacement industries and economic activity, site and land remediation, public-private partnership selection, and many other aspects of deal making. Give-and-take surrounding defense conversion planning is not an isolated event but is ongoing given the task of comprehensive site conversion that encompasses "mini-cities" rather than a single site, a district, or small-scale, mixed-use projects. It therefore requires strong, collaborative governance and leads to several important questions: How do community members know they are getting a good deal? How is risk distributed? What public goods are being delivered and at what cost? Who gets to be a part of the deal-making process? How do communities select the best option? This is especially controversial because "communities" means different things to different people. Differences in what constitutes community influence who is included in conversion processes as well as the desirability of outcomes. These issues are difficult to address in broad, generalizable terms because of each community's distinct context and goals. However, focusing on community negotiations in specific contexts illuminates many of the issues above in a more tangible way.

Negotiating defense conversion in California provides some answers to questions of value, risk, and distribution of redevelopment benefits to various publics. The California experience highlights two central preservation conflicts: open-space demands for environmental preservation and values around memory and historic preservation. Conflicts around open-space demands are common in planning and take on new forms in defense conversion. Conflicts not only stress the bases' aesthetic location along a waterfront or near another protected open-space area. Rather, the negotiation of defense conversion plans also speaks to an ongoing discussion about whether a publicly funded base should become a privatized redevelopment project. How different groups conceive of and prioritize public space and public goods thus informs their preferences surrounding adaptive reuse.

The question of what public space entails is a particularly controversial issue in preservation, an area that is often overlooked in planning and urban development. Public memory or memories of former bases encompass many different users and uses: base members and their families formerly stationed on the site, local citizens who lived nearby and visited the base, military visitors, and more. Many bases preserve these users' memories by employing traditional preservation strategies, including monuments, signage, and tours. But other community members also seek to preserve bases' open space, the public nature of these bases, and their physical infrastructure as memorials. Different interest groups espouse these different preservation values, which different policies and processes support. The planning and place-making question remains: what do we preserve, whose preservation ideas win out, and how do we negotiate these different memories? The way that the planning process incorporates these interests determines how communities answer the previous questions.

Conversion on all three California cases included contestation over public land and place-making priorities. Open-space proponents fought hard to prevent redevelopment for private interests and to protect Fort Ord's Monterey Bay waterfront. NTC San Diego contested several lawsuits over what public buildings should be protected, how much open

space should be made public, and how to keep as much of the base as protected as possible. LandWatch Monterey, a planning watchdog group, regularly made its redevelopment objections and suggestions public through
its website, mobilized local support, and pressured local officials to tailor
plans to LandWatch's perception of the Fort Ord region's environmental
needs. In Alameda there was significant debate about how to clean up the
polluted water near the base so that it could be used for public transportation and parkland. Nearby, Crown Beach users and the county have raised
concerns about the potential point-source contaminants from Alameda
NAS in local waters (Davis 2007).

The three California cases also highlight issues of power and territory.
Place-making scholars sharply criticize the planning process for favoring
certain well-funded groups and organizations over low-income residents
and community groups. These concerns also align with evidence on defense conversion and reuse. Many interest groups called for equitable
development in the face of what they perceived as practices that favored
developers. As with most planning processes, formal public participation is part of planning defense conversion and offers opportunities to
address questions surrounding the beneficiaries of redevelopment. However, formal planning documents do not refer to equitable development
as a planning priority or community value. According to Patton, "The
base reuse plan has fundamentally failed. The group as a whole didn't
discipline. It was horse trading. It was a failure of planning. It was a real
estate–based economic development plan. But what I remember thinking
about was that Seaside was going to get this. Even Delray Oaks is going
to get something. Monterey got a little something. The county got the
biggest single local government share. Marina got a share like the barracks, which is a net loss. There was a landgrab mentality in order to
make this all work" (2013). Community members therefore justifiably
question the extent to which defense conversion serves public, place-
making interests or simply functions as corporate welfare for real estate
developers.

Planning for Interim Uses

The long-term nature of base redevelopment also creates challenges in
the interim between closure and conversion. Several different vacancy

periods mark defense conversion: the abrupt or phased federal with-drawal, the lengthy planning process, the ebbs and flows of markets, the glacially slow process of environmental bargaining and remediation, and changing public policies at each level all foster differentiated con-veyance timetables for parcels on former bases. Many of the bases have therefore experimented with temporary uses to generate revenue and serve publics while awaiting full conveyance to set permanent conver-sion plans in motion. Yet these temporary uses are not always perceived as temporary uses or as "pop-ups" as planning and urban studies liter-ature describes (Ashley 2015). Temporary uses on former bases are an-chored to conversion projects for decades, they require at least some infrastructure support, they become identity markers for these bases, and they are also innovation engines for small business and local eco-nomic development.

Alameda relies on a wide variety of temporary tenants, including those manufacturing racing boats or producing beer, wine, and spirits to attract tourists and generate revenue. Additionally, these tenants help prevent some deterioration of the site caused by vacancy while waiting for various governmental entities to arrange financing and address plan-ning challenges. However, governing these temporary uses requires deft skills and a combination of short- and long-term visions. Alameda did not fully promote temporary uses or serve as their allies in transform-ing temporary uses into permanent conversion. Jennifer Ott, director of Base Reuse and chief operating officer for Alameda Point, elaborates: "Temporary uses were a huge benefit to us, but we're hesitant to do long-term leases. No one is going to spend money without a long-term lease, and so the buildings deteriorate. We don't do a lot for tenants like give them tenant improvement allowances. It was our own policy deci-sion" (2013).

Temporary uses thus provide benefits in spite of Alameda's preferences, not because of them. Nevertheless, nimble communities can benefit from temporary uses and should consider how to govern them based on what temporary uses they want, how these uses further local conversion ambi-tions, whether short-term uses are compatible with site characteristics and site quality, how to incentivize deals conducive to community benefits, whether local infrastructure and marketing capacity can support these activities, and what a transition strategy from temporary to permanent use might entail. Incorporating temporary uses into local planning culture may be challenging, but temporary uses offer potential payoffs not seen on most former defense sites.

Planning Cultures and Case-Study Context

The three California bases all closed in the 1990s, which is when more than three-quarters of all installations closed under the national BRAC framework. The cases are representative of the broader pool of base closures under BRAC from a temporal standpoint. Bases closing in the earlier BRAC rounds have now had up to twenty-five years' worth of redevelopment planning, governance, and redevelopment outcomes against which to gauge their performance. Yet the conversion experience in the three cases is not meant to be representative of all bases closed under BRAC, as discussed in the introduction. It is unlikely that the three cases will be fully representative of defense conversion experiences in communities where bases close in the future. Such communities will face many new challenges, and the specific political, economic, and social contexts in which communities will face these challenges are unknown. However, the long-term redevelopment process will still include governance challenges in many areas that are common across almost all former defense communities—for example, land conveyance, environmental remediation, and financing thorough conversions. The three California cases also represent a point of departure for communities with current and future base closures that complements the book's quantitative contribution.

Exploring these three cases uncovers causal mechanisms driving redevelopment processes in wealthy, coastal California, where one might expect defense conversion to proceed smoothly. Yet conversion has been anything but smooth in each case, an outcome stemming more from governance challenges than from local market conditions. Table 9 presents summary data on the structure of how each community governs redevelopment, each community's need for environmental remediation, and the difficulty in conveying land as well as general redevelopment outcomes and costs on each base. The following sections describe how planning processes and governance structures contributed to these redevelopment outcomes.

TABLE 9. Planning authority and redevelopment performance on three former bases: Naval Training Center San Diego, Fort Ord, and Alameda Naval Air Station

	BRAC round	Redevelopment governance	Environmental-remediation needs	Conveyance status	Preservation	Redevelopment outcomes and costs
NTC San Diego	1993	Public-private partnership with master developer	Relatively light contamination and low remediation costs	No-fee conveyance with all land transferred	Historic district with overlapping arts district. Some sight lines and open space preserved.	Mixed-use redevelopment with broad community benefits: $300 million in estimated costs.
Fort Ord	1991	Regional redevelopment authority with formal representation for more than one dozen neighboring communities	Extensive contamination, $100s of millions in remediation costs (remediation is ongoing)	No-fee conveyances, but slow as the extent of contamination became clear.	Open space preserved in large, contaminated parcels. Remediation is ongoing. Few structures preserved.	Partial, mixed-use redevelopment; community benefits surpass expectations; ongoing redevelopment: more than $1 billion in estimated costs.
Alameda NAS	1993	Several failed master-developer partnerships prior to current master-developer arrangement	Superfund site, intermediate levels of contamination. Much less costly than Fort Ord.	Alameda was caught between federal policy shifts: government demands for $110 million stalled conversion.	Historic district preserved, but some preserved sight lines and structures may not remain following redevelopment.	Stalled, mixed-use redevelopment; narrower community benefits; ongoing redevelopment: $150 million in estimated costs.

NTC San Diego

San Diego's conversion of its Naval Training Center was relatively rapid and generated benefits for a relatively broad set of community stakeholders. Mixed-use redevelopment with residential, commercial, educational, and recreational uses—housing, schools, shopping centers, parks, and a historic arts district—represents the high end of the national redevelopment spectrum. Good market conditions, good policy timing, and limited environmental contamination made the redevelopment planning process *relatively* smooth for the NTC, as opposed to Fort Ord and Alameda, where full conversion and outcomes with broad community benefits faced serious challenges and decades-long delays.

The NTC lies entirely within the city of San Diego, but many other horizontal and vertical jurisdictions overlay the site and challenge the city's primacy on redevelopment issues. Disputes between the city and different entities such as San Diego County, citizens' groups, and the California Coastal Commission (CCC) were common. Nevertheless, San Diego's experience reflects *relatively* few barriers to conversion and *relatively* good governance compared to other bases; the city of San Diego and McMillin and Co., the site's single master developer, navigated these governance challenges to achieve redevelopment outcomes that were superior to those at Fort Ord and NAS Alameda.

San Diego has a rich history of military presence and defense investment stemming from Spanish settlement (1769–1821), Mexican possession (1821–1846), and U.S. incorporation (1848–present), as have many California communities. Defense installations emerged across the city and expanded in size and scope from World War I onward. Civic boosters coveted defense investment and partnered with a willing contingent of federal elected officials to encourage a military presence in San Diego. The warm climate, waterfront location, and clustering of different military activities that needed a Pacific base for the manufacturing of defense goods, training of military personnel, and protecting growing international interests attracted military officials situating bases. Figure 2 shows encampments at San Diego NTC, where new recruits stayed during their training in the 1920s, and figure 3 presents an aerial view of NTC San Diego in 1957.

Once an isolated part of San Diego, NTC San Diego increasingly urbanized as the base expanded and urban population and investment grew around it. Today, the former base is located 2.9 miles from downtown San

Figure 2. Tent camps at San Diego NTC for incoming new recruits, 1922. Photo by Amanda Ashley, historical exhibit at Liberty Station, 2014.

Figure 3. Aerial view of NTC San Diego, 1957. Photo by Amanda Ashley, historical exhibit at Liberty Station, 2014.

Diego, sits adjacent to the wealthy Point Loma neighborhood and the San Diego Lindberg International Airport, and is near several other Navy installations. By the early 1990s, NTC spanned 550 acres with 300 buildings and 3 million square feet of space, and contributed $80 million annually to San Diego's economy. As Judy McDonald, a member of the NTC Foundation's Board of Directors and of San Diego's Arts and Culture Board, put it, "NTC was a very important site for San Diegans and for people who came through here. It was a memory builder" (McDonald 2014). Map 3 shows NTC San Diego and other military sites in the greater San Diego area.

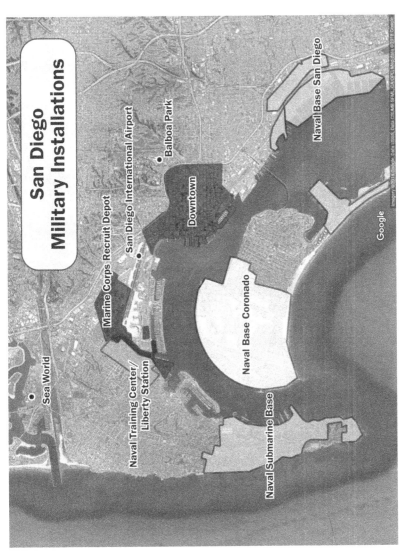

Map 3. Former NTC San Diego and its proximity to other military sites

In 1993 President Clinton approved the closure of the Naval Training Center, much to San Diego's surprise. Many had expected the NTC's strategic and symbolic nature to guarantee continued operations: the base was a favorite of the Navy because of its low cost, central location, and prime Pacific access. Moreover, the NTC was relatively small compared to many other high-profile closures, and featured more manageable environmental contamination. The NTC's closure hit the community hard for symbolic reasons as the base represented the "core of the Navy's presence in San Diego, making it seem as if the sky was falling" (Raffesberger 2013, 1). The decommissioning process occurred over a four-year period until 1997, two years earlier than anticipated, by which time the base represented a ghost town filled with "weeds, feral cats, and an eerie vacantness" (Raffesberger 2013, 1).

Public officials debated how to convert and reuse the site for several years. Planning governance took the form of the city as designated lead redevelopment authority (LRA), although San Diego's redevelopment agency, with the City Council as its board of directors, authorized the Development Disposition Agreement (DDA). San Diego's redevelopment authority then took the lead on planning and visioning. Mayor Susan Golding formed the twenty-seven-member NTC Reuse Planning Committee in 1993 to formulate recommendations for site reuse for the agency and city council. The committee adopted the following vision for NTC after a public comment period: "Create a center that celebrates San Diego's maritime history and opens public access to a waterway linking San Diego and Mission Bay. This community will anchor revitalization of the North Bay region. It will also support education, training, and research and development programs that attract new industries to San Diego and strengthen the region's performance in international trade from Mexico to the Pacific Rim" (City of San Diego 1994).

The following is a developmental time line for Liberty Station, NTC San Diego:

1993 BRAC announces closure of San Diego NTC.
1993 NTC Reuse Committee begins work on Reuse Concept Plan.
1994 San Diego Port Commission votes to request that the Navy transfer title to 120 acres of land and 55 acres of water

adjacent to the western border of Lindbergh Field (one-third of the project site). The city of San Diego opposes the request, citing the commission's unwillingness to work through the city's NTC Reuse Planning Committee.

1995 San Diegans pass referendum removing the "Future Urbanizing" designation from the General Plan.

1995 City reaches a master lease agreement with the Navy for interim use.

1996 Reuse Planning Committee and city complete Reuse Concept Plan.

1996 City Council approves Reuse Concept Plan.

1996 The city signs an agreement with seven local homeless service agencies to provide $7.5 million for housing the homeless on offsite locations, later approved by HUD.

1996 The city and the San Diego Unified Port District agree to allow the airfield to expand to meet the port's needs.

1997 The Navy officially ceases operations on the base.

1997 San Diego Redevelopment Agency adopts the NTC Redevelopment Project Area Plan.

1997 San Diego City Council adopts the NTC Redevelopment Plan.

1998 The city and the Navy reach a memorandum of understanding (MOU) to dedicate a seven-acre parcel within the fifty-nine-acre military family housing site to be used as an elementary school, at no cost to the school district.

1998 The San Diego City Council certifies the environmental-impact report (EIR).

1999 The city issues a request for proposals (RFP) for a master developer/partner.

1999 The Navy grants final approval of the Reuse Plan and certification of the environmental-impact study (EIS).

1999 President Clinton asks Congress to pass legislation to expedite military base conversion through no-fee conveyances.

1999 The city of San Diego submits its economic conveyance (EDC) application to the Navy.

1999 The city selects McMillin as its master developer.

2000 DDA signed between Redevelopment Agency and McMillin.

2000 The city, McMillin, and local arts groups establish the NTC Foundation to rehabilitate and operate twenty-six historic buildings within the Civic, Arts, and Cultural Center (CACC) district on the base.

2000   The San Diego City Council approves the NTC Precise Plan.
2000   The California Coastal Commission requires modifications to the proposed NTC Local Coastal Program Land Use Plan and Implementation Plan, and changes are approved.
2000   The Navy applies to the National Register for Historic Places.
2001   California awards San Diego with a Local Agency Military Base Recovery Area (LAMBRA) to attract investment through tax incentives.
2001   Save Our NTC files suit against the city, McMillin, and the CA Coastal Commission to stop development from exceeding as stipulated by city statute; state Supreme Court refuses to hear appeal.
2002   Save Our NTC files lawsuit alleging illegal termination of Tidelands Trust protection at NTC.
2003   City Council approves NTC Foundation's request for loans to advance the reuse of the CACC, now named "Promenade Center."
2007   The NTC Foundation completes Phase One of the rehabilitation.
2011   California Technology, Trade and Commerce Agency awards NTC with Local Agency Military Base Recovery Area (LAMBRA) designation.
2012   California Assembly dissolves redevelopment agencies, including the city of San Diego's with NTC. NTC is turned over to the city of San Diego's authority.
2014   California Assembly dissolves LAMBRA program.

The NTC's conversion did not happen in isolation but was part of an ongoing state-level conversation about policy mechanisms to accelerate redevelopment processes and stimulate economic growth. These policies are outside communities' control and thus demand collaborative governance to ensure flexible, incremental approaches to conversion. In 1993 Governor Pete Wilson convened the California Military Base Reuse Task Force, which Mayor Golding chaired when NTC's closure was announced. The task force investigated ways to expedite conveyance for local private economic development and culminated in a widely read report that recommended federal and state policy changes in conveyance, environmental restoration, and governing processes across different political jurisdictions (Perry 1994; California Military Base Reuse Task Force 1994). In 1996

California legislators created a standardized set of policies to make rede-velopment easier for future base closures. However, the policy shift failed to address the unique needs of the state's thirty closed military installa-tions, and discussion continued surrounding how to help former military communities. In response, Republican Assemblyman Ted Weggeland in-troduced a popular bill that made conversion easier by expanding the criteria for blighted conditions under California's Community Redevelop-ment Code.

At the local level, Mayor Golding convened a five-member citizen com-mittee in 1999 to select a master developer for conversion projects on the NTC and to prepare for land conveyance. The finalists were Lennar, a na-tional developer with base conversion experience, and McMillin Compa-nies, a local developer with deep ties to San Diego's political community. Although the citizen committee picked Lennar, the City Council selected McMillin unanimously. The McMillin conversion proposal included 361 acres with 349 homes, 2 hotels, 7 office buildings, an educational district, a 46-acre park, and a civic, arts, and cultural center. City Council mem-bers argued that their decision rested on supporting the local development community rather than on claims that McMillin "paid to play."

A fortuitous federal policy toward land valuation at the time of rede-velopment made the NTC project relatively more attractive and less risky than on many former bases. Previously, two options existed for convey-ance: public conveyance, which was free but mandated public use, and an economic development conveyance, which allowed private use and profits but required fees for conveying the land.

The Clinton administration passed no-fee conveyance legislation for projects that focused on economic development and job creation. How-ever, the federal government remained an important player in the NTC's conversion even after it agreed to a no-fee conveyance. President Clinton selected the NTC as one of the four regional headquarters for the Na-tional Civilian Community Corps, housing 250 members on a 72-acre site as a public-private venture, with 59 acres for housing and 13 acres for support facilities (City of San Diego 1998). Later, the city of San Diego and the Department of the Navy entered into an MOU to dedicate 7 acres within the 59-acre military family housing site to be used as an elementary school—at no cost to the San Diego Unified School District (City of San Diego 1998).

Collaborative governance to resolve conflicts across multiple sectors remained important as conversion advanced. The San Diego Redevelopment Agency and McMillin filed the development disposition agreement (DDA) outlining the details of their public-private partnership in June 2000. The district concept, each with its own LLC, set the stage for future development, beginning with a residential district. Yet significant local unrest over land-use issues occurred before, during, and after the pre- and post-conveyance process, despite the city and developer's excitement to move forward. Point Loma neighborhood residents were concerned about traffic from the new development, and affordable housing activists decried efforts to limit affordable housing on former bases.

Environmental contamination was relatively light on the former NTC, but environmental remediation still presented serious governance challenges. In this case the community was upset by the Navy's seemingly careless attitudes towards leaving decrepit buildings and contaminated areas unremediated. The original reuse plan called for a canal connecting Mission Bay to the San Diego harbor to create a San Antonio–style riverwalk promenade with shops and restaurants. This portion of the original plan was eliminated nearly from the beginning of the project because of high levels of contamination in the soil at the bottom of the channel next to the NTC. Save Our NTC, a local activist group, sought to preserve open space on the base as well as historic memory. Save Our NTC eventually brought four lawsuits against the city to preserve buildings and sight lines, and maintain development restrictions based on environmental stipulations in the state's Tidelands Trust.[1]

Criticisms of San Diego's conversion efforts were common across several different issue areas, particularly the value of land to be conveyed and the unscrupulous nature of the development. A 2007 federal audit disclosed that McMillin had overcharged for technical service that it effectively provided itself through a separate entity (U.S. Federal News Service 2007). In critics' view, not only did the city deliver public land to a private entity, but it was also complicit in making zoning changes, creating unbalanced marketing reports, and receiving political campaign contributions from private interests with the most to gain from the NTC's redevelopment. As San Diego journalist Neil Morgan noted, "Too often, we have awakened too late to win land-use battles that shape our city. The most recent and tragic instance was the debacle by the developer Corky McMillin at the Naval Training Center. We lost the chance to create a Balboa Park on the water, beside that historic base" (Morgan 2006).

Project champions and stakeholders also highlight NTC San Diego's conversion successes in its transformation and adaptive reuse of historic infrastructure for local economic development. Now marketed as Liberty Station (see figure 4), the 361-acre project includes 52 buildings listed on the National Register of Historic Places and is district-focused, including a retail and commercial district, a promenade focused on nonprofit activities, an educational district, a residential district, a hotel district, an office district, a 46-acre park, and 125 acres of open-space area along a boat channel. The master plan is approximately 90 percent complete, with all districts implemented or close to implementation. Critics suggest that redevelopment outcomes represent a bare skeleton compared to the DDA's promises, but redevelopment on the former base is extensive and surpasses that on most former defense sites around the country (City of San Diego 1998). Map 4 depicts redevelopment on Liberty Station and its land-use zoning.

Figure 4. Dance and arts building at the redeveloped Liberty Station. Photo by Michael Touchton, 2014.

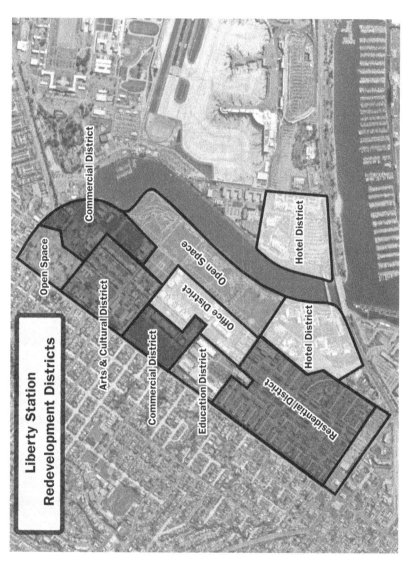

Map 4. Liberty Station divided by land-use districts

The San Diego case demonstrates the ways that intra-local and regional conflicts still occur over land conveyance, remediation, and conversion benefits, even when redevelopment progresses relatively smoothly. The NTC lies in a coveted location in terms of market and recreational perspectives, and other local interests sought to capitalize on the prospect of large, lucrative federal land transfers. Multilevel governance for defense conversion can negotiate collaborative redevelopment agreements in defense conversion and mitigate conflicts, but many conflicts still occur, even in the best of circumstances.

Fort Ord

Fort Ord's conversion represents an intermediate outcome between NTC San Diego and Alameda NAS. Fort Ord is only partially converted, with much of the base still in need of environmental remediation before redevelopment and reuse are possible. However, some conversion outcomes provide strong community benefits in the form of educational opportunities (California State University, Monterey Bay [CSUMB]), a VA hospital, a shopping center, a beachfront park, and a national monument. These outcomes are unexpectedly positive given the high levels of environmental contamination and the planning and governance challenges associated with dozens of overlapping local, regional, state, and national jurisdictions encompassing the former site. Exceptionally strong regional governance generated positive redevelopment outcomes surrounding Fort Ord's conversion, which covered conversion planning, ongoing environmental remediation, implementation, and project financing. Strong governance cannot completely overcome many of Fort Ord's conversion difficulties, but it has resulted in conversion outcomes that far surpass expectations: an uncommon achievement in military redevelopment.

Fort Ord's redevelopment planning began with the organization of a nascent governance structure through a grassroots collective consisting of a small group of local and regionally influential organizations that formed after the base closure announcement. These local groups formally organized as the Fort Ord Economic Development Administration (FOEDA) in 1991. This transition marked the evolution of the central redevelopment body from a community-driven initiative to a joint authority between the municipalities of Seaside and Marina and Monterey

County. The number of participants in the fledgling body grew when the Army allocated property to the cities of Monterey, Del Rey Oaks, and Sand City. The renamed Fort Ord Reuse Group (FORG) lasted only a short time because of concerns that the coalition did not represent a sufficiently wide range of interests. State Senator Henry Mello introduced Senate Bill 899 to create the Fort Ord Reuse Authority (FORA) and address these concerns in March 1993. Governor Pete Wilson signed the Fort Ord Redevelopment Act, which created a regional redevelopment body in 1994.

California created FORA to avoid political battles, govern redevelopment processes, and incorporate different authorities' interests into policy decisions. The Fort Ord Redevelopment Act also endowed FORA with certain governing and financing powers. For instance, the bill authorized FORA to act as a "state corporation similar to a coastal commission" and to create a redevelopment plan, ensure that projects reflected the plan, and raise money. FORA was designed for collaborative governance and includes permanent, voting representatives from the surrounding political jurisdictions as well as ex-officio members representing stakeholders from throughout the community. The legislation further stipulated the creation of a thirteen-member multi-jurisdictional board with different levels of representation for different entities depending on the strength of their perceived connections to the site. For instance, FORA gives cities adjacent to the site a greater share of voting rights in redevelopment decisions than communities that do not share geographic boundaries with Fort Ord.

FORA currently includes five voting members from Monterey County, two from the city of Del Rey Oaks, four from the city of Marina, two from the city of Monterey, four from the city of Seaside, and two each from the cities of Salinas, Sand City, Pacific Grove, and Carmel-by-the-Sea. Ex-officio members include representatives from U.S. congressional, state senate, and state house districts; CSUMB; local school and transportation districts; and the U.S. Army. All members have the power to propose, deliberate, oversee, and evaluate elements of Fort Ord's redevelopment. Voting members ultimately approve or deny conversion actions through a committee system that is divided into an executive committee, a board of directors, and up to ten other thematic committees such as environmental restoration, transportation, and financing. The executive committee and other committee meetings are all open to the public and occur approximately once per month (Fort Ord Redevelopment Act 1994).

The Fort Ord Redevelopment Act also gave FORA extensive land-use, planning, and financing powers. It authorized the board to acquire and dispose of existing real property and facilities; to plan, finance, and construct new public capital facilities; and to levy assessments, reassessments, special taxes, and development fees/bonds to finance projects (see figure 5). Moreover, the law authorized FORA's board to study, evaluate, and recommend cleanup of toxic and explosive substances within the territory and to broker agreements to mitigate Fort Ord's reuse impacts on rare and endangered species. As FORA's director, Michael Houlemard, sees it, the mission is "replacing the 36,000 in population that were here when the Fort Ord military installation was fully up and operating. There were 15,000 soldiers, thousands of civilians, and their families that were on this base every day that occupied the nearly 6,000 buildings on the former Fort Ord" (Almanzan 2014). Houlemard identified significant delays in the environmental restoration of the site, particularly because of munitions abatement, that might not be complete until 2025 (Houlemard 2013). Moreover, full conversion and reuse on the site might not occur until the 2030s, up to forty years after the base closed.

Figure 5. New housing on Fort Ord. Fort Ord Reuse Authority. Photo by Amanda Ashley, historical exhibit at Fort Ord, 2014.

Governance of local politics and interactions with regional, state, and federal agencies dominated efforts to convert Fort Ord. As Houlemard argues, "BRAC is set up to benefit the federal government, not structured to help local communities. We've dealt with sixty agencies that have their own way of thinking within their own stovepipe. The acronymical linguistics are mind-boggling, but to translate between national, state, local agencies requires an extraordinary amount of training that we do not have" (Houlemard 2013).

Fort Ord's interactions with the federal government are more important for its redevelopment outcomes than for the other California cases. Leon Panetta's leadership role and his federal connections contributed greatly to the creation of CSUMB, along with several other successful aspects of Fort Ord's conversion. In this case, Panetta organized community leaders to workshop redevelopment options from his position as a congressman representing Monterey County and the Fort Ord area in the 1980s. Panetta also pushed for specific conversion efforts surrounding education to set the stage for long-term, regional economic recovery.

The Fort Ord Task Force also sought public input and generated some early redevelopment successes, including the conversion of one 1,300-acre parcel into a new university campus in partnership with the California State University system (Munitz 2013; Houlemard 2013). The University of California system turned down Panetta's request for a new campus, but he successfully approached the California State University System and negotiated the reuse of some of Fort Ord's buildings for educational facilities: "This was an opportunity for a great experiment: whether base conversion could be used to increase capacity in an environment with reduced expenditure. We would never be able to make this work if we had to deal with the entire base at once—too large, too complicated, and the environmental-impact reports would be impossible to achieve. Bullets on the ground, oil from the tanks, endless EIR problems" (Munitz 2013).

Conveyance of land and structures for the new campus occurred quickly, even though remaining parcels on the site could not be conveyed because of dangerous contamination (see figure 6). The new campus, CSUMB, is one of the first U.S. campuses to use entirely renovated buildings for its facilities and opened in 1995 with 3,000 students. Fortuitously, President Clinton appointed Panetta as the head of the Office of Management and Budget (OMB) in 1993, giving Fort Ord's biggest champion even more access to federal resources.

Despite CSUMB's success (see figure 7), communities surrounding Fort Ord have struggled to redevelop their sites because of the difficulty of governing lengthy environmental remediation and the difficulty in reaching remediation agreements across such a broad group of stakeholders. Fort Ord's conversion began well largely because of Panetta's involvement but slowed as the thirteen local jurisdictions surrounding the former base and the many regional, state, and federal entities with authority over the site were reluctant to fund remediation or advance conversion plans: "CSUMB was seen by the community as a real positive thing. They had good leadership, good community relations. They got significant private donations from agriculture powers that be in Monterey. They did reuse structures that had pros and cons rather than leveling everything. That evoked a positive response—the community liked changing old things and making them new. They had better planning, and community acceptance comes from their own intelligence. The university is a positive whereas development isn't—more traffic, more people, more power" (Patton 2013).

Figure 6. Former military housing in need of demolition because of lead and asbestos contamination. Photo by Amanda Ashley, 2013.

Figure 7. California State University, Monterey Bay

Incredibly, one of the options for converting Fort Ord was to build a German military base because of Monterey's good weather for flight training, which the German military lacked at home. The Pentagon even had talks with the German government about this possibility: "At one of our meetings we asked if we had a choice between the German Army and the IRS, could we vote for the German Army?" joked Dick Goblirsch, Sand City's city manager (Corwin 1991).

Eventually, the members of FORA approved a national monument that preserves a large percentage of the base as open space, a state park, a VA hospital, and new commercial areas. Fort Ord National Monument and Fort Ord Dunes State Park represent the largest nods to environmental preservation on the site. Much of the national monument remains inaccessible because of unexploded ordnance, but dozens of miles of trails are open to the public, and some of the inaccessible areas provide rare, uninterrupted habitat for flora and fauna on the central California coast. The historic Presidio of Monterey remains an active military enclave, so the U.S. Army oversees that aspect of historic preservation on the base. Fort

Ord thus demonstrates broad collaborative governance that contributed to sporadic, unexpected conversion successes, given the many roadblocks to conversion on the site. Following is a developmental time line for Fort Ord, and map 5 depicts redevelopment on Fort Ord and its land-use zoning.

1990   EPA declares Fort Ord a Superfund site because of groundwater contamination.

1991   BRAC announces Fort Ord's closure.

1991   Cities of Seaside and Marina, and Monterey County, assemble the Fort Ord Economic Development Administration (FOEDA) as a joint authority to seek public input and reuse recommendations. FOEDA becomes the Fort Ord Reuse Group (FORG) and expands to include the cities of Monterey, Del Rey Oaks, and Sand City, which also receive properties following the closure.

1993   FORG submits its Initial Base Reuse Plan to the Army.

1993   The Army completes its EIS.

1993   The 7th Infantry Division (Light) leaves Fort Ord, relocating to Fort Lewis, Washington.

1993   Secretary of Defense William Perry declares that the reuse efforts at the former Fort Ord will serve as a national model for defense conversion.

1993   The DOD issues the National Environmental Policy Act Record of Decision, selecting alternative 6RM as the most likely reuse scenario.

1994   FORG publishes the initial Habitat Management Plan, reserving 15,000 to 17,000 acres for conservation under the U.S. Bureau of Land Management and 1,000 acres for coastal zone conservation under California Department of Parks and Recreation jurisdiction. The plan designates another 2,692 acres for recreational land. The U.S. Department of Commerce gives $15 million to California State University to assist with the conversion of 1,300 acres into a university campus.

1994   The California State legislature passes Senate Bill 899, authorizing the creation of the Fort Ord Reuse Authority (FORA) to replace FORG with an expanded multi-jurisdictional governing structure.

1994   Fort Ord officially closes.

1995   CSUMB opens.

1996   FORA completes the Reuse Plan and Environmental Impact Report and receives the APA award for best comprehensive planning by a small jurisdiction.

1997   FORA publishes a revised Habitat Management Plan.

1997   The Army accepts the comprehensive FORA Base Reuse Plan with the expectation that 35,000 people will be living on Fort Ord by 2015.

1998   FORA and the Army commence negotiations for the EDC.

2000   FORA and Department of the Army reach an MOU for the free transfer of 5,300 acres under the EDC.

2000   The Army completes Coastal Dunes remedial activities and revegetation.

2001   The City of Del Rey Oaks selects the Martin Group of San Francisco as the developer for a hotel/golf course site, replacing DBO of Monterey, which had withdrawn from the project.

2002   The Army completes landfill consolidation and placement of groundwater cap.

2004   FORA and the Army initiate discussion on an environmental-services cooperative agreement to provide funding for dedicated munitions remediation with oversight by the U.S. Environmental Protection Agency and the California Department of Toxic Substances Control.

2007   The Army transfers 3,340 acres contaminated with military munitions to FORA, which is responsible for munitions-response actions. All other contamination issues remain the Army's responsibility.

2008   Capital improvements continue for transportation and water.

2009   Fort Ord Dunes State Park opens on the former base.

2010   Imjin Office Park opens.

2011   Building removal and environmental rehabilitation continue across the site.

2012   President Obama designates the 14,650-acre Fort Ord National Monument.

2015   Groundbreaking for Veterans' Cemetery.

2015   Announcement of VA clinic.

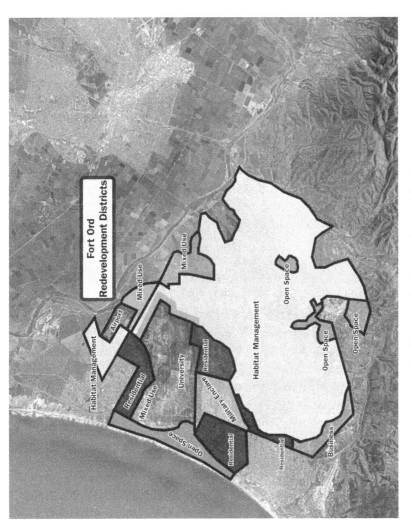

Map 5. Fort Ord divided by land-use districts

NAS Alameda

The redevelopment of Alameda's Naval Air Station (NAS) highlights the ways that strong market conditions are not enough to generate strong conversion outcomes, particularly when governance is relatively weak and plans fall through the cracks of federal policy shifts. The city of Alameda partnered with several master developers to pursue mixed-use redevelopment on the former NAS, which falls entirely within the city of Alameda's borders. The master-developer strategy and the location within the city's jurisdiction both parallel San Diego's conversion experience, and many observers expected redevelopment to proceed equally quickly and smoothly. Yet Alameda's redevelopment outcomes to date are the worst of the three cases: delays in environmental remediation and conveyance led to a stalled conversion process that advanced in earnest only in 2013, sixteen years after the base closed. Alameda's experience shows how best practices in planning and governance cannot overcome many external, uncontrollable factors, such as national policies surrounding conveyance.

The Naval Air Station's history as a military site dates to 1927, when the city of Alameda created an airfield by filling wetlands on a peninsula extending into the San Francisco Bay. The Army began using the airfield in the 1930s, and the city ceded it to the federal government in 1936. The Department of Defense began efforts to convert the airfield into a naval air station in 1938. The NAS became operational in 1940 and served as a base for two carrier air wings thereafter. Alameda retained important status in the Pacific through the Cold War, and carrier groups used Alameda as a home base well into the 1990s. The Navy considered Alameda unnecessary in the post–Cold War military drawdown and included the base in the BRAC closure list in 1993. The base formally closed in 1997, and the city of Alameda began actively planning the base's redevelopment in 2000. The following is a developmental time line for NAS Alameda, and map 6 shows NAS Alameda while in operational use in 1976.

1992   Parts of the Alameda Naval Air Station (Alameda NAS) are placed on the National Register of Historic Places.
1993   BRAC recommends closing Alameda NAS.

1993 Alameda's City Council establishes the Alameda Base Reuse Advisory Group to advise the City Council concerning base conversion issues and to provide a forum for public participation in the reuse planning process.

1994 The city and county of Alameda form the Alameda Reuse and Redevelopment Authority (ARRA) to ensure the effective transition from federal to local ownership, including planning and financing functions.

1996 ARRA adopts the Alameda NAS Reuse Plan.

1996 Department of the Navy prepares an EIS.

1997 ARRA modifies the 1996 Reuse Plan by adding office and commercial uses to the center of the air station and reducing the amount of property dedicated to educational activities. The new plan also identifies land for transfer to the U.S. Fish and Wildlife Service.

1997 The U.S. Department of the Interior includes the Oakland Inner Harbor Jetties portion of the NAS in the Federal Channel Historic District and places additional land on the National Register of Historic Places.

1998 The Alameda Annex closes.

1999 The Navy distributes EIS.

1999 The EPA declares the base a Superfund site.

2001 Alameda selects Alameda Point Community Partners (APCP) as the master developer for the property.

2003 ARRA begins process of formulating preliminary development concept (PDC).

2006 City of Alameda and the Navy agree to a $108 million purchase deal.

2006 APCP elects not to move forward with the development plan identified in the PDC and withdraws from the project.

2007 City of Alameda selects SunCal Companies as the master developer and reaches an exclusive negotiating agreement.

2010 City rejects developer- and city-initiated ballot measure to increase project density by an 85 percent margin.

2010 The Alameda City Council terminates the exclusive negotiating agreement with SunCal and halts its proposal for the former Naval Air Station.

2010 SunCal sues the city of Alameda for more than $100 million.

2012 Alameda City Council settles with SunCal and agrees to pay $4 million in damages.

2012   The California State Supreme Court dissolves ARRA. The city's planning agency takes over redevelopment administration.

2013   Alameda Planning Board begins year-long process of creating a draft EIR to help establish a foundation for entire Alameda Point redevelopment.

2013   The Navy and Alameda agree to a no-fee conveyance and new redevelopment plan.

2013   The city takes possession of 1,400 acres of land and water.

2014   The city of Alameda approves EIR, zoning, master infrastructure plan, and general plan amendments.

2014   Navy turns over land for VA hospital.

2014   City selects developer for commercial/residential site.

2015   Plan approved for 800 homes and 600,000-square-foot commercial space.

2016   City accepts more land from the Navy.

2016   Groundbreaking on residential, commercial, affordable housing development.

2016   Wrightspeed (vehicle power trains) situates billion-dollar manufacturing facility on former base.

2016   City breaks ground and dedicates ferry operating facilities.

The Navy partnered with the city and county in the early stages of Alameda's redevelopment and created the Alameda Reuse and Redevelopment Authority (ARRA) as the body responsible for developing an interim reuse strategy to take title to base lands and to implement the community reuse plan. The federal and local partners worked quickly together in the early phases of redevelopment: Alameda had an approved plan by 1996, and the Navy issued the EIS for the disposal and reuse of the Naval Air Station and the Alameda Annex the same year. Alameda's redevelopment authority even secured a master developer in 1997, by the time the base ceased operations. However, changes in the land-transfer agreement after President Clinton left office along with shifts increasing the size and scope of National Historic Registry properties halted this initial momentum. Most damning was the EPA's announcement designating NAS Alameda a Superfund site, with extraordinary amounts of polychlorinated biphenyl (PCB)–laced oil present in twenty-five areas on the former base (Alameda Point 2011). The EPA required site rehabilitation before the Navy could

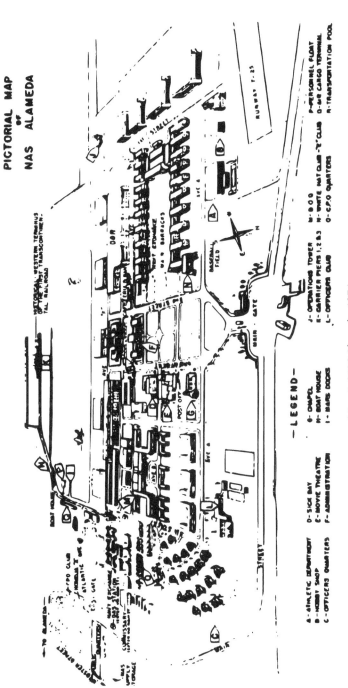

Map 6. NAS Alameda, 1976

transfer property, thus complicating any potential transfers even if a no-fee conveyance had been possible (United States Environmental Protection Agency 2013).

Oversight from California environmental agencies tangled redevelopment plans in a series of California Coastal Commission and California Environmental Protection Agency requirements and stymied development (see figure 8). Alameda's now-dissolved Community Redevelopment Agency could not assist the city in surpassing these regulatory barriers. The Navy and the California SHPO signed a MOA to "avoid or mitigate adverse impacts on eligible structures" before conveying the land to ARRA. It ultimately took more than ten years for the Navy to transfer some land. The rest of the site remained relatively dormant until recently, with the exception of some interim uses.

Alameda's redevelopment experience resembles San Diego's in the sense that Alameda must contend with many overlapping political jurisdictions even though the site falls within one city. However, a key difference between the two cases centers on Alameda's significant governance and

Figure 8. Abandoned lots awaiting redevelopment on Alameda Point with San Francisco skyline in the background. Photo by Amanda Ashley, 2013.

planning challenges surrounding environmental contamination and preservation. Alameda NAS is a designated Superfund site with contaminants
in groundwater, surface water, and soil/sludges. Tours of the former base
made it clear that every parcel had some form of pollution that would
require remediation prior to conveyance and conversion. The first round
of contamination occurred before the Navy acquired the land in 1936,
when a borax processing plant, oil refinery, and airport occupied the site.
The Navy then introduced new activities that created more-profound environmental problems. According to the EPA (United States Environmental Protection Agency 2013, 1),

> Wastes generated at the site included industrial solvents, acids, paint strip-
> pers, degreasers, caustic cleaners, pesticides, chromium and cyanide wastes,
> waste oils containing PCBS, radium associated with dial painting and strip-
> ping, medical debris, and inert and unexploded ordnance. Wastes discharged
> to the Seaplane Lagoon and the two on-base landfills pose a threat to the
> surrounding San Francisco Bay aquatic life and liquid plumes at two former
> major industrial buildings pose a potential long term human health threat.

The level of oversight, regulation, and negotiation for environmental remediation is important and entirely understandable. However,
environmental-remediation hurdles further exacerbated the antidevelop-
ment climate and hindered the Alameda redevelopment authority's ability to execute its reuse plan. Jennifer Ott notes that the city now uses an
"incremental approach" toward redevelopment: "We just haven't been
in a place to make some of the longer-term decisions [until now] because
things were so up in the air" (Hegarty 2012).

Several key conflicts at the local, regional, state, and federal level
heightened tensions surrounding redevelopment politics and showcase
the need for stronger governance. In part, redevelopment conflicts with
regional and state agencies stemmed from the location of the base and
its close, almost overlapping, proximity to neighboring jurisdictions. Alameda extends a mere 12.4 square miles over Alameda Island and Coast
Guard Island, both adjacent to the city of Oakland and San Francisco
Bay. A 624-acre runway, the San Francisco Bay, the Oakland Estuary,
and a local Main Street bound the site. Across the estuary is the Port of
Oakland, with its extensive facilities and infrastructure. As local resident

Gordon Lai describes the base, "It's prime property with views of San Francisco Bay. It can be a real tax generator. But you can't have gentrification and push poor people out, either" (Hegarty 2013). Others, such as Alameda's Mayor Bill Winthrow, disagreed: "This is a ridiculous situation. Our first priority should be to create jobs so that people have work. We should not be using these facilities to warehouse the homeless population" (Hanson 1994).

At a minimum, Alameda must negotiate with several regional agencies as it pursues redevelopment because any redevelopment project may easily affect neighboring communities and potentially harm neighboring interests. Conservatively speaking, Alameda's redevelopment must comply with the regulations of the city of Oakland, the county of Alameda, the San Francisco Bay Regional Water Quality Control Board, the San Francisco Bay Conservation and Development Commission, the Association of Bay Areas, and Bay Area transportation authorities. Laura Thomas of Renewed Hope Housing Advocates and other residents requested that the city promote affordable housing and work with HUD to provide housing for the homeless: "I support a mix of housing," said local resident Katie DeLeon. "But what scares me is traffic. It's already bad sometimes on Webster Street in the mornings and evenings, and it could get worse as Alameda Point is developed. It needs to be planned right" (Hegarty 2013).

Nearby municipalities and special-purpose authorities' different interests and motivations created significant governance and planning challenges for Alameda's conversion. Oakland sued Alameda over an "inadequate" environmental-impact report that did not account accurately for traffic impacts in 2003. These concerns about development intensity continued to grow until 2010, when Alameda citizens voted down plans to increase residential density to finance base conversion. The community's decision led Alameda to fire the master planner, SunCal, which later sued the city for $100 million for bad-faith practices. Although the suit was settled for $4 million, it underscores the ongoing difficulties the city has experienced with the master planning process: one consultant after another left because of the financial difficulties of site redevelopment.

The most significant challenge for redeveloping NAS Alameda has been the inability to convey *uncontaminated* Navy land to the city. Alameda's redevelopment got caught between the shifting priorities of two different presidential administrations and missed the window to capital-ize on the Clinton administration's no-cost EDC. Instead, the George W. Bush administration changed policy to extract financial value from the land through a heavily one-sided negotiation over the conveyance price. For example, the Navy proposed a purchase price of $108 million to the city of Alameda, thus continuing to make the site costly and difficult to develop. This policy remained in place for much of the Obama adminis-tration, and Alameda was not granted a no-fee economic development conveyance until 2013.

The inability to find a price that was acceptable to both Alameda and the federal government slowed the redevelopment process considerably and made it nearly impossible for master developers to move forward until 2013. For example, SunCal, the most-recent (former) developer, postponed a contentious ballot measure to increase population density and advance redevelopment plans because of the lack of a land deal be-tween the city and the Navy (Jones 2011). A subsequent failed ballot mea-sure in 2010 and increased public acrimony led to deteriorating relations

Figure 9. Adaptive reuse on Alameda Point, hangar to distillery. Photo by Amanda Ashley, 2013.

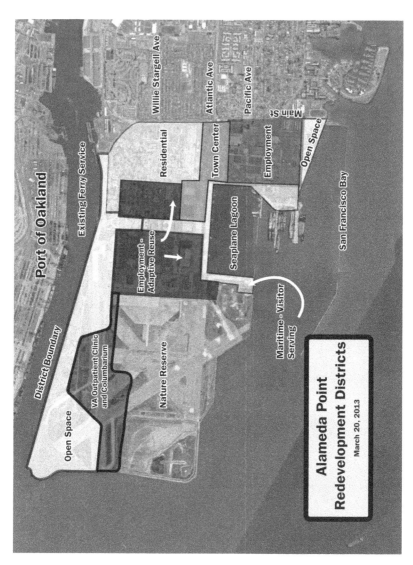

Map 7. Alameda Point divided by land-use districts

with SunCal and the city. As Vice-Mayor Doug deHaan remarked, "They thought we were just bumpkins. That we were just urban, city bumpkins that they could roll through."[2]

The city ultimately terminated its development agreement, and SunCal sued the city for undercutting its ability to negotiate with the Navy (Alameda Point 2013). Thus, Alameda had to restart the planning process from scratch, including the creation of a revised master plan and a new EIR, which reflected a protracted development partnership with the federal government. Alameda completed its deal with the Navy in 2013, thirteen years after NTC San Diego and Fort Ord were conveyed (Jones 2013).

The city of Alameda has experienced some one-off successes through smart short-term leasing strategies (see figure 9), but a good portion of the land remains undeveloped, as illustrated in map 7. More than 2.3 million square feet of property is vacant, with 1.8 million square feet occupied temporarily by tenants promoting arts/entertainment/recreation, storage, civic and nonprofit uses, marine uses, midsize manufacturing and repair, specialty beverage and foods, and transportation and warehousing (Keyser Marston Associates 2012). These tenants generate revenue to maintain the site, but they do not reflect Alameda's larger plans for making new places through conversion. As noted above, temporary uses make Alameda Point attractive in a lot of ways, but they cannot generate larger permanent investments in community because most of the interim tenants are still designated as temporary users.

Converting Holy Loch, Soesterberg, and Abrams Army HQ

This book applies directly only to former defense communities in the United States. However, U.S. bases have also closed at high rates in Europe and East Asia following the end of the Cold War. Converting these bases presents great political, economic, and social challenges. These overseas bases' redevelopment experiences fall largely beyond this book's purview but are interesting and instructive because of the different institutional, economic, and sociocultural environments in which they are embedded. Conversion experiences on U.S. bases overseas are also important to a wide variety of countries because of their relevance to host countries' economies and security. We therefore include selected redevelopment experiences from three former European bases to identify the ways that defense conversion occurs across distinct international contexts.

Defense conversion and redevelopment on three former U.S. bases in Europe provide extra, international insight into the redevelopment process. The U.S. Naval base in Holy Loch, Scotland, the Air Force base at Soesterberg, Netherlands, and the Abrams Army Headquarters in Frankfurt, Germany, all closed following the end of the Cold War and have all been converted for a variety of uses and beneficiaries. The former Abrams Army HQ is now the central campus for Von Goethe University in the heart of Frankfurt, and the former Soesterberg Air Base is now one of the largest nature preserves in the Netherlands. Soesterberg also houses The Netherlands' National Military Museum, as well as recreational activities such as cycling on former runways, pilot training schools, and boot-camp–style fitness programs. Holy Loch has been redeveloped the least of these three bases but now serves as a port for local timber operations, a small commercial marina, and the home of a sailing school.

Defense conversion on former U.S. bases in Europe occurs in different institutional contexts from one country to the next. Additionally, supranational European Union (EU) policies contribute an added layer of funding relative to the U.S. cases, along with added regulation and oversight. The geographic context of a declining European compact-city tradition also informs the ways that former military communities convert and integrate bases. European cities have become increasingly diffuse since the 1990s, when many bases closed, without consistent urban policy governing this diffusion (Sega 2015; Indovina 2016). Yet many EU bodies pursue consistent policies to maximize the bloc's economic potential and spread benefits of growth to peripheral areas within member states as well as peripheral member states within the EU. For instance, the European Union's Committee on Spatial Development (1999) has embraced the concept of polycentrism to promote economic potential and maximize EU economic competitiveness overall. Moreover, the committee has requested extra funds and regional planning associated with urban dispersion and conversion of former areas of production into other uses (Stead 2014).

The European shift toward polycentric city-regions has largely been rhetorical; consistent supranational and national policies to create polycentric city-regions have not emerged. Pursuing the Spatial Development Committee's vision is difficult without funding, planning, and support. The EU has therefore not realized a consistent policy surrounding polycentrism. Beyond EU policy, revitalized city cores are increasingly attractive because of their employment opportunities, while suburbs offer lower cost of living and potentially higher quality of life. Former military communities surrounding Holy Loch (Scotland) and Soesterberg (The Netherlands) have therefore been converted into bedroom communities for Glasgow and Utrecht, respectively, rather than being their own centers for economic productivity.

Commuting from outlying military communities to urban centers was unusual when U.S. bases were operational and regional transportation networks were much more limited. Now, the extension of rail, ferry, road, and cycling options near Soesterberg and Holy Loch allows residents to maintain employment in the city cores along with a lower cost of living in new suburbs. National and regional transportation funds supported the conversion of former military communities into bedroom communities for larger cities. However, the towns near the former military bases have yet to rebound as centers of economic activity.

Frankfurt has made redeveloping closed military installations a centerpiece of its efforts to add air-travel capacity, reinforce the city's expertise in banking and finance, and diversify into many other aspects of the knowledge economy. Most importantly, the German government, the state of Hesse, and the city of Frankfurt worked together to convert the former Abrams U.S. Army Headquarters into the new, central campus of Von Goethe University. The university is a highly regarded institution in Frankfurt's core and now offers a myriad of graduate and professional degrees in subjects that are potentially important from local, regional, and national economic perspectives. Much as in *Cities of Knowledge* (O'Mara 2015), national, regional, and local governance allowed a strong university to grow and develop. The new campus is attractive to top scholars and students alike: it is within walking distance of Frankfurt's center, with historically significant sites and access to recreation areas on the Main River. The faculty members and students who join Von Goethe University gain access to one of the largest banking and finance centers in Europe, which could provide capital and expertise in bringing innovations to market as well as jobs for graduates. The mutually beneficial, complementary aspects of redevelopment of the Abrams Army HQ complex can, in turn, produce an economic, social, and cultural multiplier effect for the region.

Ultimately, defense conversion and integration have helped to drive Frankfurt's economic growth and to some extent Germany's economic growth.

Governing the planning process is critical for defense conversion and sets communities on redevelopment trajectories that can be difficult to alter. Redevelopment with community benefits for a broad set of stakeholders then depends, in part, on how communities govern the planning process. Collaborative governance promotes defense conversion with community benefits: it helps to streamline environmental remediation, achieve conveyance, resolve conflicts over preservation on the bases, and generate redevelopment outcomes that communities support. Experienced planners are accustomed to dealing with different stakeholder groups, but base conversion requires collaboration well beyond local stakeholder groups because planning governance is not just a local issue. The breadth and depth of sublocal, local, regional, state, and national partnerships and the subcategories within each structure frequently conflict and dramatically complicate decision making in planning conversion.

Identifying possible avenues toward improved planning for defense conversion does not represent our own set of "best practices" per se. Instead, each community's unique planning history and culture influence conversion outcomes. Understanding this influence can then lead each community to leverage its planning assets, expand its role in converting former bases, and do so with community benefits in mind.

Realistically, the road to redevelopment is far bumpier than many expect, and success is in the eye of the beholder. Redevelopment success changes depending on one's vantage point; even the most thorough conversion outcomes represent a spectrum of success from different perspectives. Success is not simply about conversion and redevelopment but requires collaborative governance to ensure stakeholder representation and *beneficial* conversion outcomes. Chapter 4 therefore develops the concept of collaborative governance and examines the three bases through this lens.

4

COLLABORATIVE GOVERNANCE

How Rescaling the State Drives Redevelopment

Collaborative governance best explains redevelopment on closed military bases. Questions of jurisdiction and the local politics of land use are highly complex. Dozens of special-use districts, redevelopment authorities, utilities boards, planning agencies, master developers, other hybrid authorities, and activist organizations govern development and redevelopment processes, even if projects are undertaken within a single municipality's territory. Many large-scale redevelopment efforts often fall across multiple jurisdictions and encompass entire regions. Important differences in territory—the political boundaries around physical space on a map—and scale—the hierarchies of political, economic, and social interaction—require communities to extend governance arrangements to the regional level to meet military redevelopment needs.

Strong governance is critical for pursuing conversion with community benefits. Governing arrangements with broad stakeholder representation makes redevelopment difficult in the short term but ultimately broadens conversion benefits. In theory, broad stakeholder representation promotes stakeholders to express their preferences and informs other redevelopment actors of community needs. It also educates stakeholders about conversion possibilities and limitations, and manages expectations throughout the process. In reality, local political power imbalances remain and influence these ongoing negotiations.

Territory, Scale, and Governance

Military bases have overwhelmingly large physical footprints, sometimes up to 120 square miles, and are not usually situated within a single municipality. However, the politics of military base redevelopment are not localized but are at the mercy of local, regional, state, and federal policies, programs, and mandates. Converting closed bases requires complex interscalar governance arrangements that former defense communities sometimes never achieve. These communities thus either cannot convert bases or achieve only marginal conversion and reuse.

There are many common explanations of how urban politics influences urban redevelopment, including theories about regimes, growth machines, and neoliberal behavior.[1] However, each of these explanatory frames is insufficient for evaluating large-scale development in former defense communities, and no amount of concept stretching works. Many traditional urban governance theories are ossified and overlook the complexities of base renewal. Instead, viewing base redevelopment through the overlapping lenses of collaborative governance, regional governance, and institutional geography does a better job of explaining what happens on the ground in military redevelopment.

Redevelopment governance does not stop at the city border; efforts to promote defense conversion occur at multiple scales that extend to the regional, state, and national levels. Without a doubt, local political institutions serve a central role in most circumstances, but extended networks of stakeholders and collaboration within vertical and horizontal governing arrangements are common and expected (Pierre 2011; Levi-Faur 2012; Torfing 2012). Higher-level state and federal rules should not be taken for granted or overlooked in local development. For example, California's decision to dissolve redevelopment authorities and eliminate their claim on local revenues represents a major shift in redevelopment policy and raises the important question of who will coordinate redevelopment efforts across different scales and territories.

Special Districts and Community Redevelopment Agencies

Special districts, local redevelopment authorities (LRAs), and community redevelopment agencies (CRAs) play critical roles in governing military redevelopment. More than 5,000 special districts extend across California's 500+ city and county jurisdictions and received $42 billion in revenues in the 2014–2015 fiscal year (California State Controller 2016). The state empowers California citizens to form special districts when demands reach "beyond the physical boundaries, the financial capacity, or the core competency of multipurpose local governments" (California Little Hoover Commission 2000).

CRAs' 11 percent share of all California property tax revenue gives them considerable financial power and fiscal autonomy to finance infrastructure projects relative to municipal governments.[2] CRAs in California and LRAs in general therefore also have considerable political autonomy to promote economic development and finance infrastructure in a way that local governments often do not. These districts enjoy the power to levy taxes and use eminent domain to help provide public services such as sanitation, health care, utilities, and transportation. Growth coalitions may use opaque special districts to govern economic development while accruing debt and avoiding public oversight.

LRAs represent another way that coalitions govern economic development. Redevelopment authorities coordinate across local governments, the state government, and the federal government; other public authorities; private interests; community advocacy groups; and the public.[3] These quasi-public organizations fund redevelopment efforts by using their taxation authority to generate their own revenue, often through the popular tool of tax increment financing (TIF). This strategy first entails drawing a border around a project area. Any future increases in property tax revenue from within a project area's borders accrue to the LRA. However, LRAs are controversial for many reasons, including their common practice of diverting revenue from other local authorities, and can lead to funding shortfalls for local service provision. For example, California's 756 project areas diverted $5.4 billion from counties, cities, and school districts to their CRAs in 2007 (California State Controller 2009).

Establishing CRAs in California was even easier than establishing a special-use district: public officials needed to request a CRA simply based on a declaration of need. Over 90 percent of California cities with more than 50,000 residents had CRAs (California State Senate, Local Government Committee 2009). California eliminated all but a few CRAs in 2012, but CRAs are still pervasive in former defense communities around the country and are common in communities in general (Blount et al. 2014). For example, the Department of Defense works directly with LRAs around the country, which the DoD now requires for conveyance of land on closed bases. Many of these LRAs also have CRA-like powers to accrue debt and finance redevelopment but do not always include broad stakeholder representation.

It is difficult for communities to achieve accountability in economic development processes in the context of special-use districts and LRAs. This is because special-use districts and LRAs are generally powerful and are often created specifically to develop infrastructure without oversight from elected officials or voters (Blount et al. 2014; Leigland 1995). Instead, governing boards are limited to appointed political operatives, technocrats, and private-sector representatives. The boards thus connect the government and the market while excluding civil society and the public (Adams 2007; Blount et al. 2014). For example, San Diego created a "shadow government" to govern development and redevelopment in the city (Erie et al. 2011, 264). This "government" consisted of a wide variety of entities, including special-use districts, redevelopment authorities, utilities boards, special districts, business organized nongovernmental organizations (BONGOs), government organized nongovernmental organizations (GONGOs), and quasi-autonomous nongovernmental organizations (QUANGOs).

Critics contend that the entities that govern San Diego's development and redevelopment processes are accountable neither to the public nor to the elected mayor and city council (Erie et al. 2011). California agreed and found that special districts are less democratically accountable than city councils and lack mechanisms for financial oversight (California Little Hoover Commission 2000). Many special districts do not feature elections, but those that do experience less competitive races that attract fewer voters than even poorly watched city council or county elections. Voting in some special-use district races is limited to landowners and weighted by property ownership (McCabe 2000). Shadow government officials are usually not elected, are far removed from public scrutiny, and may be difficult to remove once appointed by a mayoral administration. Private developers can thus often capture the development process and pursue their own profit over necessary public investment.

The proliferation of governing entities involved in economic development may also complicate redevelopment efforts because of the presence of authorities with jurisdiction over redevelopment processes that predate redevelopment governance structures, even within single municipalities, such as San Diego. These authorities multiply rapidly when one moves beyond a single municipality to former bases whose physical territory crosses numerous regional, state, and national jurisdictions. Regional authorities, such as utilities and regional development agencies; state authorities, such as coastal commissions, environmental agencies, and historic preservation offices; and federal authorities, such as the DoD, the National Park Service, and the Environmental Protection Agency; are not intended to circumvent local public oversight and accountability. However, coordinating across these authorities creates considerable problems for policy implementation and redevelopment action.

Scale and territory take on new relevance in terms of special-use districts, LRAs, and authorities with jurisdictional claims over redevelopment processes that predate base closures. Navigating the challenges that these authorities create becomes crucial to achieving any redevelopment at all, much less redevelopment in the public interest. Thus, incorporating special districts and LRAs into governance theories is essential for explaining redevelopment outcomes on former military bases. In practice, CRAs often lead redevelopment processes and therefore present a critical dilemma for converting former bases in a way that produces broad community benefits. LRAs require authority to plan, finance, and implement projects, and the autonomy to do so over many electoral cycles, business cycles, and shifting political and economic winds. Yet LRAs tend to be less accountable than elected officials or easily identifiable public agencies for the reasons discussed above. Striking a new governing balance among redevelopment authority, autonomy, and accountability then becomes essential for defense conversion with community benefits.

Infrastructure and the Geography of Governance

Political institutions and governance are especially important for infrastructure development and redevelopment. Infrastructure represents one of the main concerns surrounding *military* redevelopment: connecting existing infrastructure on the former base or constructing new infrastructure to connect and integrate the base into the surrounding community is one of the chief tasks in defense conversion. As with many aspects of defense conversion, converting existing infrastructure, integrating it, and laying the groundwork for future infrastructure is particularly difficult when revenues fall because of base closure.

The local economic development network is critical for accessing and channeling investment toward infrastructure for regional economic growth (Cox 2010). This network emerges across different scales. For instance, gas and electric utilities operate at regional scales and coordinate with chambers of commerce and local governments in different municipalities within the region. The extent to which this coordination occurs across the site-selection and permitting process frequently determines whether private firms enter the region and, in turn, either promotes or undermines economic development.

Analyzing redevelopment processes at the regional scale and beyond offers clear advantages over trying to fit unwieldy, inter-scalar arrangements into purely city-focused or locally focused conceptual categories. The military redevelopment experience provides support for the argument that collaborative forms of governance *may* emerge to promote "city-regional" economic development but that the city-region does not necessarily represent a new political or economic authority. Instead, governance of the city-region is fluid and reflects the rescaling and re-territorialization of the state. Moreover, the city-region is not a stable or uniform entity but is constructed and evolves over time. It is also based on powerful actors' political and economic imaginations across space and at scale, which may be path-dependent (Jonas and Ward 2007).

The discussion above does not imply that specific governance arrangements, such as CRA versus master-developer–led conversion processes, are necessarily better or worse for communities. Instead, it shows that understanding military redevelopment requires new, broader concepts of governance, territory, and scale. By extension, redevelopment practices that leverage a broader understanding of collaborative governance at scale will produce superior defense conversion outcomes for broader arrays of stakeholders than those that do not. The case studies also show how local agency explains considerable variation in redevelopment outcomes among former defense communities operating in similar structural environments. Structural governance theories still offer insight into redevelopment processes, but communities have agency to create their own inter-scalar governance arrangements that intersect broader, existing structures and condition redevelopment outcomes.

Governance and Redevelopment on California Bases

Redevelopment in California occurs in a fiscal environment with limited federal assistance and strict control of state and local debt following the passage of Proposition 13 in 1978 (Kirkpatrick and Smith 2011). California growth coalitions deployed a web of quasi-public mechanisms to bypass electoral and state constitutional oversight to raise funds for infrastructure projects in this environment (Erie 2004). In turn, city governments faced demands to both provide firms with necessary infrastructure and satisfy public demand for services, many of which may not promote capital accumulation (Piven and Friedland 1984). Military redevelopment falls in between these demands and into a governance vacuum, with negative implications for many local stakeholders.

Redeveloping closed military bases tends to exacerbate the challenges associated with California's constrained fiscal environment. For instance, former defense communities often find themselves starting from a "reverse infrastructural trap" (Kirkpatrick and Smith 2011), where infrastructural deficits are embedded in the local political economy for decades. Furthermore, cities with closed bases frequently face a deficit in political capital and limited resources and experience for upscaling governance to engage entities with local, regional, and national jurisdiction over redevelopment. In contrast to many other forms of development and redevelopment, the federal government plays an outsize role for defense conversion in a way that creates many additional barriers to development but also offers considerable resources that California cities would otherwise not have because of strict state control of local debt.

California's redevelopment experience also highlights redevelopment authorities' importance because it offers the opportunity to observe redevelopment with and without specific agencies designed to govern the redevelopment process across multiple jurisdictions. CRAs took the lead in defense conversion in many cases and channeled TIF resources toward conversion projects. However, California's state government dissolved these agencies in 2011 to better fund schools and county services such as police and fire departments at the local level. The CRAs' dissolution returned locally generated revenue to schools and other public goods, but it also eliminated the main source of inter-scalar governance and slowed defense conversion.

NTC San Diego

Each of the three cases faced governance problems caused by the scale of redevelopment. San Diego used a master developer with high levels of authority and autonomy to address governance challenges surrounding defense conversion. The conversion of the former Naval Training Center San Diego resulted in a mixed-use site with residential, commercial, educational, recreational, corporate office, and arts districts. The master developer, McMillin, and the relationships that it developed with the city of San Diego, San Diego County, the California Coastal Commission, the State Historic Preservation Office (SHPO), and several local nongovernmental organizations all contributed to a relatively quick conversion with relatively widespread community benefits. Converting the NTC posed the fewest challenges with regional governance as opposed to the other two cases, partially because the base is contained entirely within the city of San Diego. That being said, redevelopment on all three former bases illustrates the considerable challenges surrounding territory, scale, and governance, even when the redevelopment parcel is contained within one city.

Conflicts over programs to assist the homeless, provide low-income housing, preserve open space, and restore the environment represent governance challenges. One clear example of the governance challenges limiting redevelopment on the former NTC surrounds the Civic, Arts, and Cultural

District (CACD), which exemplifies many of the problems that arise when economic interests and constraints unexpectedly collide with the pursuit of other public interests that outside entities govern. In this case, SHPO requirements conflicted with the community's economic and cultural redevelopment goals.

The CACD sits on the northwestern part of the former NTC, and its twenty-eight acres make up half of the National Historic District (designated in 2000). It contains twenty-six mission-style structures built from 1921 to 1938, many of which were contaminated or in severe disrepair. McMillin assigned the nonprofit NTC Foundation to operate and manage the CACD in 2005. The developer overcame significant public opposition to various aspects of the NTC's conversion by working with the DoD to obtain the historic designation and by creating an arts and cultural district.

So far, the NTC Foundation has restored only ten buildings in the district. Each of these buildings now houses a mix of arts, creative nonprofit, and for-profit businesses, which reflects an evolution of the foundation's and the community's original goal. The restoration has gone much more slowly than planned because the foundation did not anticipate the high restoration costs or fully understand how the restoration process worked. This lack of real estate development knowledge left the foundation in the precarious position of trying to balance preservation and redevelopment, which created tensions with its arts directive. As the director of the NTC Foundation put it, "We are the historic heart, but historic preservation isn't our mission. I am not in the business of history. I am in the business of arts and real estate development" (Roux 2014).

The involvement of numerous public actors from local jurisdictions to state agencies to federal oversight made every building change subject to multiple levels of required approvals. The foundation was not prepared for this level of oversight and the regular delays it generated in the conversion process. Nor was the foundation prepared for the loss of political and public support as costs mounted and the restoration process slowed. Next, the foundation lost a valuable source of rehabilitation funding and political support when the state dissolved California's redevelopment agencies in 2011 (Ashley and Touchton 2016). Judy McDonald, NTC Foundation board member, elaborates: "Has the redevelopment authority dissolution been a problem? Absolutely. We don't have money coming through, or advice or concern or promotion. The city has not taken it over. The political leaders have not embraced it" (McDonald 2014). Worse, the county decided in 2011 that the foundation must pay property taxes on its profit-making ventures (which the city has so far paid). McDonald explains: "Early on the city and mayor were champions. Now, we are just problem ridden and bring problems to them. The tax thing was a one-shot thing. It was a shock" (McDonald 2014). There was a steep learning curve for the foundation, the developer, and the State Historical Preservation Office in leveraging much-needed federal historic tax credits while managing their strict requirements. These extra time and resource costs made it extremely difficult for the foundation to meet its original vision.

The CACD example shows how a redevelopment goal to set aside a small portion of the former NTC San Diego for nonprofit, arts-based redevelopment can face hurdles from a wide variety of entities with jurisdiction over how the former bases are used, not just from private-sector capture of the redevelopment process. In this case, these entities range from the local (the county and "Save Our NTC") to the state (SHPO) to the national (DoD and National Park Service). Alan Ziter, deputy director of the NTC foundation, describes the process: "We spent the last ten years focusing on building renovation and making the projects pencil out. It cost $100 million more than we anticipated. I don't know how they got their initial estimates. I don't think they knew the full scope of what it would take to get a city permit. . . . I don't think it was clear. To get it, all hazardous material has to be remediated. There are so many other agencies involved and so many rules. We added sprinkler systems. It had to be ADA accessible plus government money was involved at each step, which brings new regulations" (Ziter 2014). This example also shows how territory is not limited to the physical geography of the former base. Understanding which entities wield authority over the base and how governments navigate these authorities' overlapping jurisdictions helps to explain what types of redevelopment occur and how they affect a wide range of stakeholders.

The Civic, Arts, and Cultural District's conversion experience also shows how the scale of redevelopment matters. The CACD represents just one project of many on the former base. It faces governance hurdles with the entities mentioned above, but the other projects on the NTC site also faced significant governance challenges that hindered development, most of them from different entities with different jurisdictional claims than those influencing redevelopment in the Civic and Arts District. A redevelopment authority, master developer, or city overseeing these efforts must resolve hundreds of issues with dozens of entities across horizontal and vertical levels. These challenges act as a barrier to redevelopment and are especially difficult to meet for communities that recently lost their largest employer and/or may not have had resources to devote to these areas even before bases closed. Nevertheless, pursuing governance at scale is essential to achieving redevelopment outcomes that benefit a wide variety of stakeholders. Theoretical conceptualizations of redevelopment must therefore consider and incorporate issues of territory, scale, and governance if they are to provide a useful framework for scholars of development and redevelopment. Moreover, resolving governance issues and endowing redevelopment entities with funding, expertise, and authority are thus also critical for achieving redevelopment goals.

The ability of the city and the master developer to navigate the proliferating governance associated with redevelopment allowed them to better pursue their redevelopment plan and forestall other options (Erie et al. 2011). This resulted in the privatization of public land and memory in a way that left few in the public satisfied during the early redevelopment stages. We draw on many of Erie's points concerning proliferating governance and the privatization of public resources. Master developers are not public entities and seek profits as their primary development goal. They may not have incentives to govern in the public interest, especially when pursuing the public interest undermines profits.

However, it is also important to view NTC San Diego's redevelopment in the broader, national context of general redevelopment. From that perspective, NTC San Diego sits near the top of military redevelopment projects that have gone furthest toward completion and have benefited the most stakeholders: public, private, and nonprofit. Liberty Station has won several awards, including one for historic preservation in development from the International Real Estate Federation (Showley 2011), the American Society of Civil Engineers Sustainable Project of the Year *and*

Project of the Year in 2007, the Base Redevelopment Community of the Year (2007) from the Association of Defense Communities, and many other local architectural, preservation, and redevelopment awards. Kim Elliott, senior vice president for McMillin, Liberty Station's developer, adds, "Liberty Station is one of the first successful, nearly complete base redevelopments in the country. We are very pleased that we blazed the trail for other BRAC communities" (Elliott 2014).

Proliferating governance raises barriers to redeveloping closed military bases. Redevelopment is more likely when an entity such as a redevelopment authority or, in this case, a master developer with support from the city can identify those barriers and pursue plans that reflect considerations at the local, regional, state, and federal levels (among others). In this sense, completed development is superior to never-ending projects, even if these projects benefit fewer stakeholders than we would like. San Diego's NTC ultimately reflects a broad community goal of mixed-use redevelopment, which results from the city's and master developer's ability to incorporate a wide variety of stakeholder interests into redevelopment plans and to execute those plans under a myriad of overlapping, frequently contradictory, regulatory frameworks.

San Diego thus provides an example of how empowering a private entity represents one possible pathway to resolving governance problems. Clearly, this is not the only pathway to governance, and empowering a master developer can create other problems with missing incentives to serve broad community stakeholders and accountability. Nevertheless, the high levels of authority and autonomy in San Diego's governance arrangement resulted in rapid, beneficial conversion relative to other cases in the analysis. San Diego's experience shows how important governance at scale is for redevelopment performance (Agnew 2016a; Jonas and Ward 2007; Ansell and Gash 2008). Simultaneously, it shows how much scholars and practitioners should make room for local agency when choices to empower, authorize, and hold entities accountable for redevelopment governance are all possible and consequential for defense conversion.

Fort Ord

Collaborative governance in practice is one of the most pressing challenges to converting and reusing Fort Ord. This project drew on political resources to coordinate a regional redevelopment process that surpassed expectations in conversion speed and community benefits. Many political jurisdictions border Fort Ord at the municipal, county, and state levels. Financing, transportation, environmental restoration, and infrastructure remediation are several of the many issues surrounding Fort Ord's conversion, crossing the entire forty-square mile region. Dozens of governmental, nonprofit, and private-sector stakeholders pursue their own interests across the region as they try to resolve regional conversion problems as well. Resolutions are therefore difficult to achieve without a regional governance perspective and a decision-making authority that engages stakeholders vertically, up and down scale, and horizontally across space and sector.

Governance of Fort Ord's conversion has surpassed expectations largely because of the community's access to federal and state resources. Specifically, many people credit then-Congressman Leon Panetta's Washington connections for securing resources for the Fort Ord project early in the conversion process, including helping to transfer land to the university system for free despite federal requirements demanding full conversion plans (rather than partial ones) prior to any transfer. Furthermore, the U.S. Department of Commerce granted $15 million to California State University in 1994 to assist with the conversion of 1,300 acres (approximately two square miles) into a university campus. As former chancellor of the California State University system Barry Munitz commented, "If you aren't lucky and well-connected, then the hill [for base redevelopment] is steep to climb" (Munitz 2013).

Panetta also helped direct resources for environmental remediation of the Superfund site at Fort Ord. Directing resources for environmental remediation began to address one of the biggest challenges in Fort Ord's redevelopment process: the presence of typical base contaminants as well as extensive unexploded ordnance. Congress passed the National Defense Authorization Act with "no-cost" economic conveyance (EDC) legislation in 1999, which "provided for no-cost transfers of EDC property to further stimulate economic redevelopment and long-term job creation and to eliminate delays resulting from prolonged negotiations over fair market value." Fort Ord's leadership leveraged this and other favorable incentives to gain no-fee land conveyances. Congressman Sam Farr (D-Monterey) noted the difficulty that many former defense communities face with remediation costs: the federal government should

"make contamination remediation a higher priority. If there is a conveyance cost, have it paid *after* redevelopment or as development becomes
profitable rather than put the money up front. Congress should pay for
toxic cleanup—they put the money in the account for cleanup through
the DoD" (Farr 2015).

The Fort Ord Reuse Authority (FORA) and the Department of the
Army entered into a memorandum of agreement (MOA) for the transfer
of 5,300 acres under the EDC in 2000 after gaining approval of their
reuse plan (Luckey and Schultz 2001; Fort Ord Reuse Authority 2013).
The no-cost conveyance may seem like a boon for local redevelopment
authorities, but it has not been a salve for Fort Ord's redevelopment
problems: "Approximately 1,200 World War II era structures are left
that do not meet civilian building codes and contain hazardous materi-
als such as asbestos and lead-based paint" (Luckey and Schultz 2001, 7).
This is consistent with Panetta's earlier rejection of the claims that a no-
cost conveyance is all that closed bases needed to thrive. More directly,
Panetta described the Army's claims as "bullshit" at the Military Bases
and Community Partnerships: Maintaining California's Edge conference on April 10, 2001, in Monterey (Luckey and Shultz 2001) because
environmental-remediation costs outweigh any benefits of receiving land
through no-fee economic development conveyance. Instead, no-fee conveyances represent *minimum* necessary conditions necessary for incentivizing conversion on most former bases, where expensive remediation
is likely.

In 2004 FORA and the Department of the Army initiated discussions
surrounding an environmental-services cooperative agreement (ESCA).
Conversations with Michael Houlemard of FORA highlight the importance of the ESCA for remediating Fort Ord. The ESCA would provide
dedicated funding for munitions disposal and remediation as well as support the U.S. Environmental Protection Agency (EPA) and the California
Department of Toxic and Substances Control's (DTSC) oversight, improve
coordination between FORA reuse activities and necessary remediation,
and ensure the safe transfer of approximately 3,340 acres to FORA (Fort
Ord Reuse Authority 2013). In 2007 FORA and the Department of the
Army completed their ESCA negotiations and executed the agreement,
with the final version allowing the Army to transfer to FORA nine parcels of land, totaling 3,340 acres, contaminated with a combination of

unexploded ordnance. According to the ESCA, FORA is now responsible for addressing all munitions-response actions for these nine parcels, while all other contamination issues, including groundwater, soil, and landfill concerns, remain the Army's responsibility. The ESCA also allows the Army to provide dedicated funding for munitions remediation on these specific parcels directly to FORA (Fort Ord Reuse Authority 2013).

Federal environmental priorities and land responsibilities also influenced Fort Ord's conversion. The former Fort Ord is not only a redevelopment site but also includes a wildlife refuge. As a result, the U.S. Fish and Wildlife Service mandated a habitat-management plan to reduce the incidental take of listed species and loss of habitat that supports those species (Fort Ord Reuse Authority 2013). The base reuse plan's land-use outline includes 18,000 acres to be reserved for conservation areas under the purview of U.S. Bureau of Land Management and 1,000 acres for coastal zone transfer under the California Department of Parks and Recreation's jurisdiction. A common misconception is that the military departs entirely when bases close. However, Fort Ord retains an active military presence on a portion of the base, with five California Army National Guard Units, a large Army data center, and the Monterey Presidio section still in operation. This occurs regularly on former bases and extends the federal government's authority over land use for decades. In Fort Ord's case, it is clear that the federal government is a central landholder, with over 61 percent of the former base under its control. The Cal State system owns 8 percent of the former base, and the Army retains 3 percent for continued, active-duty use. Taken together, these parcels total 71 percent of the former Fort Ord that the local community *does not own* under the FORA system (Lewis 1997). Thus, local agency is important for Fort Ord's redevelopment, but local authority exists for only 29 percent of the base.

Fort Ord's experience demonstrates the importance of local agency in terms of political resources to create functional governance structures for redevelopment at scale. The Fort Ord community leveraged political capital to release federal and state resources and promoted relationships that are not common in former defense communities. A strong regional governance structure and federal support mitigated the redevelopment challenges associated with massive environmental contamination on the former base and reconciled the needs of dozens of bordering and overlapping local, regional, state, and federal jurisdictions. The Fort Ord Reuse Authority's regional, collaborative redevelopment governance also speaks to the theoretical discussion surrounding territory and scale (Agnew 2016a; Jonas and Ward 2007; McCann 2003; Ansell and Gash 2008). FORA had to develop the very same new, broad, conceptualization of governance to promote conversion with community benefits; the community surpassed redevelopment expectations as a result.

NAS Alameda

The federal role in constraining redevelopment and disputes over the value of the former military site combined to slow conversion of NAS Alameda relative to the other bases. Approval to begin permanent conversion in pursuit of residential, commercial, and recreational redevelopment materialized only in 2013, even though the base closed in 1997. The conversion experience on the former NAS site also showcases how the challenges associated with governance, territory, and scale can limit redevelopment, even in cases where strong market conditions and local financing are available. In this case, federal policy stymied redevelopment plans even though governance arrangements were similar to those on the other bases and local authorities acknowledged the needs for expanded concepts of collaboration. In this sense, Alameda's conversion experience demonstrates the importance of national- and state-level policy structures that the local need to make redevelopment choices and devise governance structures may not always overcome. Redevelopment structures are eminently malleable in this sense and depend on the agency of actors beyond local borders. Unlike Fort Ord, Alameda lacked the political resources to gain special treatment at the state and national levels. Conversion choices were therefore subservient to federal policy, which stalled redevelopment for more than sixteen years.

President Clinton pledged a "speedy clean-up of contamination and hope for economic development" within months of the BRAC Commission's decision to close NAS Alameda (Clinton 1993b). Unfortunately, the site's redevelopment has been the antithesis of speedy and hopeful. Alameda's failures result from major policy shifts that contributed to redevelopment processes that have taken much longer than for the other California bases. The adoption of a fee-based federal land conveyance policy to extract market value from surplus federal property in 1999 and the dissolution of California's redevelopment authorities in 2011 both undermined the city of Alameda's ability to reach redevelopment deals with private-sector partners and efficiently engage local, regional, state, and federal agencies to clear conversion hurdles

The federal government's land-valuation policy is not the sole cause of Alameda's inability to advance its development process. In fact, city representatives have been outspoken about how the Navy and the city are on the same side: "We have good relationships with the Navy. Having a positive working relationship is key. It is [in] all of our best interests to get along," said Jennifer Ott, Alameda director of Base Reuse and COO of Alameda Point (2013). Rather, the point is that the federal policy on fee-based EDCs places communities in a deeper redevelopment hole than they would otherwise be in as they marshal their redevelopment resources. In Alameda, federal insistence on exchange value for the site rendered even private-sector development (for housing) untenable relative to redevelopment plans designed primarily to attract jobs over "use value" for residents. Governance challenges in this case extend across the federal government. The EPA, the National Park Service, and the White House all have jurisdiction over critical elements of NAS Alameda's redevelopment.

Alameda and its redevelopment authority have barely begun to address local and regional redevelopment governance challenges because of federal barriers and the city's difficulty in navigating relationships with the federal government and private-sector master developers. The lack of collaborative governance at scale and the lack of political resources show how the absence of these factors are critical for explaining Alameda's lack of progress. Thus, the cases show support for expanded concepts of governance from both positive and negative directions: empowered, autonomous, redevelopment authorities that promote collaborative governance arrangements at scale in San Diego and Fort Ord generated relatively quick defense conversion with relatively broad community benefits. The absence of these arrangements resulted in conversion delays and an inability to convert a former base altogether in Alameda, where redevelopment authorities also lacked agency.

Governance and Conversion at Holy Loch, Soesterberg, and Abrams Army HQ

Holy Loch, Soesterberg, and Abrams HQ were converted rapidly and at a minimum cost for residents, at least by U.S. standards. The extent of cooperation across different levels of government explains these outcomes. Multilevel cooperation is expected in a unitary system of government, such as The Netherlands, where fewer levels of governments involved in the conversion are likely to make collaboration easier than in federal systems with additional government layers. The Dutch government retained possession of the Soesterberg Air Base following the U.S. Air Force's departure and redeveloped it with national, not local, needs in mind. Yet the national government worked with the municipal government to fund and execute simultaneous redevelopment of the village adjacent to the base. The plan revitalized the village of Soesterberg's main street with new, pedestrian-friendly, visually attractive commercial and recreational development. Defense conversion complemented this revitalization as visitors to the new national military museum or the national park on the site could patronize the revitalized village, thus replacing some of the revenue and jobs lost when the base closed.

Of these European bases, the most surprising conversion outcome occurred in Germany, where the federal government, the state of Hesse's government, and Frankfurt's government worked with Von Goethe University to convert former military facilities. The new central campus situates Von Goethe's world-class facilities within walking distance of downtown Frankfurt. The new campus renders the university much more attractive for students and faculty, and it supports Frankfurt's position as a European capital of banking and finance as well as its new forays into other industries. It was therefore in the city, state, and federal interest to convert the former military facilities strategically. However, this type of conversion does not occur in many U.S. contexts.

Conversion outcomes on European bases are not all uniform or even desirable: less than 10 percent of the revenue and jobs that left with 4,000 American service personnel have returned to Dunoon, Scotland. The UK is not a federal system of government, although Scottish devolution brings it closer to federalism. Holy Loch and the nearby town of Dunoon were left largely on their own relative to the German and Dutch experience.

However, regional governance and Scottish national spending have extended rail and ferry service so that residents of the town of Dunoon could commute to work or shop in Glasgow, across the Firth of Clyde, only thirty-five miles away by car or bus.

These three base conversion experiences show how the structure of national political systems is not destiny for governance of base conversion. Collaboration and strategic, long-term planning can occur despite the challenges of coordinating across additional layers of government in federal systems. Similarly, unitary systems *may* make redevelopment governance easier, but they will not always lead to broad defense conversion, even in affluent democracies.

Complex, inter-scalar governance arrangements are necessary to advance redevelopment processes. Unfortunately, these arrangements are often opaque, leave little room for public engagement, and add to the general lack of accountability in local infrastructure development. Communities also choose to structure redevelopment processes differently and pursue many different conversion goals for different stakeholders, which suggests that local agency in military redevelopment is present at greater practical levels than many might think. This is an important component of defense conversion from a theoretical perspective as well: broad governance theories under-specify local agency, which is critical for explaining individual outcomes and important to consider for theorizing redevelopment governance.

This chapter speaks to the question of what level of government should have primacy in the revitalization of the base. As a rule, most planners would advocate for the empowerment of those most likely to be directly affected, and defense conversion most directly affects local communities. However, too often these local communities are ill-prepared to tackle the enormous redevelopment issues that they face. These communities frequently also define redevelopment issues downwardly and view the universe as the borders of their town. The federal presence in redevelopment forces communities to reconsider this view. Absent successful lawsuits, the DoD usually gets its way over the community in terms of critical considerations of which bases close, when they close, and their condition at the time of conveyance. But federal involvement also comes with resources and redevelopment support. Ultimately, communities would benefit from more agency in the redevelopment process but would suffer from the lack of resources such agency might bring.

The impact of base closures often crosses into communities many miles away, and base closures are instances where "values larger than local" should prevail. Redeveloping closed bases in a way that benefits local communities in a sustainable way is simply not possible without engaging multiple jurisdictions horizontally (all of the cities bordering the base, cities where residents commute through those bordering the base, those downstream, etc.) as well as vertically (county, regional, state, federal). Additionally, many authorities exercise control over redevelopment processes, but these might not be classified as easily, such as voting districts, coastal commissions, school districts, and commercial districts. Values larger than local entail accommodating the needs of many of these stakeholders in addition to laying a foundation for a sustainable local community following a base closure.

The defense conversion experience shows how the nature of local power relations conditions redevelopment governance and outcomes. Communities choose how to structure specific governance arrangements and redevelopment policies, and there is considerable variation in how they address the next challenge of connecting sites that may be physically central in communities but suffer from economic, political, and cultural isolation. Thus, local agency and redevelopment control remain possible in former defense communities even if communities' general strategies and policies diverge in many areas.

5

THE PURSUIT OF INTEGRATION

Centrality and Isolation in Defense Conversion

Defense conversion turns the concept of centrality on its head. Many former bases are physically central to major urban areas but have been isolated economically, politically, socially, and culturally for decades. Bases were largely off-limits to the public while in operation and were designed to be self-sufficient in many respects. They were governed separately from the local community and acted, at least in part, as their own isolated ecosystems. Many of these bases were once physically isolated by design, but regional growth encroached on military space. Local infrastructure to support this multi-jurisdictional growth tends to develop around the bases, rather than through them, and in most cases bypasses the bases altogether. Base infrastructure is standardized to military specifications, not local or state building codes and environmental regulations. Much of the infrastructure on former bases is therefore incompatible with that of the surrounding city-region. Military communities also often act in isolation in terms of service provision while the bases are active and have their own road and water systems, communication infrastructure, and electric grids. Former bases' economic, physical, and political isolation ultimately reflects decades of independent, exclusive operations and local successes in creating networks that work around the bases, not through them. Many bases thus represent walled-off spaces that are technically public land but act as private enclaves: "One of our problems is signage and way-finding. This place was not meant for the public; it was not supposed to be easy to find," said Jennifer Garey, president of Art and Antiquities and former preservationist at Liberty Station (2013).

After a base closes, integration becomes the utopian ideal and one of the largest challenges in defense conversion. But integration represents a long-term, incremental process rather than a dichotomous outcome. A wide variety of challenges slows economic, political, and social integration, which advances more quickly in some areas than others. Partial, selective integration then becomes the norm throughout the defense conversion process, which itself is not a terminal state but ongoing, like development in general. Changing goals of what constitutes ideal end states further complicate the challenges of partial integration. The goal in this chapter is therefore to provide a view of integration based on these processes as opposed to simply characterizing bases as integrated or not.

Pursuing economic integration and development is a key aspect of redeveloping closed bases. Recentralizing geographically central sites and connecting geographically isolated sites are essential for many redevelopment projects on former bases, such as those with educational, industrial, and commercial components. Military bases and the defense industry represent their own clusters and drive regional economies. Former military shipyards or weapons-testing grounds can be converted for defense contractors' use, but most former military bases are not well-suited for private defense use. Additionally, these sites are rarely aligned with local industries in ways that allow for easy clustering in defense conversion. Geographic integration and economic integration are important, but the concerns for redevelopment on former military bases are not limited to these areas. Pursuing political, social, and cultural integration with communities and city-regions is also of great importance for governing redevelopment, retaining and attracting residents, attracting capital, and creating a meaningful sense of place. These challenges extend far beyond traditional notions of community redevelopment because former military bases are also isolated from communities' political systems, social networks, and cultural lives. Long-term redevelopment on former bases is thus unsustainable from the perspective of providing economic benefits to broad groups of stakeholders without simultaneous pursuit of political, social, and cultural integration.

Reversing this isolation to begin to integrate the former bases is costly and difficult because allowing physical access to the base after its closure is not enough. Additionally, conversion occurs through distinct, simultaneous processes, and one often sees elements of successful and unsuccessful integration within the same project and across different projects on the same parcel. Communities converting closed bases thus almost always still have decades of economic, political, social, and cultural exclusion with which to contend. The result is a paradox of centrality: potentially high-value real estate within sight of large, vibrant markets is difficult to develop or redevelop, requires considerably more money than similarly large projects might otherwise take, and regularly falls short of expectations. Bases in rural areas are even more difficult to convert in the face of similar integration challenges because of their much lower market values. The challenges of integration demonstrate that closed bases are deceptively difficult and expensive to convert, even though many appear central and possess ostensible assets. The level of integration into the surrounding city-region thus represents another factor explaining how bases are converted and for whom.

Economic Isolation

Regional-growth scholarship frequently includes a measure of both geographic and economic centrality. Geographic proximity to supply chains and markets, and the ability to collaborate using the same physical space, promote economic productivity and growth. Researchers employ network analysis to show how important economic and social linkages are for economic development (Jackson 2008; Rakodi 2014; Moss and Marvin 2016). Even physically centralized bases are isolated from these networks, except for the provision of services, such as retail shopping outlets and food delivery, for troops stationed on the base.

Economic activity in defense communities is not trivial: military bases employ troops and support large service sectors that surround bases with housing and retail options. Military bases also coordinate DoD Prime awards, which provide contracts, grants, and research and development agreements to many local firms and nonprofit organizations in the surrounding region. Small-business support programs also operate through bases and thus expand economic networks to serve the community as well as provide opportunities for local businesses to expand. Former defense communities thus begin the conversion process with some economic advantages that former industrial communities do not usually have (Markusen et al. 1991). Still, rural military bases are not aligned with agrarian economies, and exurban, suburban, and urban bases are only rarely aligned with manufacturing sectors or services in environments with more diverse forms of economic activity. This disconnect with surrounding economic activity makes integration difficult because of extra costs for infrastructural conversion and the challenge of creating new economic networks that include the former base rather than bypass it.

The infrastructure that city-regions build to attract investment and support market activity skirts bases while they are in operation or is integrated with the bases only in a piecemeal fashion. However, this is because military bases develop an independent infrastructure to suit their own needs that does not always extend to local networks outside of the base. This creates isolated infrastructure on former bases that is often designed for very different purposes than the infrastructure surrounding the base. For example, the infrastructure necessary for providing water for thousands of personnel living in concentrated barracks on a rural base may not integrate easily into the irrigation systems of a farming and ranching community. Additionally, much of the infrastructure on former bases is standardized to military specifications, not local codes. That makes converting existing infrastructure or adding new infrastructure to integrate former bases very expensive.

Despite the expense, integrating local transportation, power, water, and communication networks is mandatory for defense conversion: enterprises require basic services and the simple ability to meet face-to-face. Moreover, modern industries depend on advanced services such as high-speed communication networks. Yet many bases are left out of the infrastructural network needed to add communications capacity as technology progresses. Attracting investment in high-value-added industries in the absence of such networks is next to impossible, and providing the infrastructure after bases close is costly. Pursuing economic integration is an extraordinary endeavor from the very beginning of the redevelopment process. Taking advantage of opportunities to form industrial clusters and generate gains from agglomeration is thus very difficult for former defense communities. There is evidence of economic gains stemming from careful defense conversion to align with existing economic activity, but this is the exception rather than the rule. However, even economic gains will not contribute to broad, sustainable conversion on the former bases if different aspects of development occur in isolation from one another.

Political Isolation

Active military bases are politically isolated because they are governed by the service branch operating the base rather than by the surrounding community. Bases do have public affairs and community relations officers serving as liaisons with local governments, but those governments do not have political jurisdiction over the base while it is active. The military branch operating the base determines the precise timetable for departure when bases are slated for closure and the precise amount of personnel and services that depart, with little direct community input. Several officers serve as direct liaisons to the community surrounding the base closure process as well, but the branch of service operating the base makes many of the decisions surrounding departure logistics.

There is an immediate need for political integration with the surrounding area after a base closes, but integration is difficult to achieve because of contested jurisdictional boundaries among surrounding communities and lack of zoning on the former defense site. Local, regional, and state authorities all vie for political influence and territory in this process, which pits governing bodies that complement one another in theory against one another in practice. Additionally, partial closures are the rule for bases that closed under BRAC, rather than the exception. It is rare that all military functions cease and all personnel depart following the official closure. Most former bases continue to host military activities and active-duty personnel for years afterward. This makes governance and political integration of former bases especially difficult because some parts of the base are transferred to nonmilitary authorities while others remain in military hands and are governed under military systems.

Integrating former military bases into the surrounding intergovernmental political environment includes both horizontal integration (neighboring municipalities) and vertical integration (within the wide variety of
state and federal entities with jurisdictional claims on former bases). In
this sense, integrating closed bases requires simultaneous region building.
Region building consists of integrating political, economic, and social processes across physical space. For example, former military communities
often join federal and statewide funding proposals to connect the bases
with public networks or to align them with other ongoing multimodal
initiatives. These initiatives rely on Department of Transportation (DOT)
resources for funding and limit redevelopment options because of the need
to comply with federal law. This example speaks to many of the trade-offs
that communities face when converting former bases: bargains that foster
economic integration often limit local political integration or add layers of
oversight that limit communities' conversion options.

Social and Cultural Isolation

Military bases are often culturally isolated from the surrounding city-
region because of the insular nature of military activities. Civilian residents are often excluded from the site because of the sensitive, potentially
dangerous activities that occur on base, and service members are not
always free to discuss their work with civilians. The transient nature of
military service promotes this isolation: many active-duty military members live on base, reside in the area for a relatively short time, and have
few incentives to integrate with the surrounding civilian community. On-
base social events are primarily designed to serve active-duty military
personnel, which generates "cultural clusters" while the bases are operational. However, those clusters change continuously as people and defense
activities evolve. These activities represent cultural barriers to integration,
particularly as groups battle over whose cultural memory to preserve in
the redevelopment process.

Military cultural clusters tend to disappear after bases close and the
cluster is no longer productive in economic or social terms. To be sure,
there are always social connections between personnel and local members
of the community, but residents are generally not accustomed to going

on base for their public services, using base territory for recreation, or crossing the base using public or private transportation. One of the results of this social isolation is that community thoroughfares, transportation networks, and patterns of community life avoid the bases. Furthermore, bases often sit empty for lengthy periods after their closure: "When we got here, feral cats and weeds had taken over the base . . . it was a ghost town, a no-man's-land," said Alan Ziter, NTC Foundation director (2014). This makes the civilian residents who remain after a base closure tend to continue avoiding the base.

Military bases are more culturally integrated with the community in rural areas that are more economically dependent on the base. These bases are often the centers of cultural activity because military personnel represent such a large percentage of the local population. However, the social and cultural relevance of the military community also creates problems for permanent civilian residents living near the base. Many residents in these areas have a difficult time preparing for closure and planning for conversion precisely because they were integrated into the military culture and will be left culturally isolated after the bases close. In this sense, culturally integrating veterans and other residents in former defense communities can mimic some of the challenges associated with incorporating other culturally isolated groups, such as immigrants, less affluent residents, or members of ethnic minorities, into the community fabric (Logan et al. 2002; Charles 2006; South et al. 2005). For example, broadening social networks beyond the military in-group and shifting the epicenter of social life from the military base to the former defense community take time and effort. Similarly, normalizing workplace and social interaction among veterans, former military service providers, and the broader civilian public is not easy because of cultural differences across these groups (Ostovary and Dapprich 2011; Zemke et al. 1999).

Many communities face a cultural division between permanent residents who are not members of the armed forces and retired military personnel. This is especially apparent in more-populous areas where members of the military and those employed in businesses serving the military represent a small percentage of the total population. Retiring near a base where one served is common, however, and military retirees frequently seek to preserve historic sites throughout redevelopment. Preserving historic memory is a laudable goal for many in the community, but it can put residents promoting redevelopment at odds with former service members who hold different collective memories that they believe are worth preserving (Barthel 1996).

Historic designations can mitigate some potential conflicts by attracting residents or commercial tenants, or offering opportunities for refurbishing structures. Furthermore, historic preservation benefits a broad array of stakeholders and community members. In this sense the historic designation that is common on former military bases can provide opportunities for financing redevelopment through tax credits and other incentives, but it can also maintain cultural isolation on the former bases—for example, by preserving memory at the cost of preventing the creation of new structures for residential, recreational, or commercial use. Despite its potential benefits, historic designation thus presents trade-offs: it potentially represents one more constraint on redevelopment.

Cultural divisions and debates about preservation are part of a broader set of disagreements about what the converted bases should be and who they will serve. The fact that much of the base area remains off-limits because of lead, asbestos, and fuel contamination compounds this set of challenges. Lawsuits that advocacy groups bring against cities, redevelopment agencies, and development partners mark conversion efforts on most former bases.[1] These challenges to certain stakeholders' redevelopment visions reflect the difficulty in integrating isolated bases from a cultural standpoint because of broad cultural gulfs across historic preservationists, environmentalists, advocates for marginalized residents, local governments, residents, and private-sector partners.

Ordinary Cities, Extraordinary Circumstances

Defense conversion reflects many of the development challenges facing ordinary cities. Much of the existing literature on redeveloping closed bases emphasizes success stories in global cities such as San Francisco or New York. Only a handful of America's former defense communities could be categorized as global or national cities that serve as important nodes in global financial and economic networks (Scott 2011). Most bases fall into the category of ordinary cities, which are intermediate or peripheral to global economic networks (Amin and Graham 1997). These ordinary cities face serious challenges in governing, becoming competitive, and engaging in global markets, especially when a military base closes and takes jobs, revenue, and services with it. This scenario is analogous to the crises of deindustrialization, suburban sprawl, and the deterioration of the urban core that many cities faced from the 1980s onward.

Reinvention or resilience is the supposed requirement for global cities to remain "the key command and control centers within the interlocking, globalizing dynamics of financial markets, high-level producer services industries, corporate headquarters and other associated service industries" (Amin and Graham 1997, 414). Ordinary cities are less able to reinvent themselves because of weak governance and limited resources. Former defense communities in quasi-urban, suburban, and rural areas may not have the wherewithal to gain resources associated with the recent focus on cities as drivers of national and international economic development, especially in the context of high levels of specialization associated with high-tech and service-based economies (Scott 2011; Hall 2000). A general lack of development experience, a lack of connections across levels of government, and little experience with sophisticated governance are the rule rather than the exception for the ordinary cities with a closed base. As a result, ordinary cities tend to lack the resources and governance structures to integrate former bases.

Defense conversion extends beyond cities to suburban and rural communities. These communities face even starker redevelopment prospects than ordinary cities as they convert closed bases, but the lenses used to explain redevelopment in ordinary cities are much closer to suburban and rural communities' experience than to San Francisco's Presidio or Brooklyn's Navy Yard. Suburban and rural communities with closed bases tend to have weak governance frameworks, at least from the perspective of collaborating across multiple levels of government and incorporating many community stakeholders. The lens surrounding how ordinary cities are governed even applies to growing urban regions such as San Diego, Monterey, and Alameda as they connect with larger, more populous southern California, San Jose and Silicon Valley, and the Bay Area.

Urban scholarly paradigms beyond ordinary cities offer insights into how governance relates to integration of former military sites. The "flexible cities" framework describes dynamic urban environments where cities constantly reinvent the ways they organize politics and economics to meet new challenges (Amin and Thrift 2002). Former military communities are forced to reinvent themselves to meet new challenges as well in the hope that policy makers, citizens, and advocacy groups can promote and govern policies to meet their redevelopment needs. Flexible cities are thus essentially thought to be resilient cities. Some communities' defense conversion experiences fall under the flexible cities rubric when the redevelopment process is governed well, but former military communities also demonstrate aspects of the so-called "crisis city" (Gotham and Greenberg 2014). Collaborative governance that could promote and harness collective action is missing in these areas, and the pursuit of individual interests precludes cohesive governance for the "common good" (Gotham and Greenberg 2014; De Rosa and Salvati 2016). The goal is to be well-governed enough to be flexible when a base closes and to achieve major economic and political change to integrate the base into surrounding networks. However, most former defense communities are "ordinary" in their governance and thus slip easily into "crisis" mode when bases close and collective action and integration do not easily progress.

Bases that are unable to reinvent themselves to compete and to govern cohesively cannot regain economic centrality, if they had it to begin with. These communities are also poorly suited to regain political, social, or cultural centrality. The departure of the military puts many communities on a crisis footing, and redevelopment challenges move many of them from ordinary cities to crisis cities, perhaps permanently. This is different for flexible and global cities, where the crisis footing is only temporary, if it occurs at all. Global or flexible cities, such as San Francisco (global) or San Diego (flexible), use governance to achieve superior redevelopment outcomes that integrate and recentralize former military sites along economic, political, social, and cultural dimensions. In contrast, many former military communities categorized as "ordinary cities" and those in suburban or rural areas fail to develop collaborative governance and exhibit economic, social, and political problems more typical of the periphery.

Clustering and Agglomeration

Physical isolation prevents or undermines "clustering": complementary industrial siting to improve competitiveness through knowledge spillovers, regional competition, labor market pooling, and supplier specialization

(Sasson and Reve 2015; Porter 1990). Infrastructure investments provide opportunities to overcome these geographic challenges and connect economic islands. Doing so fosters the cluster mechanisms that are so important for competitiveness. Decreasing the spatial gradient for economic interaction thus increases regional economic cohesion and unlocks cluster benefits. However, public policy often determines which regions join economic networks and which remain isolated (Sasson and Reve 2015; Porter 2008; Sölvell et al. 2003; Wilson 2012; Musterd and Ostendorf 2013). Of course, this is not to suggest that all potentially complementary clusters will realize economic success (Porter 2008; Zettinig and Vincze 2012). Challenges in terms of ensuring competition among firms, integrating private firms into clusters, and balancing trade-offs between capitalizing on existing opportunities and researching and developing future opportunities abound and can easily limit benefits from industrial clusters (Sölvell et al. 2003; Ferreira et al. 2012; Niu et al. 2012). Nevertheless, connecting formally isolated cities, industries, and firms offers more potential for success through clustering than if each entity remained isolated.

Cluster benefits may result immediately from integrating economic islands into the local and regional economies. However, the extent to which previously isolated markets result in cluster benefits and create value for residents depends on the extent to which these markets complement one another. It is entirely possible that some cities specialize in unrelated areas that do not complement one another under the clustering framework. Any increase in value resulting from integration under such circumstances will be limited to a reduction in transportation costs (Jacobs 1969); cost savings from serving a larger population, such as economies of scale in producing and delivering utilities; and increased urbanization (Glaeser 2011).

The creation of value through clustering increases as the previously isolated areas' economic specializations come to mirror one another. Many studies have shown that this type of clustering produces a large proportion of economic value and drives economic growth in many regions. Agglomeration and cluster analyses in labor market economics, urban economics (Behrens et al. 2014), and regional economics (Sasson and Reve 2015) support these conclusions. Thus, the desire to create economic clusters and increase regional competitiveness frequently drives regional economic planning and policy.

The clustering concept applies to former military bases as well. These sites are commonly isolated from comprehensive regional economic networks, even though they may be geographically central. Yet military sites lie at the center of different kinds of clusters. The bases support extensive service industries through local contracting and procurement. They also support extensive research-and-development networks that extend across private, public, and nonprofit sectors. In this sense, defense communities fall under the concept of military industrial districts, where government funding and resources drive local economies (Markusen et al. 1991; Markusen 1996). The challenge for former defense communities lies in transitioning from one established type of industrial clustering to future, unknown clusters that complement local or regional economies.

Military bases have distinct suppliers, service providers, and infrastructure, resulting in economic islands that are difficult to integrate. Unfortunately, former military sites rarely complement clusters of economic activity in the surrounding region. The benefits of connecting these former sites to local infrastructure networks are thus lower than in many other redevelopment contexts. Arguments in favor of integration are therefore difficult to sustain and funding for integration difficult to achieve, particularly in the face of a need to financialize infrastructure and service delivery (Sasson and Reve 2015). Former military communities are thus likely to miss out on the higher capacity for entrepreneurship, competition, and innovation in the marketplace that stems from complementary clustering as infrastructure helps to integrate isolated economies. In turn, relatively poor economic performance is less likely to attract individuals and firms from outside of the region, which begets continued poor performance and creates a vicious circle. The outcome for former military communities is missed opportunities for job creation and higher productivity for enterprises that remain after a base closes.

Cluster theory has serious practical implications for former military communities. Larger clusters will create more economic value than smaller clusters, and complementary industrial clusters will create more value than unrelated industries situated physically close to one another. Larger clusters often occur in cities and can drive economic growth from an industrial perspective, even in the knowledge economy (O'Mara 2015). Infrastructure works to promote growth and foster the development of complementary industrial clusters only when isolated, potentially dynamic industries exist in the first place (Sasson and Reve 2015). Connecting one economic island to another can still be beneficial, but it might not be very cost-effective if the industries are not complementary. In this sense, rural, geographically isolated, *and* economically isolated former military communities are at a severe redevelopment disadvantage relative to other communities.

Agglomeration is not likely for industries in many former military communities because there are few industries to speak of following military base closures. The likelihood of complementary industries existing in close enough geographic proximity to take advantage of clustering is low. The prospects for clustering on rural bases is thus also low. Nevertheless, many bases in urban, suburban, and exurban areas have more opportunities to take advantage of complementary clustering and fit themselves into dynamic local economies. Public policies designed to promote clustering in former defense communities by harnessing existing knowledge and industrial experience can help. For instance, California State University, Monterey Bay (CSUMB), is physically close to Silicon Valley and has achieved some complementary clustering in the knowledge economy. CSUMB allows scholars to take their research innovations to market, meets the demand for an educated workforce, and partners with private firms to provide students with direct work experience prior to graduation. Other examples of clustering on former bases include creative-company corporate headquarters near production and distribution centers at the Philadelphia Navy Yard and even the integration of San Diego's former Naval Training Center into the local arts-based cultural economy. Alameda has high potential for clustering with the tech industry as well but has thus far failed to make targeted investments to realize this potential.

Integration as Conversion for NTC San Diego, Fort Ord, and NAS Alameda

Most former defense communities are ordinary cities, but the three California cases do not belong purely in this category. Instead, their integration challenges resemble those in communities with higher property values and stronger connections to vibrant, urban economies, at least in terms of the extraordinary region in which all three cases lie. The discussion of ordinary cities and how they address challenges surrounding integration is thus intended for the national defense conversion audience. However, the integration challenges in the three cases demonstrate the difficulties in this area, even for cities with strong market conditions. The wide economic, political, and social diversity of the regions surrounding the three cases is an additional reason why strong market conditions in some communities near former bases do not always promote integration in defense conversion. For example, Carmel, California, is a bastion of coastal wealth near Fort Ord, while Salinas is an agricultural community. They both help to govern Fort Ord's redevelopment, and it is important to note their varied interests, needs, and resources as they do so.

NTC San Diego

San Diego's NTC was the least physically isolated of the three former bases. It was also the most conducive to economic integration of the three cases, but not necessarily because of its physical centrality. The former NTC San Diego sits on the northern shore of the San Diego Harbor, surrounded by the Point Loma community. It is less than a mile from the San Diego International Airport, two miles from the southern shore of Mission Bay, and four miles from downtown San Diego. Strong general market conditions for waterfront property in San Diego, economic growth throughout the 1990s, and a real estate boom until the mid-2000s made economic integration cost-effective and desirable from the developer's, residents', and tenants' perspectives. As a city, San Diego is the least "ordinary" among the cases. It has considerable administrative capacity and serious resources to bring to bear on defense conversion. Far from destitute after the NTC's closure, San Diego's other, active bases buoyed its broader economy, which has remained relatively strong and flexible throughout the time frame of the study compared to other communities with closed bases. Thus, San Diego's conversion experience at the high end of the redevelopment spectrum is at least a partial result of San Diego's position as a city with extraordinary resources and consistent insulation from economic crisis.

The base was built in 1923 and updated over the years from an infrastructural standpoint. Nevertheless, buildings on the base were not generally suitable for occupation or connection to local infrastructure (electricity, water, sewer, transportation) without full renovations. Older facilities are not suitable for integration on most former bases, but the NTC San Diego is the smallest geographic parcel of the three former bases and one of the smallest in the national database. Its small size and its physical proximity to established infrastructure made it less costly to integrate than other bases. For instance, the cost of the new streets, water, sewer, and electric lines necessary to connect new educational, residential, recreational, corporate, and retail redevelopment sites on the base with existing networks was lower for the NTC than on other, more physically isolated bases. Furthermore, the structures on the former base could be demolished outside of the historic district, and new construction for residential, corporate, and retail use could then progress rapidly on other parts of the base. These advantages spared the master developer great expense in terms of building new infrastructure or renovating existing buildings to integrate Liberty Station with the surrounding economy.

Governance poses some of the greatest integration challenges in defense conversion. However, the governance structure for converting the NTC posed fewer challenges than for Fort Ord and NAS Alameda, and it reflects a *relatively* easy integration process. This is partially a result of the former NTC's geographic location, contained entirely within San Diego. Despite this advantage, challenges surrounding territory, scale, and governance plague integration efforts even when the former defense site lies within one city. A large number of other horizontal and vertical jurisdictions overlay NTC San Diego and require collaboration and negotiation on many redevelopment issues. For example, converting the NTC required simultaneous arts development and historic preservation: "We are the historic heart, but historic preservation isn't our mission. We are a nonprofit real estate developer. That's exactly who we are," said Whitney Roux, program director of the NTC Foundation (2014). Also, according to Judy McDonald, a foundation board member, "One of the tensions is combining real estate development with the arts side of it. Making sure the talents of the people who are driving are able to cope with both sides" (McDonald 2014). And Timothy Brandt, of the California State Historic

Preservation Office, says that "what we warn—no project is done until it is reviewed—it is done at their own risk—local approvals and entitlements do not mean approval for tax credit review" (Brandt 2015). But San Diego's governance of defense conversion in the form of a master-developer partnership resulted in relatively quick dispute resolution between the city and different local, regional, state, and federal stakeholders and authorities.

Strong market conditions and the return of the compact-city tradition also aided economic integration. Future residents quickly purchased new housing on the former base to live near downtown San Diego, the airport, the harbor, and Mission Bay. Corporate, commercial, and educational tenants found the site similarly attractive: McMillin (the master developer) moved into its new corporate headquarters on the site early in the conversion process. Commercial and educational tenants began occupying buildings upon completion of construction and renovation, which created a new, economically integrated, mixed-use community that has won more than a dozen international, national, state, and local development awards, including for architecture and historic preservation. Other cities around the country increasingly see demand for adapted former factory spaces and warehouses that are converted into residences and other public spaces, such as universities and museums. The scale of these former sites of production is large, much as with former military bases, and many are environmentally contaminated. Conversion in this area is therefore relatively rare outside of strong market conditions and not always feasible (Sega 2015). Yet San Diego's market conditions were strong, contamination was relatively light, and the transformation of warehouses, barracks, and other large structures into public spaces did occur.

Politically integrating the NTC was easier than for many other communities because the base fell within the city of San Diego's political territory on many dimensions. Yet simmering conflicts still occurred because of county taxes, state historic preservation requirements, the state Coastal Commission authority, the airport authority, and Point Loma neighborhood advocacy groups. Many of these entities claimed jurisdiction over the former site, but redevelopment still advanced through a carefully managed partnership between the city and McMillin. Some Point Loma residents argued that the public-private partnership and political integration that followed came at the expense of residents' rights. However, the group has been working more closely with McMillin and recently awarded the developers its Lighthouse Award for supporting the Point Loma Association mission and its "visionary development of Liberty Station" (Point Loma Association 2016). These voters and members of community advocacy groups objected to new residents, new visitors, and the new traffic that might accompany them. Political integration can therefore have a downside that reflects the ability to advance the redevelopment process over the objections of local groups. The NTC San Diego redevelopment partnership's success in this area thus suggests that the former base *is* well-integrated into a local political environment. However, this is a political environment where city hall dominates neighborhoods in a way that also benefits private developers (Erie et al. 2011). Whether integrating former defense sites from a political standpoint benefits the community then depends, in large part, on the broader political context in which integration occurs.

Social integration at the former NTC occurred as new residents moved in and new schools, theaters, and recreational spaces opened. Soon the former base had 349 new housing units. The historic church on the base became a coveted wedding site, with ceremonies booked for years in advance. The recreational parcels and forty-six-acre waterfront park on the site now receive tens of thousands of visitors annually. Hundreds of students attend one elementary, two middle, and two public charter high schools on the site; the Rock Academy, a private Christian school, is also located in Liberty Station and serves students in grades K–12. This and other enterprises are controversial to some in the community because of the privatization of public land. Nevertheless, private enterprises thrive on the former base: eleven restaurants offer spaces for socialization, a movie theater offers entertainment, and grocery stores provide relatively easy options for food shopping. McMillin and other companies' employees who work in Liberty Station offices regularly remain on the site after hours to shop, dine, and socialize, and many community members use the former base after work and on the weekends.

Social integration followed economic and political integration relatively rapidly but left open questions of how to prioritize social benefits for the community. Land is in short supply on the relatively small NTC, and each land-use decision comes with opportunity costs. For instance, educational, recreational, and some commercial uses have social benefits but also come at the potential expense of museums and the preservation of historic memory through sight lines and building configurations. Preservation also has social benefits, but for different community stakeholders that did not feel their interests were represented in the conversion process (Save Our NTC 1995). John McNab, of Save Our NTC, refers to the conversion as "continuing to give away valuable land for Liberty Station . . . more good money being thrown into a bottomless pit of broken agreements. The public has given McMillin too many concessions without getting anything in return. It is time instead to demand our buildings and land back" (Save Our NTC 2003). These sentiments are common in defense conversion, as many feel that former military space should revert to the public rather than have it privatized through a master-developer–led process.

Cultural integration represents one of the greatest points of contention in the conversion of San Diego's NTC. The NTC is the oldest of the three cases and was one of the older bases in continuous operation in the country at the time of its closure in 1992. The base's long history carried cultural value for many residents in the area and for many others who trained on the base or whose parents or grandparents trained there. Community stakeholders pushed for historic preservation through maintaining sight lines and open space as well as maintaining many of the structures on the site, which were eligible for historic designation. Military preservation proponents were disappointed with the redevelopment plans, but they did have their interests represented in the historic designation of a 56-acre National Historic District on the 550-acre NTC site. Yet ending the redevelopment efforts with historic preservation alone would have left this portion of Liberty Station culturally isolated.

In addition to preservation, the redevelopment plan for portions of the base near the historic district included mixed-use spaces for residential, educational, recreational, and commercial activity. These provisions made cultural isolation in redevelopment a prime point of contention. Integrating the redeveloped NTC into the surrounding community from an economic perspective included new construction (in the style of the buildings in the historic district) and new sight lines. Many community stakeholders who served on the base argued that these new structures destroyed their memory of the site. However, members of the surrounding Point Loma neighborhood, new residents on the former base, and private-sector developers were often at odds with preservationists. Development proponents believed that the preservationists acted against the community's best interests when they opposed housing, commercial centers, recreation areas, and signage in areas designed to serve the public, such as the arts district on the base. However, as noted above, the Point Loma Community Association and McMillin have largely mended their relationship and now work together on many aspects of Liberty Station's operation.

The Civic, Arts, and Cultural District within the NTC's historic district serves as a cultural centerpiece for the community and integrates formerly isolated cultural space with the broader arts culture in San Diego. Yet creating and sustaining the arts district remain one of the greatest conversion challenges surrounding the NTC. The district has overcome many unexpected hurdles associated with redeveloping former military bases and operating in historic buildings. The expense of refurbishing buildings, the limitations on signage that come with historic tax credits, and the need to attract for-profit as well as nonprofit tenants to continue redevelopment all slowed conversion and cultural integration efforts. The costs of converting and integrating existing structures for reuse were greatest for the stakeholder that could least afford it: a nonprofit arts foundation. The arts foundation was originally seeded with capital from the master developer but was left to raise money for refurbishing buildings on its own after the expensive tax burden and conversion costs became clear.

The corporate, retail, residential, and educational districts in Liberty Station benefited from new construction in the sense that they could be created and inexpensively integrated into local markets and social networks. The master developer could also profit immediately from corporate, retail, and residential development in a way that the nonprofit arts foundation could not. By that same token, the historic and arts districts are prominent in Liberty Station's branding: "I wanted to emphasize the arts on this campus. Others believe you fill it up with who you can get so we can pay our bills. Both of us are right" (McDonald 2014). McMillin and the city *did* emphasize the arts from a marketing standpoint and *also* emphasized revenue-generating redevelopment from the standpoint of sequential timing to pay the bills. This reflects another integration trade-off from a cultural perspective: arts and historic districts help to preserve and create place. They are therefore attractive for corporate and retail tenants, for fulfilling an educational mission, and for residents and visitors.

But arts and historic districts are the least directly profitable of redevelopment options on many former bases and are thus underfunded or ignored in favor of economic redevelopment that might not integrate former bases into the cultural fabric of the community.

Social and cultural integration also includes community access to public space. Proponents intended the Civic, Arts, and Cultural District to support San Diego's artistic community through below-market studio and gallery space. However, the high costs of raising revenue to support building restoration and refurbishment forced the NTC Foundation to moderate this goal. The foundation sought market-rate tenants to offset restoration costs and diverged from its original vision of a low-cost artistic community. Still, the arts district now boasts ten refurbished, historic, mission-style buildings and receives more than 100,000 annual visitors. The district hosts regular events such as gallery nights, fund-raisers for the arts in San Diego, live music, and other cultural activities. Preserved memory is thus integrated with local cultural desires in a way that makes Liberty Station an attractive place to live, work, and visit. Yet the challenges surrounding the creation of the arts district suggest that cultural integration with a strong preservation component is expensive and should be undertaken only with a thorough understanding of the limitations that it places on redevelopment. Given such an understanding, San Diego's efforts can serve as a model for other historic base communities and a cultural anchor for conversion for a wide variety of stakeholders.

Fort Ord

The former Fort Ord is the most physically, economically, socially, and culturally isolated of the three cases. It thus presents some of the greatest redevelopment challenges among the three cases. The large physical size of the base presents immediate economic challenges in terms of connecting the base to local infrastructure. Laying cables, pipes, electric lines, and building roads is costly across the site's 28,000 acres. Even maintaining the hundreds of miles of roads that existed at the time of closure is an expense that the surrounding cities do not want to share. The former base is located directly in between many regional destinations, but local roads also take travelers around the base rather than through it. As it stands now, travelers go miles out of their way to reach destinations across the Monterey Bay region. This extra time costs residents and firms millions of dollars a year in lost productivity and inefficiencies when residents commute, travel for meetings, or ship goods to market.

Most of Fort Ord's structures cannot be reused to support economic integration because these structures were built to military standards, not California standards, and had deteriorated badly by the time of conveyance. Using lead and asbestos in construction was commonplace at the time the Army built barracks, offices, and other structures on the site. Lead and asbestos abatement would have been cost prohibitive for Fort Ord's hundreds of contaminated buildings, even if the surrounding communities could afford the expense and agree on how to extend electricity, water, sewer, trash, fire, and police services to the site. Michael Houlemard, executive director of the Fort Ord Reuse Authority (FORA), describes these challenges: "Not all of the records were kept, they didn't always trace where they did training, they might never have checked where sewer/water were all in the same place. It was expected that these sites would remain for military use. We don't have a lot of information. The information you do have [on contamination] will scare you to death" (2013). Demolition became attractive once abatement was ruled out, but demolition is cost prohibitive as well: structures with lead and asbestos must be disassembled by hand and sent to expensive facilities with the capacity to safely dispose of contaminated material.

The cities surrounding Fort Ord are many and varied, from ordinary, primarily agricultural cities such as Salinas, to wealthy enclaves such as Carmel, to smaller municipalities with few resources such as Marina, Seaside, and Sand City. Monterrey is the regional hub from an economic standpoint and represents an ordinary city as far as coastal California goes. These cities' interests and their capacity to pursue them also vary dramatically, and redevelopment collaboration fights emerged immediately after the closure announcement. The state of California therefore created FORA, a regional, multi-stakeholder body to govern Fort Ord's conversion and integration into the surrounding community. The authority formally represented more than a dozen local jurisdictions' interests and created a mechanism for financing conversion through local tax revenue. The authority also provided a forum for dispute resolution and integration efforts that included dozens of regional, state, and federal authorities as well as stakeholders across public, private, and nonprofit sectors. This structure forced some flexibility on many cities whose ordinary status and varied interests might have led to conversion stalemates. Instead, FORA navigated governance challenges to integrate the former base at a level that surpasses expectations, thus far, given the high levels of environmental contamination on the site, the base's large physical size, and its location bordering many local jurisdictions.

Economic integration has been slow and costly for Fort Ord but has been more extensive than observers familiar with defense conversion on other bases might have expected. Fort Ord's perimeter now includes a shopping center and a VA hospital designed to serve several communities near the former base as well as military veterans who live in the area. The costs of developing these peripheral sites was much lower than for any sites in the interior, where the distance from existing infrastructure would raise costs and new development would likely suffer from a lack of consumer and user traffic. Commuters and residents already pass by sites on the edge of the base as they use existing transportation networks and can thus access the new commercial centers.

The creation of California State University, Monterey Bay (CSUMB), is Fort Ord's primary success story and represents the best example of how redevelopment integrated the former military site into the broader community from economic, social, and cultural perspectives. The new university opened in 1995 on a portion of Fort Ord where existing structures could be renovated in a cost-effective way and where physical isolation helped to create a sense of community, as on many university campuses. CSUMB is a rare example of excellent timing, access to resources, and leadership that can overcome and even leverage isolation on former military bases in pursuit of redevelopment. Demand for a new state university in the region was high because of rising populations and Silicon Valley's need for labor. Programs designed to train students to work in the valley's tech firms were a natural fit: demand for skilled employees and the presence of qualified applicants interested in remaining in the area made for agreement among the local congressional delegation, particularly Congressman Leon Panetta, the president of the California State University system, and business interests on the desirability of a new campus. The new university was also designed to take advantage of its location near Monterey Bay, offering programs in marine biology, oceanography, and climate science to accommodate excess student demand that had led to oversubscribed programs on other campuses in the California state system. Coupled with the new Monterey Bay Sanctuary, the Monterey Aquarium, and several dozen local research institutes, CSUMB has become part of the "Blue Silicon Valley" that emerges from the "Serengeti of the Sea" (City of Monterey 2016).

University research produces regional economic benefits. Laboratory science and engineering tend to generate spin-off commercial applications that can act as a regional economic multiplier. University spin-off enterprises now create new jobs, bring investment capital to the area, and fund additional research. Once again, the campus's location near Silicon Valley places it within the valley's venture capital and tech funding orbit. Attracting strong faculty, graduate, and undergraduate students then becomes relatively easy compared to other California universities created from scratch during the same era or elsewhere in the country.

CSUMB enrolls 7,000 students per year and had graduated over 10,000 total students by 2016; many of these students remained in the greater Monterey Bay region. A large percentage of students at CSUMB major in tech-related and marine-related fields, which take advantage of the school's proximity to local markets and field sites and prepare students for regional, high-value-added employment. Students and faculty now participate in regular "start-up weekends" to create business plans and secure venture capital, with many of the participants creating spin-off companies upon graduation. The university thus goes far to replace lost consumption and lost revenue for surrounding communities as the students, a transient population like the military, spend money locally and sometimes put down deeper roots as well. This is not to say that 7,000 students at Cal State Monterey Bay can replace the estimated $500 million impact of losing 15,000 active-duty Army personnel and families at Fort Ord, only that the university and its students help to convert and remake place following the military departure in a way that is as rare as it is desirable.

CSUMB also promotes social and cultural integration between the base and the surrounding community. University buses transport students to the shops, museums, and cultural attractions of downtown Monterey. The university attracts residents in the surrounding communities to the former base through regular cultural events and speaker series at the Leon Panetta Institute for Public Policy. Social and cultural integration also occurs through university agricultural programs, which connect students to the nearby agrarian communities. CSUMB thus serves to connect new residents to existing activities in a way that surpasses the social and cultural isolation on Fort Ord when it was operational.

Fort Ord was especially isolated relative to the other bases because of its active, live-fire exercises and bombing ranges. Unexploded ordnance throughout the former base thus discourages social recreation on a large portion of the site. The creation of the Fort Ord National Monument mitigates some of this isolation by preserving a large portion of the base, which is consistent with many of the values of the local community, and providing trails for horseback riding, hiking, and mountain biking. Still, much of this space is unsafe for visitors and thus remains closed to the public. The cost of remediating the area is so high that the prospects for fully opening the former base and the national monument to recreational use are very low in the short to medium term. In the long term, FORA's estimate is for full munitions clearance by 2030: thirty-six years after the base closed. The length of time that environmental restoration for integration takes at Fort Ord thus shows that integration can require decades and suggests that public officials should plan conversion and reuse with this timetable foremost in their minds.

There are some areas where public services benefit from the physical isolation. The local police and fire departments use a few former bombing targets and live-fire training sites on the base for their own training and practice. These activities are often dangerous and noisy, and might disturb residents or commercial activity if the training sites were located closer to residents or commercial sites. Being isolated allows the SWAT teams to use explosives, the police to fire guns, and the fire department to set buildings ablaze without fearing for the safety of others in the area. These examples reflect creative reuse of isolated areas, but they do not reflect extensive community integration. Rather, they reflect a community that makes the best of a bad situation and extracts at least some value from otherwise unusable assets.

Some stakeholders would prefer that Fort Ord remain isolated to preserve its wild environments. Fort Ord includes thousands of acres of coastal dunes, grassy hills, and forests. Local environmental groups opposed economic integration on Fort Ord in order to protect these areas from resort development, strip malls, big-box stores, and other commercial activity that could threaten the wilderness. Keep Fort Ord Wild is a local environmental group that sued FORA over munitions clearance and environmental restoration, as did the Sierra Club. Both groups advocated for a different, environmentally focused vision of a converted Fort Ord, which promoted at least some public support for creating the Fort Ord National Monument. Fort Ord Access Alliance (FOAA) is another local group that fought for ballot initiatives to bypass FORA's authority, preserve specific parcels on the former base, and place them off-limits to commercial developers. In this case, the alliance proposed a ballot initiative to oppose pari-mutuel horse racing on the former site. As FOAA spokesman Jason Campbell said, "So many people think Monterey Downs is a bad idea. . . . That's probably the No. 1 thing we heard" (Molnar 2013). The alliance and LandWatch Monterey sued the city of Seaside to prevent the project, and the city's private-sector partners ultimately abandoned their proposal. These examples are two of many where groups oppose integration on former bases and demonstrate that not all community stakeholders desire economic integration. Additionally, economic integration can be at odds with local cultural and social values, such as maintaining wild areas.

Politically, Fort Ord is also the least integrated of the three cases. The large number of political jurisdictions bordering the former base at the municipal and county level led to expectations of political battles surrounding conversion and redevelopment. FORA is designed for co-governance with permanent, voting representatives from the surrounding political jurisdictions as well as ex-officio members representing other community stakeholders. Its current composition includes five voting members from Monterey County, two from the city of Del Rey Oaks, four from the city of Marina, two from the city of Monterey, four from the city of Seaside, and two each from the cities of Salinas, Sand City, Pacific Grove, and Carmel-by-the-Sea. Ex-officio members include representatives from U.S. congressional, state senate, and state house districts; CSUMB; local school and transportation districts; and the U.S. Army. All members propose, deliberate, oversee, and evaluate aspects of Fort Ord's redevelopment, with voting members ultimately approving or denying redevelopment actions through a committee system divided into the executive committee, a board of directors, and up to ten other thematic committees, such as finance, transportation, and veterans' affairs. The executive committee and other committee meetings are all open to the public and occur once a month, on average.

Fort Ord is by no means fully redeveloped, and FORA still governs redevelopment on the former base. Disagreements among local municipalities and counties therefore currently play out through FORA. Yet it is unclear how land, residents, and commercial activity on the former base will be integrated into local political jurisdictions once FORA's mission is complete. For example, it is unknown whether parts of the former base will be absorbed into the county or neighboring cities, or will create their own unique jurisdictions. Will revenue from economic activity on the former base continue to be shared across the region? Who will pay to extend and maintain infrastructure, particularly if residential conversion occurs on the former base following environmental remediation? Fort Ord is easily twenty to even fifty years away from addressing some of these contingencies, so speculation on how political integration may or may not proceed is premature. Strong regional governance institutions simply must adapt and, in many cases, give way to new imperatives surrounding former bases' economic and political integration as conversion continues. There are currently no plans for whether and how this adaptation will occur, which highlights how political integration could still confound, slow, or halt future conversion efforts.

NAS Alameda

NAS Alameda represents the best example of the paradox of physical centrality and shows how integration is dependent on market dynamics. The former base is located on San Francisco Bay, next to prosperous, thriving communities in Alameda and Oakland, and a short, scenic ferry ride across the bay to San Francisco. Strong market conditions might have convinced some observers that redevelopment there would be easy. The high-value waterfront property in the Bay Area, the desirability of living and working in the region, and the NAS falling entirely within the city of Alameda's political boundaries all point toward relatively easy conversion with few potential governance problems compared to other bases. NAS Alameda is not physically isolated, and the distance from existing infrastructure that would need to be bridged to integrate the base from an infrastructural standpoint is very short. Yet there has been very little permanent redevelopment on the former NAS Alameda since the base closed because of federal rules and environmental-remediation costs.

Alameda's context as an ordinary city also influences its conversion process. It is tempting to equate Alameda with San Francisco because of their proximity, but this would be a mistake. Alameda has strong market conditions and lacks much of Oakland's impoverished areas. However, Alameda is a small city with relatively few resources compared to San Francisco or even San Diego. Alameda has a much smaller administrative staff than does San Diego and has a much lower level of concentrated community resources to draw from, such as private foundations devoted specifically to Alameda, as in San Diego, rather than to the Bay Area in general. Alameda is also too small to have established extensive connections in Washington or the ability to lobby for a smoother, more favorable conversion with federal assistance. In this case, Alameda's ordinary status could not prevent the federal government from placing a high conveyance cost on the property to reflect its presumably high market value. Furthermore, investments necessary to clean up the site and prepare for new residential and commercial construction were not made for almost twenty years after the base closed in 1994; the first phase of redevelopment was set in motion only in 2013. These investments would have been extensive at any time during the preceding twenty years, but the city of Alameda and master developers were understandably inflexible: they were not willing to make such investments and also pay a high federal conveyance fee. Conversion, redevelopment, and integration stalled as a result.

The environmental-remediation costs and the conveyance fee isolated NAS Alameda from an economic standpoint and precluded development. The *potential* market value for development on the former base is indeed high. Yet it was not high enough to overcome the high conveyance cost that the Bush administration placed on the property because of the administration's anticipated but unrealized redevelopment windfall. The other costs associated with redevelopment were also high because fuel, lead, and asbestos remediation are not covered under Superfund legislation.

This means that the federal government has no legal obligation to clean up these pervasive types of contamination on the site through the EPA. The site remains largely unconverted.

The 2008 global financial crisis and recession altered Alameda Point's redevelopment prospects. Paradoxically, weak market conditions in the short term may have improved long-term redevelopment prospects. The limited economic growth during the Great Recession, the difficulty of connecting or converting existing infrastructure or building new infrastructure, and costly, lingering challenges with environmental remediation led many to question the property's value. Environmental remediation in the tens and potentially hundreds of millions of dollars made many developers skittish about partnerships with the city or led them to demand plans with large numbers of residential units and very high density to overcome potential environmental costs, as in the original partnership with SunCal. As City Manager John Russo noted, "I think there were some misunderstandings about the value of property in the Bay Area in general. If that property couldn't be developed in a boom, then what's it worth in a bust?" (Jones 2011). Rather than further isolating the former NAS Alameda, the Navy dropped its demand for a fee-based conveyance in 2011 and agreed to turn the parcel over to the city of Alameda for free.

The conveyance officially occurred in 2013, sixteen years after the base closed and after two previous development plans had fallen through. The city's current plan includes efforts to integrate the former base into the surrounding community with the city serving as the master developer. Alameda's plan now provides for 1,425 new residential units and 5.5 million square feet of commercial space, including hotels, restaurants, retail shops, office space, condos, and affordable housing units. The plans also include a ferry repair site, a VA clinic, and a waterfront park with open space (Johnson 2015). Adding more commercial space raises the city's redevelopment costs but also brings an estimated 1,500 new, permanent jobs to the site in the first redevelopment phase (Alameda Point, 2013). William Carsillo, the Navy's real estate consultant for Alameda Point, says that this combination of jobs, affordable housing, and less residential density convinced the Navy to drop its fee and allow conveyance to move forward (Jones 2011). In recent years, economic integration has regained momentum on Alameda as residential, commercial, and recreational development advances.

Politically, Alameda Point falls within the city of Alameda's purview and did not face the same challenges of coordinated governance to integrate former land into the surrounding political network as on many other former bases. Instead, the city faced opposition to its earlier development plans at the ballot box. In 2010 Alameda voters rejected SunCal as master developer of 4,800 residential units by an overwhelming margin of 85 percent to 15 percent. Voters' concerns were numerous, but the largest objections were to increases in population density and traffic, and the strain on services that new residents would bring. From an isolation standpoint, the voters rejected the private master-developer model that seemed to distance the base and its governance from voters' political and policy preferences. The redevelopment plan implemented in 2011 was not subject to a direct popular vote but reflected popular dissatisfaction with expensive conveyance fees and predominantly for-profit land use.

The subsequent redevelopment plan was much more sensitive to residents' concerns, with disincentives to build more than the 1,425 planned residential units contained in the proposal. For instance, the city agreed to pay the Navy $50,000 for each additional market-rate unit over 1,425 built on the property (City of Alameda 2011). Yet the new plan also contained provisions designed to prevent another referendum that might challenge the agreement. Thus, the city and the Navy incorporated public preferences into the new plan but also limited public oversight. The result is a compromise agreement that is amenable to the city, the Navy, a new master developer, and Alameda residents. Only with this compromise solution has permanent conversion moved forward.

Advancing defense conversion is good news for Alameda, but the city also made the best of a bad redevelopment situation while it awaited a solution. For example, the long time frame for land conveyance on NAS Alameda allowed for some small experiments in social, cultural, and economic integration. The Navy permitted the city of Alameda to lease former hangars and other structures on the base to pay for the site's maintenance while awaiting conveyance and permanent redevelopment. Tenants occupying these hangars offered a variety of products and services, from craft-distilled spirits, wine, and beer to tech firms, environmental-consulting services, piano repair, a church, a theater, and indoor sports facilities. A variety of museums also operated on site and ranged from those covering naval operations, such as the decommissioned *USS Hornet* docked on site, to those housing antique pinball machines. The former base also hosted some recreational tenants, such as the America's Cup team, other boat racing teams, and boatbuilders, and hosted regular recreational events, such as road races, as well. These groups formed a sense of community and currently have options to remain tenants in Alameda Point and drive economic, social, and cultural integration as conversion continues.

Planning for temporary use is an important part of building community in Alameda. Thousands of visitors shop, dine, and recreate among the hangars, roads, and runways on the former base each week. These visitors and their activities promote integration in social, cultural, and economic senses. Leases are temporary on the site, but temporary is relative: Google signed a three-year lease for office space in 2015 and an additional four-year lease in 2016. This investment is technically for temporary use, but it has stimulated the creative economy on the base and brought hundreds of jobs to the site: "We think this is a very good deal for the city. This lease brings jobs to Alameda, and it acts as a catalyst for high tech jobs," said Nanette Mocanu, Alameda's assistant community development director (*East Bay Times* 2015; McDermid 2016). Creating place from temporary uses is thus not only possible but desirable for integration, as an emerging community can help transition from temporary to permanent uses.

Lessons from the Bases

Integrating geographically central but economically, politically, and socially isolated former defense sites is easier when collaborative governance steers this process. Integration is also easier near attractive urban centers with strong market conditions. This is a planning and zoning question as much as it is a political and economic one. Living on the former NAS Alameda is desirable because of its waterfront location and proximity to Oakland and San Francisco. Similarly, living on the former NTC San Diego offers residents easy access to the airport, downtown, the San Diego Harbor, and Mission Bay. The return of the compact-city tradition and the use of mixed-use zoning to convert bases into new urban places represent unique opportunities for defense conversion under strong market conditions. Planning and zoning are integral parts of collaborative governance and are therefore key to harnessing market conditions in favor of integrating closed bases. In contrast, the return of the compact-city tradition does not foster integration on many suburban and rural former bases. Fort McClellan, near Anniston, Alabama, is physically distant from urban areas and much less attractive to potential residents. Collaborative governance would help integrate these bases, too, but sophisticated planning and zoning may only aid integration on the margins in communities with little economic activity.

Clustering in the city-region also offers opportunities for economic integration. CSUMB helps to integrate Fort Ord into the regional knowledge economy. But founding a university is not the only way forward for integrating converted bases into the knowledge economy: Alameda could potentially follow Fort Ord's lead and lease some of its new office space to tech tenants to take advantage of the industry's concentration in the Bay Area. Nor is the tech industry the only option for clustering. Former defense communities should pay careful attention to city-regional clustering opportunities in a wide variety of areas as they pursue economic integration. The problem here is that ordinary cities with ordinary governance are not well-equipped to take advantage of these opportunities because of their weak governance. San Diego as a cohesively governed, flexible city, and the Monterey region as flexible through its leadership and governance, show how integration can advance despite significant hurdles, especially in Fort Ord's case. Alameda lies in an extraordinary region and has clustering opportunities in every direction. Yet Alameda did not develop the multi-scale connections to take advantage of these opportunities, and the state eliminated its redevelopment agency, which further undermined some of its governance capabilities. The result is an island of low economic activity in a vibrant, flourishing region.

Redeveloping and recentralizing former military sites may entail creating entirely new industries. The decline of manufacturing in city cores offers some opportunities in this respect because manufacturing has left the city over time, in many cases because of spatial reasons. For example, tensions between urban transportation and transportation of goods have shifted much manufacturing and general production out of the city center. Drawbacks to certain production processes, such as noise and air pollution, prevent them from remaining in the city center (Sega 2015). Add high land values in city centers, and industrial and manufacturing processes flee the city.

Little traditional manufacturing appears in the three cases. However, Alameda Point does have some light manufacturing and industrial workshops as temporary uses. Fort Ord's large physical size would also make it a good candidate for new manufacturing sites if the base were not so heavily contaminated. There are fewer general barriers for situating manufacturing on former military sites relative to compact cities, especially geographically isolated ones. In this sense, manufacturing may also aid the development of polycentric production precisely because manufacturing is often seen as incompatible with the traditional compact city. Where to situate manufacturing is a significant issue facing city-regions and one that is continually negotiated. Well-governed former defense communities have opportunities to pursue industrial conversion and leverage the physical isolation on former bases, but they will have to deliberate and proceed carefully because locating production on former bases may preclude integration in other areas.

The post-Fordist context of a declining "real economy" makes understanding cities in terms of production difficult because urban development may now depend more on financial governance and fiscal limits (Harvey 2003). But the prospect of decentralization of production to the periphery of city-regions may still attract workers away from the city center and toward some former bases. Attracting manufacturing to former bases may be especially relevant as some overseas manufacturing returns to the United States. These firms and those that never left are now shifting production from northern states with stronger unions to southern states with lower labor costs and lower costs of living. Former military sites in rural areas with low costs of living and inexpensive land may become increasingly attractive as this trend continues and manufacturing grows in some parts of the country. Industrial defense conversion is exactly what isolated former bases pursue—often providing at least some economic integration into the surrounding community—which is noteworthy given the many constraints facing isolated former military communities. Achieving this type of conversion also requires strong, collaborative governance to attract manufacturers from around the world, entice (primarily domestic) workers to move to the area, and expand services so that they will stay.

Integration of converted defense sites offers some lessons for integrating former *nonmilitary* industrial sites around the country. Integrating former industrial sites is likely to be easier than for former bases because of the access to local infrastructural networks that these sites enjoyed during their operation. Of course, updating and refurbishing these sites will still be required for integration into local economic, political, and social networks. Additionally, these former industrial communities lost jobs, revenue, and residents and likely face considerable financial constraints. Maintaining services while integrating the former sites, no matter the form their conversion takes, will therefore require significant governance, planning, and long-term financing, just as in former military communities.

Former bases' physical centrality is misleading because these sites are usually isolated from the surrounding community. Decades of isolation from economic, political, social, and cultural standpoints makes for costly, challenging redevelopment. Governing conversion to integrate bases from an economic perspective is a tall order for many former military communities. Lost population, jobs, and revenue all make governance for integration, including planning, funding, implementing, and adapting economies, difficult enough on its own. Adding political, social, and cultural integration in ways that promote a broad distribution of benefits, sustainability, and equity is a challenge that few former military communities have met. Still, the experiences of San Diego, Monterey, and Alameda with defense conversion suggest that communities have options for reversing military isolation and integrating former defense sites into surrounding communities.

Communities must be both lucky and good to integrate former bases. Communities must be lucky because of the long redevelopment time frame and the importance of timing surrounding market conditions and government policy. They must also be "good" in terms of collaborative governance across sectors and at scale, and access to resources, leadership, and creative problem solving. Lacking either of these two elements can easily result in long-term underdevelopment or redevelopment limbo. Having both luck, in terms of resources, and good governance will not create paradise or even convert bases in a way that broadly satisfies all stakeholders. However, it will likely integrate former military communities in a way that is more satisfying than many alternatives.

Integrating former military communities into global financial markets represents a final, unique challenge in defense conversion. Chapter 6 describes why globalized financial processes are influential for local redevelopment choices and how local financing options can decrease risk and increase community benefits. Thus, local agency and redevelopment control to integrate communities into the international marketplace also carry prospects for a range of outcomes: from positively leveraging market conditions and financing redevelopment to capture by savvy international investors.

6

FINANCING THE DEAL

Leveraging Global Resources for Local Conversion

Defense conversion depends on optimizing limited resources and managing relationships outside of the immediate geographic area to leverage and access even more resources. These resources are available from local, regional, state, national, and even global outlets. The level of community integration into the financial marketplace at each level and the community's ability to navigate channels far beyond local borders through redevelopment governance often determine the extent to which communities achieve their conversion goals. Capital markets' strong connection to industries that provide essential services, such as health care and education, also means that the level of integration into the marketplace influences residents' well-being through access to health care, education, housing, and government programs. This consistent drive for redevelopment capital occurs in competition with other communities, which is why engaging global financial markets is critical for securing conversion financing.

Marshaling financial resources is very difficult to govern and achieve in practice. Redevelopment is an unstable, long-term process that tends to cost much more than communities expect. The fluctuating costs of environmental remediation, infrastructure integration, and changing market conditions all led to cost overruns in the first rounds of base closures following the end of the Cold War. These conversion efforts had to react to and follow the neoliberal movement in infrastructure financing, where privatization of some infrastructure, local project funding and management, and limited prospects for raising taxes preclude paying for projects through the general fund or through property tax revenue.

Defense conversion occurs as a response to an economic and civic crisis, where lost jobs, revenue, and resources limit communities' ability to respond to financing challenges. Financing development deals for redevelopment is also often more complex than for earlier projects because of the large number of political jurisdictions that former bases cross and the stakeholders involved. Communities lack governance structures, knowledge, and resources to design and maintain financing arrangements to complete projects, sustain fiscal health, and continue to provide services to residents. Meeting these challenges is integral to achieving redevelopment goals but, as with other areas, very difficult to achieve in practice.

Communities finance defense conversion through several different tools that have evolved over time. Local governments' financial options are no longer limited to general obligation bonds. Traditionally, municipalities would issue bonds to fund projects and use tax and other revenues to pay interest to investors. More recently, limited municipal ability to raise property taxes and public opposition to issuing debt have spread much of the responsibility for financing development projects from a municipal government across redevelopment authorities and special districts. Local governments and other authorities now use a wide variety of arrangements to finance large projects and are not the only ones issuing debt or extending credit. These authorities issue public debt but do not always issue debt through traditional financing arrangements. Instead, *financialization* of local assets and revenue streams is an increasingly common alternative to traditional financing. Cities, regions, special districts, and redevelopment authorities borrow money to fund infrastructure and other development projects by issuing bonds, as in traditional financing arrangements. These authorities then pledge future revenue from development projects or other public assets to pay interest on bonds. Thus, these projects and assets have been financialized. Although this issue may seem too technical to matter, it is the future of municipal investment, especially for infrastructure, and an area where strong collaborative governance offers significant returns.

Governing financing for defense conversion is difficult. Former defense communities tend not to be particularly sophisticated or experienced in how they engage with global markets. Many also lack collaborative governance structures that can overcome legal and political constraints on raising taxes and issuing public debt while also maintaining transparency and accountability. For instance, financialization strategies are designed to surpass political and legal barriers to debt issuance, but they also suffer from a distinct lack of democratic transparency and accountability. Special districts and LRAs that financialize public assets are not elected and often operate outside of public view. Residents are not usually aware of what revenue streams special districts and LRAs harness and what liability taxpayers may have if these assets fail to generate expected revenue. Transparency is rare in financing defense conversion as well, and there is very limited public information available about the debt that special districts and LRAs issue.

Different stakeholders and ostensible redevelopment partners at the local, regional, state, and federal levels may not even be aware of what financing deals that LRAs, special districts, or cities themselves may be arranging. Similarly, dozens of overlapping, long-term financing deals for different district, municipal, and regional development projects make it very difficult to discern the issuing authority, the risk to the taxpayer, or the opportunity cost in terms of services that could be funded with the same revenue. The complexity of financing arrangements and their lack of transparency then limit opportunities for oversight and accountability when collaborative governance is absent. When financialization goes poorly, the result can be expensive debt servicing and drastic cuts in services to avoid municipal default (Kane and Weber 2015; Baker et al. 2016).

Global Financial Markets and Redevelopment

A Keynesian policy framework of major federal support for infrastructure projects marked the U.S. development landscape in the 1950s and 1960s. By the 1980s, the perceived failure of Keynesian infrastructure policy and the welfare state ushered in neoliberal models of local control and responsibility for development funding. For neoliberals, economic growth stems from free-market resource distribution, where private-sector–driven growth is more efficient than state-directed or regulated distribution and ultimately benefits everyone (Harvey 2007). Yet many critics point out that neoliberal assumptions about competitive markets, property rights, access to information, and impartial enforcement almost never hold. Critics therefore contend that neoliberalism empowers the private sector at the expense of residents: local governments socialize debt and repayments while firms privatize profits (Harvey 2007; Leitner et al. 2007a). Governments subsidize private firms against residents' interests, regulate the private sector in a way that limits competition, and redistribute wealth upward through international markets. Privatization of public utilities and other entities is one way this occurs, while financialization of state assets is another.

Converting closed bases now generally occurs in a neoliberal context where local governments increasingly have access to and are integrated in global financial markets. Neoliberal financing challenges drove many communities to better govern their financial practices and become more entrepreneurial, more accepting of risk, more savvy in negotiating project deals, and more experienced (Altshuler and Luberoff 2003; Weber 2010; Kotin and Peiser 1997; Sagalyn 1990, 1997, 2007; Fainstein 2001). Yet the neoliberal funding environment for infrastructure and other large projects poses enormous challenges for military redevelopment. Redeveloping closed bases requires large-scale, regional efforts for integrated redevelopment, something cities and regions are ill-equipped to attempt *de novo* because they largely spent the previous few decades eschewing these strategies in favor of more simplistic, established methods. Military redevelopment, almost by necessity, occurs during times of fiscal stress. Former defense communities almost always face high environmental-remediation costs and loss of jobs, residents, and revenue. In turn, revenue losses prevent communities from using the general fund to convert closed bases, and remediation costs are often too high for private-sector developers to bear.

The combination of common revenue losses and high redevelopment costs drives former military communities toward financing conversion projects, which other communities already tend to do for large projects in general. Financialization is not essential, but it is a more politically attractive option among few palatable alternatives in the context of revenue losses and economic contraction when military bases close. Financialization is also risky in this context and therefore dangerous for communities unless they have the resources and administrative capacity to negotiate financing deals. Ultimately, opportunities *are* present to strike good financing deals, but they depend on collaborative governance to achieve and are site-specific, rather than present in a general, best-practices framework.

Financialization of (Re)Development

Financialization refers to the creation of investment vehicles for a dispersed, global group of investors based on income streams from a variety of local and regional assets (Weber 2010). In this case, cities, regions, special districts, and redevelopment authorities borrow money to fund infrastructure and other development projects by issuing bonds. Then cities or other entities pledge future revenue from development projects to pay interest on bonds, often based on increases in property values. Bondholders can then rapidly transfer ownership of these investment vehicles around the world as opportunities appear elsewhere and markets rise and fall. Capital can thus enter and exit projects rapidly in cities and regions, which increases volatility in financing. Financialization has integrated local governments and financial markets to the extent that issuing debt is now the preferred method for financing infrastructure projects (Weber 2010), including those associated with military redevelopment. The three California cases used different financial arrangements to convert former bases that were specific to each site and the political environment of each community, but financialization is the most common form of redevelopment funding strategy around the United States.

Opinions are mixed as to the desirability of the expanded, internationalized financialization of development projects. Marxist economists tend to see bubbles in financial assets based on a search for ever-higher returns and the absence of strong, direct investment opportunities (Harvey 2003). The U.S. financial industry took advantage of the federal government's retreat from infrastructure investment and regulation to assert control as owners of capital across the entire economic landscape under this framework (Dumenil and Levy 2004; Lawrence and Stapledon 2008; Page et al. 2008).

Investors' chief imperative is for bonds to be honored, and the financial and political costs of honoring these bonds are of little concern to investors. Similarly, social dislocation resulting from service cuts to make debt payments does not sway bondholders from demanding payment (Kirkpatrick and Smith 2011). The ability to extract bondholder payments before funding public services or to promote shareholder value over wage increases in the private sector reflects these arguments. The local growth consensus can suffer when market conditions deteriorate because utility companies and public employees' unions are some of the first groups of stakeholders to experience cuts associated with falling revenue (Sbragia 1983). Of course, the quality of residents' lives also suffers if bond payments are made but public services are not funded. This raises questions concerning equitable development practices that surround defense conversion—in this case, concerns for selling the public's financial future to potentially convert bases for private benefits. The prospects for inequitable outcomes are arguably greatest when the local government cedes control over financing to global markets.

Many economists hold a more positive view of financialization. In this outlook, financial expansion allowed for greater oversight of shoddy municipal governance and efficient distribution of capital toward the greatest returns around the world, especially prior to the 2008 financial crisis (Ter-Minassian and Craig 1997; Fischel 2001). Globally shared economic risk is also desirable from this perspective because it allows municipalities to weather an economic downturn much more easily. This is because economically growing areas may buoy economic contraction, declining profits, layoffs, and suspended projects in another area. The global nature of the current financial landscape will thus smooth the peaks and troughs in local business cycles to make more capital available, for more communities, more of the time. Furthermore, market requirements for consistent returns and transparency will drive municipalities to improve governance of local assets and development projects. The resulting expectation is that improved governance will spill over into other areas and improve service provision and quality of life. From this perspective, communities are understandably enthusiastic about the prospects of harnessing whatever assets and revenue streams they have in pursuit of attracting more international financing.

Cities and other authorities have some agency in how they channel global finance and embed it into local redevelopment projects. It is incumbent on the municipal, regional, and other authorities to create their own investment vehicles to become active participants in financial markets, rather than passive recipients of capital. Communities also have the authority to create new underlying assets and decide which to commodify. For instance, cities can gain independence and finance development by creating new asset classes (Leyshon and Thrift 2007; Weber 2010). Strict political control, as in Chicago under the Daley administration, may be necessary to establish these asset classes, but it *is* possible to do so (Kane and Weber 2015; Weber 2010). Recognizing that cities have many assets that are unusual and thus not fully legible to investors is also key here. For example, real estate represents one such asset class that can be used to attract investment funds after investors and rating agencies understand its potential to generate future income streams (Clark and O'Connor 1997). All of these strategies require strong financial governance, of course, which few former defense communities possess.

Local governments with strong governance can benefit from demonstrating their political control over their assets. Ratings agencies and global investors privilege stability in this and other areas and thus channel investment capital to communities with stable income flows. Investors also weigh the risk of income shocks and assess this risk based on the credibility of local policy commitments, the valuation of the underlying assets, and the income streams they generate (Keefer and Stasavage 2003; Touchton 2016; Weber 2010; Kane and Weber 2015). This is a challenge in an area where transparency surrounding asset values is low and investment vehicles are novel. Nevertheless, making credible policy commitments through collaborative governance may counteract some of the accountability problems associated with opaque special districts, LRAs, and their abilities to accumulate public debt through complex investment vehicles.

Tax Increment Financing

Local and regional authorities frequently use tax increment financing (TIF) to finance new infrastructure projects, including those on former military bases. TIF functions by creating investment vehicles from local property tax income or other revenue streams. TIF first requires the city or CRA to establish a project area. Then any future property-tax increases within that area accrue to the city or the CRA. Thus, the tax increment (the increase) goes toward financing the redevelopment project. However, this strategy can be risky, especially for former military communities whose revenue has contracted sharply. This is precisely why financialization and TIFs are attractive, but they divert new revenue from schools and other local services when property values rise. In contrast, cities are forced to curtail existing services to service debt and pay bondholders if property values stagnate or fall. Former defense communities with low administrative capacity, weak governance, and little experience in financing deals then potentially put the entire community at risk in order to pursue defense conversion.

Local governments and redevelopment authorities issued increasingly large amounts of debt through TIFs during the property boom of the 2000s (Hitchcock 2006). For example, California had 756 Community Redevelopment Agency (CRA) project areas in 2011, including some on former military bases (Kirkpatrick and Smith 2011). TIF channeled $5.4 billion in property taxes toward CRAs and away from school districts, cities, and counties in 2007 (California State Board of Equalization 2007). This diversion represents 11.4 percent of all California property taxes, a percentage that has grown since California's Proposition 13 was passed in 1978 (Kirkpatrick and Smith 2011). At the city level, several studies estimated recent revenue diverted from municipal spending on services or other areas to redevelopment at considerable levels. For instance, California's Municipal Officials for Redevelopment Reform (MORR) estimated Los Angeles County's diverted annual redevelopment revenue at $380 million between 1978 and 1994, and $2.6 billion by 2002 (MORR 2002). California eliminated its CRAs in 2011 and limited the prospects for using TIF to fund development projects under CRA auspices, but a 2014 law (State Bill 628) encourages continued TIF arrangements for infrastructure projects around the state by creating "enhanced infrastructure financing districts."

Tax increment financing is risky because it relies on local governments' placing big bets on increasing property values in a concentrated geographic area. TIF projects designate an area as underdeveloped or blighted, and then local governments sell investors on growth potential in that area. Yet property values are primarily outside of local government control, thus making this debt instrument particularly risky (Ashton 2009; Weber 2010; Baker et al. 2016; Weber and O'Neill-Kohl 2013). Local governments risk default on debt payments if taxes from the designated property do not appreciate at a pace that investors demand. Rather than default, municipalities frequently divert funds from services to maintain debt payments, which harms residents. Some cities, such as Chicago, can manage property values in TIF areas to their benefit through strict political control of property assessment, sequencing of debt, and release of information (Weber 2010; Kane and Weber 2015). However, there are equity issues here, too: Illinois state law limits TIFs to blighted areas, but Chicago uses them in expensive downtown districts, which can subsidize taxes for already-wealthy corporations (Associated Press 2016). Even though this option leaves a lot to be desired from an equity perspective, most local governments, including those of most former military communities, lack the collaborative governance strength, political control, resources, and expertise to perform this trick. They are therefore at risk of losing funds for services if their bets on property values do not pay off.

Local governments face default if projects are not completed, property values fall, or tax revenue is less than anticipated (Weber 2002, 2010). Failure to complete projects is very common in military redevelopment because of the difficulty of governing at scale; the loss of local revenue, residents, and expertise; and changing market conditions over the course of these long-term projects. Issuing debt through TIFs is therefore especially worrisome for military redevelopment projects because there are no profits to back the bonds if the redevelopment plans are not completed. Bond payments must then come out of the general fund, where they are most likely to undermine services and harm residents. Options to avoid default then include reducing services, increasing tax rates, or selling assets, none of which are politically popular or even feasible in most former military communities because of job and revenue losses, already-poor services, and relatively few assets, on average. The best-case scenario under these circumstances is that local governments can use their general fund to make debt payments to avoid default, which squeezes out desirable services. This is usually what happens because cities can capture taxpayers' funds to cover TIF obligations in a variety of ways, all of which come with opportunity costs in terms of services (O'Toole 2011; Kane and Weber 2015; Weber 2010; Baker et al. 2016; Weber and O'Neill-Kohl 2013).

TIF carries additional downsides in the context of economic expansion and project completion. Communities have to be very well-governed financially to successfully pursue desirable outcomes through TIF programs. Unfortunately, most governance arrangements are not particularly strong in this area, which raises the prospects that money that might have gone to support public services, such as health care, education, or housing, goes instead to LRAs or whichever entity issues debt through TIF. This leads to disproportionate burdens placed on less affluent communities, whose underperforming schools and public services can ill afford to lose future revenue (Dardia 1998). Such trade-offs are rarely popular from a political, economic, or social perspective and result in a lack of support for LRAs at the state level. LRAs have therefore been dissolved in places with relatively high levels of public accountability associated with their creation and use, as in California. Yet TIF arrangements and the authorities that use them are often not accountable to elected officials or to the public for a wide variety of reasons.

Democratic Deficits in Financing

The range of financial services available to cities, the high levels of municipal debt, the privatization and securitization of public assets, and the concern for serving investors before local citizens all reflect democratic deficits in governance as financialization spreads across urban policy arenas (Weber 2002, 2010). As discussed above, financing redevelopment frequently occurs through "backdoor" debt instruments, where hybrid municipal-regional authorities issue bonds and take on debt without any direct authorization from elected officials or public oversight (Perry 1994). Financialization is not exactly a best practice, but it is a common practice that many communities unknowingly pursue through subtle, opaque processes and special authorities. These authorities can fall under the collaborative governance framework when other stakeholders can influence, monitor, and publicize their activities. However, these special authorities are often isolated and autonomous in practice, which limits oversight of their activities and accountability to the broader public.

Special districts issue debt and hold considerable assets. For example, California's special districts made payments on $8.2 billion of long-term bonds in 2015, which is greater than the total of the current municipal bond market in the state (California State Controller 2016; California State Treasurer 2016a, 2016b). Redevelopment authorities are often empowered to issue debt in the same way that other quasi-municipal authorities, such as bridge commissions, port authorities, or water-treatment districts, have done in recent decades. In many cases this kind of financing splinters growth coalitions and limits prospects for traditional financing of development or redevelopment. This is an especially serious concern in California, with its constitutional limits on municipal debt and public opposition to taxes.

Special-use districts and LRAs also avoid public scrutiny and electoral accountability. Appointed officials, not elected ones; opaque operations; and deep connections to the private sector all make special-use districts and LRAs attractive for circumventing political and legal limitations on financing development and redevelopment. Well-funded, private-sector actors then gain increasing advantages over the public in terms of what type of development that cities finance and how they finance it. For instance, scholarship on the city of Vallejo, California, demonstrates how shifts from serving a public constituency of local citizens to a private one of bondholders occur in the context of financing development projects. By extension, these trends also aid private-sector capture of what redevelopment occurs on former bases as opposed to public benefits (Adams 2007). Base closures break up local power structures. The fear of financializing assets to fund redevelopment projects in these communities is that the newly empowered will be international bondholders, with no regard for the community, its values, or its continued existence as long as their debt is serviced.

LRAs do not always fall prey to private-sector capture, but they are still heavily insulated from direct public oversight. CRAs in California can contest the location of new sales-tax-generating enterprises in neighboring cities, subsidize commercial development in some areas over others, and increase competition for investment among municipalities in their jurisdictions without municipal input (Kirkpatrick and Smith 2011; MORR

2002). In terms of financing development and redevelopment, this prospect highlights the need for or at least the consideration of collaborative regional governance, like that seen for the former Fort Ord, to manage inter-municipal competition and distribute the benefits of redevelopment investment equitably. Additionally, guaranteeing no-fee conveyance would limit some of the financing risk: "The no-cost conveyance options are important and free communities from some of the financing pressures [of defense conversion]," said Bryant Monroe, downsizing director, Office of Economic Adjustment, Department of Defense (2014).

The imperatives of financialization can also divert public resources to private interests by privileging short-term, "self-funding" projects at the expense of integrated regional projects with many beneficiaries. Integrated, regional public works projects are often public officials' and outside investors' last choices. Instead, these actors prefer piecemeal projects that can pay for themselves through user fees and other generation of local revenue, such as bridges or toll roads. This observation explains many cities' preferences for sports arenas over parks and toll roads over light-rail systems (Sbragia 1983). This also explains the overarching decrease in public infrastructure investment, coupled with an increase in investment subsidies for individual projects in cities experiencing economic growth (Graham and Marvin 2001). The fragmentation of infrastructural financing then promotes infrastructure projects based largely on short-term economic cost-benefit analysis rather than long-term benefits for a range of citizens and private-sector investors (Pagano and Perry 2008).

Pursuing short-term "self-funding" projects undermines city competitiveness. Cities that lack public transportation networks, public space, and strong public services, such as health care and education, are less attractive as places to work and live than are cities or regions that invest in these areas. Investors may then avoid devoting capital to new projects that would bring jobs and revenue to the underdeveloped, under-integrated region. This logic extends to private firms, real estate developers, and bondholders. These groups will not encounter the benefits of place, market conditions, and finances that are conducive to investing in businesses, developing commercial or residential property, or supporting debt in areas that fail to support integrated projects. This concern becomes especially relevant during economic downturns, when the cities that have embraced neoliberal infrastructure investment strategies suffer the most. Financialization's risks thus have the potential to undermine community health in a wide variety of ways. Well-governed former defense communities will consider these risks very carefully before financializing assets to support redevelopment. In contrast, former defense communities without collaborative governance arrangements will likely strike bad deals, both for the cities and for their residents.

Contesting Financialization

The financialization picture is not entirely bleak for less affluent cities in need of redevelopment financing. Capitalism can disrupt traditional community organization and render collective action increasingly difficult by fragmenting communities (Saegert et al. 2011). Yet this fragmentation also creates new spaces for institutional creation and interaction among citizens that might not otherwise overlap in regional and social geographies. In turn, new spaces create new opportunities for collective action to resolve common issues and remake communities following external shocks (Fields 2015). The redevelopment struggle on former bases can thus potentially foster new communities that help to make redevelopment processes accountable. The same integration into global markets, capital mobility, and labor mobility can, at least in some instances, therefore offer opportunities for democratic, accountable governance.

TIFs are a risky proposition for financing redevelopment, but here are several instances where communities have modified TIF requirements to better fund local services. For example, public school districts in many California communities generated support for "pass-through" agreements that send future revenue back to school systems after passing it through redevelopment authorities. Consensus on what policy areas merited "pass-through" arrangements was rare and therefore occurred in only a few domains (Althubaity and Jonas 1998; Kirkpatrick and Smith 2011). Similarly, California state requirements for a 20 percent pass-through to support low-income housing were not enforced in practice (Kirkpatrick and Smith 2011). Only 2 percent of the pass-through ever supported low-income housing, with much of the revenue supporting "mixed-income," market-rate development that investors deem much more attractive (MORR 2002).

Pass-through provisions were politically popular when they worked and represented California CRA proponents' chief evidence in support of CRAs' equitable, short-term desirability. But diverting financing to CRAs, with limited democratic accountability and oversight, was also unpopular enough to warrant their dissolution in California. LRAs still exist in most former military communities outside of the state, however, and tax increment financing through redevelopment authorities still represents the primary means of funding redevelopment projects. Of course, this raises normative questions surrounding the beneficiaries of redevelopment, particularly when redevelopment financing comes at the expense of new revenue for schools and health care. The danger that defense conversion advances as a form of corporate welfare is very real in these and many other cases. Generating collective action to oppose deals that ultimately harm residents is difficult, but Alameda's voter-revolt experience provides a blueprint for improved financing through democratic accountability.

Struggling against financialization doesn't necessarily make sense for military redevelopment because redevelopment might not occur without some sort of financialization of assets and revenue streams in many former military communities. Instead, these communities should focus on governance structures that promote transparency to raise awareness of unsustainable debt and provide a forum to pressure public officials to control the financing process. In that sense, alternative knowledge production and carefully engaging international financial markets may be feasible. Then, at least, communities could place pressure on private-sector investors to provide public goods (Weber 2002; Fields 2015).

California Conditions for Redevelopment Financing

There are several challenges associated with financing defense conversion in California. De facto austerity policies caused by limited taxation authority, slow growth, dissolution of CRAs, and political opposition to higher taxes all impact redevelopment financing in the three cases (Davidson and Ward 2014). However, California serves as a policy pioneer in many respects, and many states have adopted similar policies that structure redevelopment financing around the country. The next section describes these structural constraints as well as the extent to which each former defense community addressed these constraints through governance processes and exercised agency to finance redevelopment.

California's tax revolt of the late 1970s placed municipalities and the state in a financing bind once bases began closing at the end of the Cold War. California is at least somewhat representative of the rest of the United States in this sense, as more than twenty states enforce similarly limiting property tax laws (Martin 2008). As discussed above, hybrid public entities were essential to promoting and financing large-scale development and redevelopment. Special-use districts and local redevelopment agencies represent the bulk of these hybrid authorities. As Kirkpatrick and Smith (2011) and Mizany and Manatt (2002) note, these authorities have been critical for maintaining California growth machines in recent decades.

Cities responded by shifting their revenue-generating focus away from property taxes and toward sales and income taxes. Cities promoted commercial development and job creation in pursuit of higher revenues through taxes in each of these areas. Commercial development takes priority in many California cities because it produces both property taxes and sales taxes that exceed those stemming from other forms of land use. This is because California's sales taxes return to the geographic point of sale, which creates competition over the location of large sales-tax-generating enterprises such as car dealerships or big-box stores. This competition is evident on former military bases, where cities within the broader former base community compete with one another to attract enterprises and capture more tax revenue than their neighbors.

California's 2011 dissolution of the community redevelopment authorities has had mixed effects on the prospects for the state's local development and redevelopment. However, its impact on former defense communities has been primarily negative because it undermines much of the established process for governing and financing redevelopment. On the one hand, dissolving the CRAs alters redevelopment options at communities' disposal because it severely limits local tax revenue for redevelopment. It also reflects a larger battle over how to finance urban development and infrastructure that pitted the state of California against its cities. In this case the cities argued that the state was unconstitutionally seizing millions in local funds. Governor Jerry Brown railed against the result of CRAs' financing strategies because the state subsequently paid a larger share of school district and county budgets that were leaner than they would have been because of redevelopment area designations. On the other hand, dissolving the CRAs may result in greater funding for schools and county services that cities did not want to fund. California's structural rules surrounding revenue thus influence financing arrangements in all communities, not just those with closed military bases. However, the following section describes how San Diego, Fort Ord, and Alameda each exercised agency to create site-specific financing arrangements for defense conversion within the overarching, statewide context.

The narratives on each base are not exclusively about financing but are also about financial issues and governing resources for incremental conversion. The three cases did not fall into crisis because of financialization or TIFs. However, financing conversion has still been difficult, especially after responsibilities were disaggregated and dispersed following the CRA dissolution and the loss of targeted administrative capacity. Savvy, professional CRA management that was part of each city's redevelopment governance structure was lost at this point. The challenge of governing resources and raising redevelopment funds was then turned over to less-experienced employees in many cases. Thus, these communities face different but overlapping challenges relative to the rest of the former defense communities in the data set.

NTC San Diego

San Diego financed the conversion of its Naval Training Center through a partnership with a master developer, as discussed previously. This form of public-private partnership spread some of the redevelopment risk to the private sector and insulated the city from the pressures of financialization in redeveloping the site. This experience demonstrates the agency that communities have to pursue alternatives to incurring heavy debt, relying on tax increment financing, and facing the prospect of cutting local programs in favor of servicing debt. Yet master-developer partnerships also have risks because master developers can go bankrupt or otherwise withdraw from projects. In this case, converting the NTC represented a much larger effort with larger risks than the company had undertaken in other projects prior to its selection as master developer. However, McMillin was a local company whose survival and reputation depended on redeveloping the site. The company also stood to realize serious private profits and corporate growth upon successful conversion of the base. The result was shared risk for the city and large financial and reputational incentives for the private-sector partner to complete the project as planned. These incentives would have been considerably limited if the city had selected a developer from outside the area or with a much larger project portfolio. In this case, the city and the developer made mutually beneficial commitments to each other that insulated the city from risk and avoided the downsides of financialization.

The partnership with McMillin still left room for financing challenges, but also for collaborative governance solutions. For instance, San Diego relied heavily on the state of California to offset financing costs in redeveloping the NTC. Specifically, the NTC Foundation, a nonprofit entity tasked with turning a historic district into an arts and cultural district, found itself in a property tax dilemma as it created a series of for-profit entities to access federal tax incentive programs. The foundation gained access to new resources but also accumulated significant property tax charges that it passed on to arts tenants who were promised below-market-rate rents. The city of San Diego, which owned and leased 27 buildings to the NTC Foundation for a 55-year period, was forced to cover $1.1 million dollars in back taxes accumulated since 2006 (Ruiz 2011; Bennett 2011).

The city and the nonprofit lobbied state legislatures to amend the state constitution to avoid future taxes and support the nonprofit's mission: "If you are capitalized property, like any other real estate developer, then you can make it happen and it is OK. We weren't. We were a start-up foundation with no resources to carry out our renovation. We are still not self-sustained because of the financing structure," said Alan Ziter, director of the NTC foundation (2014). Local Democratic State Senator Juan Vargas introduced Senate Bill 314 in 2011, and it passed in 2012. The bill used the state's "welfare exemption" to justify a tax levy (Vargas 2012):

> This bill would provide that property used exclusively for charitable purposes and located within the former Naval Training Center in San Diego and leased by the City of San Diego or the Redevelopment Agency of the City of San Diego to a nonprofit entity or to an entity controlled by the nonprofit entity shall be deemed to be included within the welfare exemption and shall be entitled to a partial exemption, as specified, in any year in which the development of the property is being financed with funds made available through specified federal tax credit programs.

The state-level support made it possible for the NTC Foundation to continue its work to support the local arts community by adapting historic structures on the former base. This outcome is the opposite of what one would have expected if redevelopment financing had occurred under a primarily local framework: in this case, the arts district nonprofit would have been forced to turn the property back over to the city without legislative assistance at the state level. This display of strong city governance in support of redevelopment financing highlights the role that administrative capacity and experienced, dedicated government officials play for redevelopment outcomes, even when a master developer finances the bulk of the project.

The city of San Diego also turned to other state agencies for economic development assistance. The state's dissolution of all community redevelopment agencies had less of an impact on San Diego because most of the conversion was already well under way by this point and because of San Diego's ability to secure offsetting state benefits. For example, in 2011 the California Technology, Trade, and Commerce Agency designated the NTC a local agency military base recovery area. This program was designed to offset job loss from base closures and gave redevelopment areas similar rights as communities qualifying for state enterprise zone incentives. That same year, the State Lands Commission approved San Diego's request for an in-base land swap that would make it easier to create denser development parcels on the inner core of the site and leave more public land available on the waterfront. These one-off interventions combine to highlight California's broader recognition that financing base conversion is not limited to issuing debt or partnering with private developers. Instead, there are many areas where strong local governance and collaboration across other levels of government can limit the amount of debt that a public entity must issue, the funds that it must raise, or the profits that a private-sector partner must realize to profit on a deal.

In San Diego, defense conversion included infrastructure for residential development, schools, and parks, rather than just commercial and corporate uses. However, it is important to note that San Diego's private redevelopment partner is a locally owned, privately held firm, which made it easier to plan for long-term conversion with a broad group of beneficiaries for several reasons. McMillin does not face public shareholder pressure for immediate profits, and its employees live in San Diego. The privately held firm can therefore take a longer view toward profits than can many publicly traded companies. McMillin's physical location also makes it beholden to the local community, at least to some extent. The company could therefore build roads and renovate buildings in ways that were not immediately profitable because residential and commercial development was so lucrative and preceded the less-profitable aspects of redevelopment. Additionally, the city of San Diego's governance of the master-developer–led process allowed for support across multiple tiers of government to secure the less profitable projects on the former base.

Fort Ord

The Fort Ord Reuse Authority (FORA) relies on local tax-revenue sharing and member dues to finance redevelopment. These are not the only sources of redevelopment financing on the base, however, as different redevelopment partners, such as California State University, Monterey Bay (CSUMB), rely on other funding sources to complement FORA's financing. Revenue generation is difficult on Fort Ord because more than 70 percent of land is designated as open space in perpetuity. Another 15 percent is already taken for other uses, such as the university, which leaves 15 percent of the land to generate enough revenue for FORA to use for maintenance and redevelopment. Each member of the FORA board contributes an annual membership fee of $15,000. FORA then splits land and leasing sales revenue with the underlying jurisdiction and distributes 24 cents of every property tax dollar from the site to the local jurisdiction as well. FORA uses the remaining 76 cents on the dollar to fund redevelopment. In this case, the collaborative governance arrangement that resolves conflicts and promotes conversion with broad community benefits also limits the amount of resources available for redevelopment. Very large, comprehensive conversion projects are therefore unlikely due to FORA's governance structure. Yet incremental, smaller-scale projects also benefit communities by limiting their exposure to risk in the international marketplace. Communities surrounding Fort Ord saw only incremental conversion on the former base but avoided the pitfalls of heavy debt and TIF risk, such as the loss of funding for social services.

The FORA Act established FORA as the lead redevelopment agency, as discussed in chapter 3, and endowed it with financing powers under the collaborative governance framework. The legislation gave FORA the authority to levy assessments, reassessments, special taxes, or development fees, and issue bonds. FORA uses a variety of these options to finance infrastructure, prepare sites for future conversion through environmental remediation, and promote commercial development on the base once sites are prepared. The state of California's elimination of its CRAs does not alter FORA's structure, funding, or authority because of this separate, important legislation that establishes a strong foundation for collaborative governance in defense conversion.

From an environmental standpoint, preparing remaining land for conversion would entail millions of dollars in rehabilitation costs that FORA and local communities would have to fund directly or finance. Thus far, governments in these communities have been unwilling to issue debt to finance this rehabilitation, which is one reason that greater conversion on much of the base has not moved forward. As Congressman Sam Farr (D-Carmel) points out, "The Pentagon's assumptions about what a community can and cannot afford to do with a base are untenable. The remediation costs are too high to support most projects, and issuing debt is unsustainable" (Farr 2015). By the same token, market conditions might not yet justify preparing additional parcels for conversion given the large amount of debt it would place on local communities. Many members of the community note the slow pace of redevelopment on Fort Ord, but the reluctance of FORA's board to move forward with expensive aspects of redevelopment or to address region-wide considerations may also save residents from unsustainable public debt in pursuit of private redevelopment that might not materialize.

California and the federal government fund other conversion projects on the base that have advanced more quickly than in areas that depend on local funding. For example, California funded the creation of CSUMB, and the federal government funded Superfund cleanup on the site, funded the Fort Ord National Monument, and funded the VA hospital. Different agencies are responsible for these different areas, which reflects many of the difficulties inherent in converting a large site with a complex set of stakeholders and entities with redevelopment authority. Local financing for the national monument and CSUMB thus was not necessary, although both projects generated large community benefits. The result for FORA and the other communities was that the governance structure forced an incremental process of funding remaining projects through shared revenue from the site rather than by financializing each city's assets. Incremental financing leads to incremental conversion, but it also insulates surrounding communities from the perils of tying assets to global markets.

NAS Alameda

Financing defense conversion on the former NAS Alameda speaks to many of the trade-offs inherent in financing defense conversion in general. Partnerships with master developers promote defense conversion in many cases, as in San Diego. However, these arrangements are also fraught with risk in long-term redevelopment processes because of limited abilities to govern financial arrangements and limited accountability. Increasing accountability by avoiding partnerships may increase the prospects for redevelopment that is acceptable to broad groups of stakeholders but may also put taxpayers at risk. Thus, redevelopment financing strategies do not lend themselves to best practices but instead to careful consideration of the benefits, detractions, and incentives in each community.

The city of Alameda created redevelopment partnerships with Alameda Point Community Partners (ACP) in 2006 and with SunCal in 2010. The original partnership disintegrated when the Navy instituted fee-based conveyance requirements for NAS Alameda and insisted on $108 million from the city prior to transfer. Such a high fee was cost prohibitive from the developer's standpoint, and ACP withdrew from the partnership. SunCal formed a more recent partnership with the city that included approximately $200 million in tax increment financing. These funds would cover the costs of public services and amenities to accompany the thousands of new residential units that the developer planned to construct on the former NAS. Additionally, SunCal would include these amenities, such as open space and recreational trails, in the project only if special property taxes from a new community facilities district funded them as well (City of Alameda 2009). This is because devoting extra portions of the site to open-space recreation would decrease the number of housing units that SunCal could potentially build and lower its profit margins. This financial arrangement put services at risk and increased local taxes: two areas that voters overwhelmingly opposed. This deal was doubly unpopular once coupled with the increased traffic and pressure on services that increased population density would bring. Alameda voters ultimately rejected this deal by an overwhelming margin in 2010 because of concerns over housing density and a poorly structured financial arrangement.

The Navy returned to a "no-fee" conveyance once the city of Alameda agreed to limit the construction of new housing units: this time to 1,425 instead of the 4,800 that SunCal had originally planned. The city now acts as master developer, which will allow for the construction of housing on a nonprofit basis and prevent another failed public-private partnership. Of course, publicly financed redevelopment also drives public debt and puts pressure on the city to financialize its assets in a way that San Diego avoided. Yet the city of Alameda is more directly accountable to voters than a master developer because of the public participation in referenda on defense conversion and the possibilities that the public will vote local politicians out of office if the city accrues too much debt. Alameda's experience represents not collaborative governance in financing but rather a financing arrangement that was transparent enough for a direct vote to govern the process and make it accountable in the absence of redevelopment structures like Fort Ord's FORA.

Alameda's conversion financing experience shows how local civil-society groups can place redevelopment questions on the ballot so that citizens may reject poor redevelopment arrangements. Passing direct judgment on redevelopment plans is rare in these cases, however, and often not possible because of the many overlapping political entities' stakes in redevelopment processes. Thus, Alameda's experience shows how oversight and accountability in redevelopment deals are possible but not always likely on former bases. Furthermore, Alameda's experience also reiterates how many factors that influence redevelopment financing lie beyond local control. The state's dissolution of its redevelopment agencies forced the city to take on more direct governance responsibility, exactly at a time when the redevelopment deal was in crisis and local expertise could best influence conversion choices. Financing is thus the area where structure explains the largest variation in outcomes relative to local agency on the three California bases and likely does so on other former bases as well.

Financing Conversion on International Bases

Financing conversion at Holy Loch, Soesterberg, and Abrams Army HQ depended on national government funds. Local governments tend not to govern financing on these bases and therefore tend not to issue debt, financialize local assets, or even spend from general funds to support defense conversion. Instead, unitary national governments control and fund conversion, either for comprehensive redevelopment in the Soesterberg case or, in a narrower sense, for some redevelopment at Holy Loch. Conversion in Frankfurt advanced with the German federal government's gift of highly valuable land and buildings to the state of Hesse. Hesse then worked with Von Goethe University to transfer the campus, convert it for academic use, and integrate it into the city infrastructure for $100 million: a bargain price for a full academic campus in the heart of Frankfurt. The university contributed $25 million to this effort, with the state of Hesse, the city of Frankfurt, and the German federal government covering the remaining funds. Thus, local governments in Europe did not shoulder the burden of defense conversion, although conversion ranged from minimal (Holy Loch) to comprehensive (Abrams Army HQ, Frankfurt).

It is not clear how much federal debt the government of each country issued to fund defense conversion on these former bases. However, national governments are more integrated with international financial markets, have more expertise in issuing bonds and repaying interest, and are more insulated from individual base closures than local governments are. These advantages likely translate to better rates for financing defense conversion and general development projects, and lower costs than if municipalities pursued financing on their own, especially given the loss of revenue and residents that base closures bring. Citizens outside of the region where bases close then pay for a portion of redevelopment costs, but this is no different than for redevelopment projects following natural disasters or industrial decline. A national redevelopment strategy means that not all bases will be converted or redeveloped. Still, those that are might be financed with less cost and risk to former defense communities.

Lessons from the Bases

Communities can minimize risk, exercise agency, and still finance redevelopment through strong governance. Cities, regions, special districts, and redevelopment authorities all face pressure to attract capital. The amount of capital they attract and the risks they run by engaging markets to fund redevelopment can be high. However, engaging markets and partnering with private firms have the potential to benefit communities if governance structures and practices are collaborative, transparent, and accountable. Partnering with private developers is one way that cities limit their exposure to risk in international financial markets. Such partnerships are increasingly common, not just on former military bases but for megaprojects in general. Master-developer strategies can also limit democratic accountability, but civil-society mobilization in cities such as Alameda worked to make such partnerships accountable to the public. Alameda voters rejected an undesirable financing deal, which does suggest that public oversight in financing redevelopment is possible. In contrast, the master-developer strategy was unaccountable and gave unnecessary profits to the city's private partner, according to critics of San Diego's redevelopment process. Nevertheless, the city avoided many of the pitfalls associated with financializing assets as it pursued redevelopment. Governance structures such as FORA's limited governments' ability to issue debt but also guaranteed less risky, incremental projects that did not endanger surrounding communities.

Some well-governed cities leverage their strong market conditions to gain independence from financial market directives and to ensure that other public agencies and private firms provide public goods and infrastructure support. Financial markets largely ignore cities that have weaker governance, weaker market conditions, fewer assets to monetize, or fewer income streams to harness. Taking advantage of financialization of productive assets is thus possible, but it is likely that the relatively well-governed, well-resourced cities, such as San Francisco and San Diego, are the ones best able to do this. Other cities with poorer governance, fewer

resources, and weaker market conditions are much less prepared to operate in the international financial marketplace, gain funding support, and
direct it toward redevelopment.

Mobile labor and capital across much of the world mean that former
military communities are now embedded in a global political economy.
As DeFilippis and Saegert (2013) note, residents of a community were
rarely born in that community, may have emigrated from another country, may send their children to school in a different country, and may support elderly relatives in a third. The globalized nature of contemporary
communities challenges their ability to govern financing for defense conversion, financialization of local assets, and other financial processes that
extend far beyond their borders and occur at different scales.

Cities face many financing pitfalls and potential trade-offs in terms of
bond ratings, repayment schedules, and funding for services in the global
marketplace. Governance to optimize the costs and benefits in these different areas represents a very tall order, to be sure, but one that is possible
and should at least be pursued if military redevelopment is to occur at all,
much less in a way that is sustainable. Organized, strategic, well-governed
communities can harness financial markets to pursue development and
redevelopment in a sustainable, equitable manner.

Financing defense conversion with an eye toward social equity is essential for completing long-term projects in a way that provides broad community benefits. Most evaluations of development and redevelopment
financing focus on how cities structure deals. "Good" deals are those that
allow the city to maintain a favorable bond rating, pay off debt, and complete the project. But financing redevelopment should serve goals beyond
paying off debt and entail more than simple partnerships with private
developers. Engaging master developers is one way to finance redevelopment without squeezing already-struggling schools and other local
services. Providing public oversight through governance arrangements
can ensure that these partnerships not only benefit the developer and the
city but also the community. Direct electoral accountability is another
path to responsible financing. Public referenda are blunt instruments of
democratic governance, but some form of accountability is necessary to
incentivize cities to look beyond their immediate financial bottom line
and negotiate for community benefits in redevelopment financing deals.

Finally, cities that demonstrate political control over their assets can also extract concessions from the financial industry, improve the prospects for a favorable debt rating, and sustain services. Strong, collaborative governance provides pathways to all of these outcomes and is critical if former defense communities are to finance redevelopment for the many rather than for the few.

Conclusion

Converting Bases in the Twenty-First Century

Base closures strain entire regions' economic, political, and social fabric, but redevelopment offers opportunities to provide community benefits by reconfiguring economic, political, and social networks. Sustainable, equitable defense conversion is rare among the bases because of all-consuming environmental, financial, and planning challenges that common governance practices struggle to overcome. A lack of community resources and preparedness to meet these challenges leaves us pessimistic about communities' prospects for fully rebounding from base closures without considerable external assistance and favorable market conditions. Optimally, communities would not only replace activity that the former base generated but also use redevelopment to improve their economic positions and residents' quality of life. However, many of these goals are not realistic in the short term for communities facing extraordinary challenges in environmental remediation, critical revenue shortages, flight of expertise away from the region, and unfavorable market conditions. Most communities are simply not equipped to address the scale of governance challenges and redevelopment hurdles that a closed base represents. The recommendations below are therefore designed for these communities to optimize their positions, no matter how grave their situations.

Transformation is possible, given the targeted conversion success evident on the ground. In these cases, internal and external forces simultaneously create conditions that make conversion progress feasible. Of course, different stakeholders within the community see success and failure very differently. But some redevelopment is better than no redevelopment under these circumstances, even if redevelopment benefits are concentrated in a few areas. It is pragmatic to assume that success will come in fits and starts, given the size and complexity of redevelopment, and it is important to remember that the early projects that appear on a former base do not necessarily reflect the long-term redevelopment trajectory.

What Is Redevelopment Success?

Redevelopment success balances the desirable with the feasible in all aspects of defense conversion. Achieving defense conversion with community benefits is not easy under the best of circumstances, given that each community has many groups that feel and think very differently about bases as public assets and public space. Success in redevelopment means completion of the project, fiscal health for the city, and benefits for the community. But these aspects of success should be weighed against expectations, given the many challenges facing former defense communities. Governing at scale, massive environmental-restoration costs, loss of revenue, and information and power imbalances relative to federal and private-sector redevelopment partners make strong redevelopment performance very difficult to achieve. Of course, some defense conversion outcomes are superior to others. However, general success entails how far a community goes toward conversion and reuse *given its starting point.* Thus, community outcomes should be compared to community circumstances, resources, and opportunities rather than to a redevelopment ideal type. This is important because the "ideal" is a moving target because of the fifty-year time line for many conversion projects.

Realizing strong outcomes is nearly impossible if the local government is forced to cover most of the redevelopment costs or shoulder the burden of transformation; these communities care about community redevelopment but are poorly equipped to achieve it alone. However, redevelopment success looks very different from the Pentagon's perspective. Success means closing superfluous, expensive bases and getting them off the DoD's books. This can mean saddling other federal agencies, such as the EPA, with large defense conversion costs. These agencies tend to operate with much smaller budgets than the DoD and may decrease their support for other areas when they take on responsibility for defense cleanup. Expanding agencies' budgets to cover costs means that the U.S. taxpayer is ultimately left holding the base closure bag. The base closure and conversion process puts communities at great risk and needs to be fixed.

National Trends

Collaborative governance structures play an extremely important role in redevelopment. A great many other factors also influence outcomes associated with defense conversion, but some are beyond former defense communities' control. The amount of environmental remediation necessary to prepare a site for conversion, the level of economic productivity in a community, and a community's proximity to metropolitan areas are difficult or impossible to alter. Communities can anticipate many of the challenges associated with defense conversion and seek outside assistance to achieve equitable, sustainable outcomes. Who partners with the city and how these partnerships function are two areas where communities do have some agency. The extent to which communities use this agency to build a redevelopment coalition and pursue values "larger than local" goes far to explain how communities pursue redevelopment, the degree to which they convert former military bases, and who benefits from this conversion.

Planning

Planning is a conduit through which governance influences the degree and kind of defense conversion and reuse. Traditionally, local governments pursue development and redevelopment goals through local planning departments. This relationship also exists in military redevelopment, but defense conversion processes require an expansion of this traditional view. Local redevelopment authorities, regional bodies, and many public officials sometimes make land-use decisions in military redevelopment without input, oversight, and expertise from planning agencies. Planning for land use in defense conversion thus not only connects inter-scalar governance to specific projects; it is also part and parcel of governance and, more specifically, collaborative governance.

How planning for conversion occurs has considerable influence on how bases are converted, and for whom. Governing authorities often make planning decisions on what temporary and permanent land uses to pursue in defense conversion without training or support from local planning authorities. Planning departments should be incorporated into negotiations surrounding important areas such as land-use mix, environmental restoration, and economic activity because they have experience in these areas. Planning departments can therefore help strike good redevelopment deals that support collaborative governance.

Regular renegotiation of redevelopment responsibilities is important to promote continued collaboration in the face of unknown, perhaps-unanticipated challenges that appear over the course of complex conversion processes. As Congressman Sam Farr (D-Carmel) says, "Congress should pay for toxic cleanup—they put the money in the account for cleanup through the DoD. There's little lobbying in this area currently—but there are former defense sites in every congressional district. For land transfers, they can go forward as long as a 'proven technology' is in place even if the land or groundwater is still contaminated. Adaptability and flexibility of local government is key. The military doesn't do this very well" (Farr 2015).

Governance

The challenges of governance, territory, and scale influence communities' abilities to "make" places through defense conversion. Cities are integrated within regions and engaged vertically with other levels of government (region, state, national, transnational) as well as horizontally with governments bordering the base, the private sector, and civil-society organizations. Marshaling resources to pursue collective goals entails building coalitions and managing those coalitions to ensure collective action. Private-sector and nonprofit partners are crucial for redevelopment governance, which extends into planning, financing, implementing, and evaluating the defense conversion. Stakeholders from multiple jurisdictions and with diverse interests should be involved in redevelopment governance as well. The Navy's goal, as Steve Iselin, the Navy's deputy assistant secretary for energy, installations, and the environment, sees it, is to better prepare communities to accept land and convert it: "Getting to where a local redevelopment authority and a community work together to pursue the same redevelopment goals is the biggest challenge" (2014).

The ways that defense conversion can benefit the community speak to questions of governance and equity in development and redevelopment. Many large-scale development efforts are regional and suffer from similar governance issues as military redevelopment efforts. New development or infrastructure projects are unlikely to be intentionally sited on brown-fields or Superfund sites, but they cross a great many political jurisdictions and require long-term planning and financing. Megaprojects and many average projects now require financing as well and often increase city debt burdens in anticipation of economic growth and revenue increases.

Many development projects feature democratic deficits as LRAs and special-use districts issue public debt to finance the programs. "Ordinary" cities that plan and implement these projects also face information and resource disadvantages compared to the private sector or other levels of government with authority over development, even when these cities lie in extraordinary regions, as with the three California cases. Nonmilitary redevelopment projects, such as those following deindustrialization or natural disasters, face very similar, often intractable hurdles to those in former defense communities. Rebounding from the loss of jobs, revenue, and community resources associated with these shocks can be quite difficult, even in resilient communities. Strong governance, outside assistance, and long-term time horizons are all necessary if these cities are to return to "ordinary" status as well.

Integration

Military sites' physical centrality is misleading: these parcels may be physically central to urban cores but have been economically, politically, socially, and culturally isolated for decades: "The challenge is having the military cooperate with the community. Access to community is sometimes a challenge. In 1988 communities and the federal government thought closures would run easily, but of course, they didn't. Now there are OEA [Office of Economic Adjustment] needs for more environmental insurance products. Communities have to presume that there are problems that communities simply won't know about," says OEA Director Patrick O'Brien (2014). Bases are designed to be self-sufficient in many respects and largely exclude the public while they are operational. Military bases act as their own isolated ecosystems in some ways and are governed separately from the local community. Former military infrastructure is therefore incompatible with that of the surrounding city-region in these cases or requires extensive refitting to align it with local systems.

Decades of economic, political, social, and cultural isolation render conversion and integration costly and challenging. In turn, achieving beneficial redevelopment outcomes is rare for former military communities. Lost jobs, residents, and revenue combine to make planning, funding, implementing, and adapting strategies for economic integration difficult to begin with. Adding integration from political, social, and cultural perspectives to the mix makes promoting community benefits through defense conversion rarer still. Nevertheless, San Diego, Monterey, and Alameda's experiences with defense conversion demonstrate several options that communities may draw on to integrate former military sites into surrounding communities.

Communities must provide persistent, knowledgeable, and experienced leadership to weather the long-term redevelopment storm and the volatility of market conditions and government policy. Communities must also quickly gain expertise in marshaling resources and solving problems creatively. Even communities with the benefit of governance, resources, persistence, and luck will not convert bases in a way that satisfies all stakeholders. However, these exceptional communities will have a better chance of integrating former military sites like NTC San Diego and Fort

Ord in a way that is more equitable, effective, and ultimately satisfying than many alternatives.

Financing

Communities use many different strategies to finance defense conversion. Creating LRAs and special districts that issue public debt are the two most common. These options regularly entail financializing local assets and revenue streams to bypass legal and political constraints on issuing public debt and raising taxes. CRA and special-district–led redevelopment also suffers from democratic deficits and a distinct lack of accountability relative to some alternative financing options. Local projects generate revenue for global bondholders and potentially forgo new funding for public services when financialization goes well. Assets fail to generate expected revenue when it goes poorly, which can lead to expensive debt servicing and drastic service cuts to avoid default. Financialization to fund redevelopment thus often harms marginalized cities and marginalized populations within cities because cities and residents are in weak financial positions when they originally turn to financing.

Communities' globalized nature challenges their ability to govern financialization strategies that extend far beyond local borders and occur at different scales. Optimizing the costs and benefits surrounding bond ratings, repayment schedules, and funding for services is difficult, but possible, and it merits pursuit. Only then can strategic, well-governed communities engage financial markets to have a chance at equitable defense conversion. O'Brien agrees with the need for much more technical assistance for financing: "Another shift would be in financing, which has become more difficult. OEA has to perform a lessons-learned program to figure out what worked and what didn't in 2005. Thirty percent of properties are still not disposed of, in part due to lack of financing for conversion" (2014).

Financing defense conversion to promote equity and sustainability is critical for completing conversion projects while also providing community benefits. Cities that demonstrate political control over their assets can extract concessions from the financial industry, improve the prospects for a favorable debt rating, and also sustain services. Partnering with master developers is another potential way to finance redevelopment without risking funding cuts for already-struggling schools and local services. Adding structured public oversight to financing deals can ensure that public-private partnerships benefit not only the developer and the city but also the broader community. Direct electoral accountability may be too blunt of a democratic instrument in the context of complex, global financial arrangements. Still, some forms of democratic accountability can prompt cities to emphasize more than their immediate financial bottom line as they negotiate redevelopment deals.

Lessons from NTC San Diego, Fort Ord, and NAS Alameda

All three bases appeared primed for successful redevelopment before they were closed and may have even been selected for closure as a result of expectations of easy conversion. However, the conversion progress has diverged despite high land values and significant community resources devoted to conversion. Instead of easy conversion experiences, the three bases show how planning, integration, governance, and finance explain distinct redevelopment performances, with NTC San Diego at the high end of the spectrum, Fort Ord in the middle, and NAS Alameda at the bottom.

NTC San Diego

San Diego's NTC achieved the most comprehensive conversion of the three California cases. Liberty Station reflects expedient, mixed-use redevelopment that benefits a large contingent of local stakeholders. Liberty Station contains residential space, commercial space, educational institutions, an arts district, green space, and corporate workspace, all in a way that goes far to preserve historic memory on the base and fit the local community. San Diego's experience ultimately parallels many of the results from the quantitative analyses. Low environmental costs, "easy" integration, strong market conditions, and a strong partnership with a master developer led to better outcomes. Liberty Station now has 350 residential units, more than 100 commercial and nonprofit tenants, a high school, a theater, 46 acres of public open space, and 9 schools. Additionally, more than tens of thousands of weekly visitors browse Liberty Station's shops, use its parks, and attend dozens of art and cultural events (Raffesberger

2013). Job and revenue estimates are relatively high for Liberty Station and resemble those for other closed bases that have been thoroughly redeveloped for mixed use.

San Diego's NTC had several advantages over other bases from a redevelopment standpoint. The original agreement to lease the base and return it to the city following the military's departure ensured a no-fee conveyance, which made redevelopment more profitable and attractive for the master developer. The comparative lack of environmental contamination on the base also made it far easier and more profitable to redevelop. NTC San Diego contained relatively little soil contamination and could thus accommodate residential, educational, and green-space redevelopment far more easily than on other bases. However, it is telling that aspects of the original redevelopment proposals, such as a waterway connecting the San Diego Harbor to Mission Bay, were not pursued because of the high cost of remediating areas that *were* contaminated, such as the bottom of the harbor near the former base. Furthermore, lead and asbestos remediation in the historic district has been one of the slowest aspects of the NTC's redevelopment.

Critics rightly deride San Diego's redevelopment process as too corporate, too commercial, and too beneficial to private investors. For many people, the NTC's conversion represents crass commercialization of public, historic space, with a superficial recognition of this space in the site's marketing. To be sure, McMillin, the master developer, gains the most from redevelopment in a direct, material sense. But this critical perspective raises the question of where San Diego lies on a redevelopment spectrum ranging from no redevelopment at all to ideal redevelopment, especially considering the many different stakeholders and interest groups involved in the conversion process. San Diego prioritized economic recovery in conversion, which it achieved relative to many other communities. Yet this achievement does not override a broad set of issues surrounding civic space and the difficulty of converting former bases with public benefits in mind. Redevelopment gains rarely accrue equitably across all stakeholders, but the conversion of San Diego's NTC still leaves a lot to be desired in terms of the balance between private and public benefits. Thus, San Diego's conversion experience looks wonderful in a relative sense, when compared to other bases, but has room for improvement in an absolute sense, when compared to an equitable ideal.

Proliferating governance raises barriers to redeveloping closed military bases. But redevelopment is more likely when an entity such as a redevelopment authority or, in this case, a master developer with support from the city can identify those barriers and pursue plans that reflect considerations at the local, regional, state, and federal levels (among others). In this sense, completed development is superior to never-ending projects, even if these projects benefit fewer stakeholders than one would like. San Diego's NTC ultimately reflects mixed-use redevelopment, which results from the city and the master developers' ability to incorporate a wide variety of stakeholder interests into redevelopment plans and to execute those plans under a myriad of overlapping, frequently contradictory, regulatory frameworks.

Fort Ord

Fort Ord's redevelopment surpassed many expectations in terms of community benefits from defense conversion, primarily because converting Fort Ord originally appeared impossible. Yet Fort Ord's conversion is nowhere near as successful as San Diego's NTC, and it is not likely replicable on other closed bases. Fort Ord began its redevelopment process with several distinct disadvantages compared to other bases. The redevelopment parcel was heavily contaminated in many different ways: from unexploded ordnance left over from its use as an artillery and bombing range to hundreds of structures with lead and asbestos that required disassembly rather than demolition. The physical size of the parcel also stretched across dozens of local, regional, and state jurisdictions, which made coordination difficult.

Yet the former base has several exemplary projects. It now contains a university campus, a national monument (much of which is closed to the public because of unexploded ordnance), a hospital, and a commercial center. These aspects of redevelopment account for more than 4,000 jobs and bring 7,600 students to the area to attend CSUMB. But the former base is generally unsuitable for residential redevelopment, even in a region with exorbitant housing costs and high housing demand. A sense of place is thus missing in many respects, even if this is improving near the university.

It is surprising that Fort Ord has enjoyed as much success as it has given its disadvantages. However, enormous assistance from Fort Ord's friends in high political places certainly helped. Most notably, Leon Panetta, former congressman, White House chief of staff, secretary of defense, and CIA head, secured federal and state funding for redevelopment projects on the base and followed through during project implementation. Panetta was a driving force behind conversion for the community. Congressman Sam Farr (D-Carmel) discusses the creation of a "Monterey Model" of defense conversion, but Panetta's presence cannot be replicated in other former defense communities. This type of assistance is extraordinary; most former military communities cannot count on direct support from the White House. Fort Ord's redevelopment performance defies expectations because of these friends in high places, and quantitative models had predicted outcomes on the base to be much worse, given its disadvantages.

Fort Ord is also a complex redevelopment project because of its size, location, and status as a Superfund site. But Fort Ord also stands out as an exemplary case because California created FORA, a collaborative governance initiative that fosters far more stakeholder agreement than if it had been absent during conversion. The state assembly chose to create a collaborative, democratic, regional decision-making body to govern Fort Ord's redevelopment. This lightens some of the redevelopment burdens facing many communities that do not have extensive redevelopment experience and want to pursue joint stakeholder interests.

NAS Alameda

Redevelopment of NAS Alameda represents the weakest performance from almost any measure of success, despite its phenomenal location. There has been relatively little redevelopment on the base in both relative and absolute terms. This is somewhat surprising given the former base's location in an area with very strong market conditions and desirable elements of place such as its location on San Francisco Bay. Much of the planned residential redevelopment on the base never materialized, and the commercial/entertainment aspects of the redevelopment are placeholders for a time when environmental remediation can be achieved and residential redevelopment can resume. Temporary uses generated several hundred new jobs on the site and brought several thousand weekly visitors to the base, but they do not come close to offsetting the 14,000 jobs lost when the base closed (Association of Defense Communities 2013). Still, this redevelopment sets the stage for a strong effort at defense conversion with community benefits: residents and visitors enjoy entertainment and consumption opportunities on the former base and can access public transportation via ferry to Oakland and San Francisco. Moreover, mixed-use redevelopment is now advancing. There are 1,425 housing units under construction as well as commercial and recreational centers on the former base.

The largest obstacle to NAS Alameda's redevelopment was the federal government's insistence on a fee-based conveyance process because of the site's large perceived market value. However, the large fee ($110 million) prevented the city and several developers from following through with redevelopment plans. Alameda was one of the only communities in America that did not contest the BRAC Commission's base closure decision; rather, local policy makers saw the closure as an economic opportunity. Despite its forward-thinking mentality, Alameda's struggle to reinvent the Naval Air Station (NAS) has been economically crippling because of bad timing, community conflict, and the instability of federal policy. Many different local, regional, state, and federal actors have tried to support and assist the development process, but they have been unable to do so for a wide variety of internal and external reasons. Redevelopment efforts were largely futile until the DoD agreed to a no-fee conveyance in 2012, which paved the way for conversion.

NAS Alameda's conversion showcases the capriciousness of federal policy on base closures and how it can harm communities. At the same time, Alameda's experience also highlights the ways that the federal government promotes equitable development. Policies and mandates surrounding environmental health (ironically), homelessness, historic and environmental preservation, and planning are all seen here. Alameda also demonstrates the possibility for local democratic accountability in the redevelopment process. The long-awaited conveyance of land followed a revised master plan that represented a victory for community-advocacy groups over earlier master-development agreements. Prior to conveyance, SunCal had agreed to develop the former NAS with 4,500 new housing units to overcome the $110 million federal conveyance fee. Existing residents feared the increased population density, traffic, and strain that such development would place on services. Community groups placed the agreement on the local ballot, and residents rejected it overwhelmingly. The new plan that replaced it featured a no-fee conveyance concession from the Navy, the city as master developer, and mixed-use redevelopment with only 1,400 housing units at its core. The new agreement met with local approval and shows how even opaque defense conversion planning and deal making can be made subject to residents' approval and, thus, more equitable.

Base Closures with Community Benefits

Defending the United States and its allies is important, and many goals surrounding closure are laudable. Military redevelopment is important for national security because the U.S. military's ability to defend the country depends, in part, on the relative ease of shifting defense spending to areas that address twenty-first-century challenges and support new methods of warfare. The large network of fixed, domestic military bases was designed to address nineteenth- and twentieth-century challenges that are less and less relevant to contemporary military preparedness. In this sense, base closures serve the U.S. public as the DoD closes bases that it deems superfluous and shifts spending to more relevant areas. Focusing personnel near mission theaters, making budgetary room for new weapons systems, and generally dispensing with surplus expenditures can all promote the military's mission. However, closing bases is politically difficult because many closures will damage communities in the short term and long-term redevelopment will be extremely challenging.

The DoD should not pay to keep unnecessary bases open, but closed bases tend to be liabilities, not assets, and conversion is expensive. Furthermore, losses from base closures are concentrated in communities, rather than in regions or states, and these communities often face redevelopment challenges without resources and expertise. It is not the Pentagon's responsibility or mission to drive the domestic economy. However, federal, state, and local governments all bear responsibility for citizens' welfare, and reconfiguring BRAC is essential to avoid the many problems that base closures foist on communities. Redevelopment costs currently fall hardest on communities that are poorly prepared and equipped to shoulder them. Base closures and subsequent conversion costs are bitter pills for communities to swallow, but these recommendations are designed to improve performance around managing complex conversion projects and, in turn, increase the chances for cost-effective, equitable, sustainable redevelopment.

Additional federal resources could produce outsized community benefits for funding redevelopment governance and planning. BRAC legislation should allocate redevelopment funds directly to staffing local redevelopment agencies, possibly with federal professionals who understand the unique challenges that former defense communities will face in redevelopment. More bases will probably close despite community lobbying to keep them open, and these communities will be at a distinct redevelopment disadvantage from a power perspective. The important thing for communities is to prepare by gaining information on designing, governing, and funding conversion. This includes knowledge of cost drivers (environmental), the redevelopment time frame (long), and the hurdles to overcome (many). Managing expectations then becomes extremely important: not every community will get a Liberty Station, like San Diego, or a Presidio, like San Francisco.

Outcomes that benefit the public might be in greater supply if the federal government financed more of the redevelopment or at least covered environmental-remediation costs for land contaminated on the DoD's watch. Funding a redevelopment agency is a good start, but technical assistance is not enough: communities have few prospects for covering their environmental remediation and overall redevelopment costs without private financing, which can lead to capture. The federal government should pay for all environmental remediation on the site; it is shameful that Superfund legislation exempts the types of contamination almost always found on former bases. New legislation specifically for BRAC sites should cover this gap to give all communities the option to pursue mixed-use redevelopment and force the federal government to fully clean up its mess.

The BRAC process solves one political problem—the inability to close bases—but causes another in terms of long-term redevelopment challenges for U.S. communities. Recent BRAC legislation and the increasing involvement of the Office of Economic Adjustment in redevelopment are an improvement over earlier iterations of the closure process. However, it is not enough: the DoD still holds expensive, surplus property and active bases throughout the United States and still desires to shutter bases. This is understandable from a military perspective, but BRAC closures create dubious cost savings at the federal level, especially as later rounds exhausted "easy" opportunities for closure and conversion. Federal costs have thus risen quickly as the extent of environmental remediation becomes clear and the lack of community resources to achieve conversion has become better known. Federal policy makers should weigh the military budgeting need against other federal spending priorities before closing additional bases; military budgets should not come at the long-term expense of communities around the country.

Communities and Defense Conversion

Jobs that disappeared when bases close are unlikely to return. Yet revenue *can* rebound, and defense conversion *can* benefit broad groups of stakeholders. Collaborative governance at scale, phased project planning, integration of isolated sites, and equitably financed redevelopment can all help to complete projects while also providing community benefits. Knowledge of the challenges that communities will face and early preparation will help with making realistic conversion plans and achieving redevelopment goals. As Fort Ord Reuse Authority Director Michael Houlemard (2013) notes, "If you think you are going to be on a list, make friends with the commanding officer at base. Find out everything you can about the installation. If you are thinking it will happen, then start preparing for it. The most important thing is to know what you are getting."

Cities can and should prepare for base closures in a variety of ways. One method is to invest in the political capital necessary to extract redevelopment resources from the federal government (DoD, HUD, Commerce, HHS, EPA). Investing in political capital entails modifying institutions, structures, and practices that would enable cities to expand choice (Savitch and Kantor 2002). Moreover, rescaling different jurisdictions and territories could assist cities. National urban or redevelopment policy would help to foster cooperation among national, regional, and local authorities. Rescaling should move upward as well as downward: link-ing the city's external bargaining position with its drive to win citizen support would enhance democratic legitimacy and expand conversion project ideas. That way, investing in political capital could pay off in an expansion of social capital.

Local and regional governments can *prepare* for base closures by iden-tifying site assets and liabilities, selecting and securing public-private part-nerships, financing project implementation using deliberative phasing, designing site use based on places' assets and liabilities, engaging commu-nity stakeholders to ensure a transparent and collaborative development process, understanding planning cultures that shape development activity, and evaluating project outcomes on a range of economic, environmental, and equity factors.

Achieving these goals requires additional staff and assistance from consultants and may seem to be extravagant expenses in the context of disappearing jobs, residents, and revenue. However, the expense of hiring environmental consultants to provide a realistic estimate of remediation costs is quite low compared to the cost of ignorance surrounding remedia-tion challenges. Similarly, environmental insurance is one way that local governments can protect themselves and their constituents from the risk of cost overruns in remediation or the discovery of new hazards, such as unexploded ordnance, that can undermine and preclude conversion plans. Insurance can also insulate communities from the legal risks associated with converting former defense sites. Policies for former defense sites are available commercially and could save communities from potential bank-ruptcy as they convert and develop former bases.

Pursuing social equity in development is essential for providing com-munity benefits along with completed projects. Ensuring community ben-efits through development occurs on two levels: how the project itself takes place and for whom, and what communities might have to forgo to fund or finance that project. Opportunity costs that harm services for remaining residents sometimes loom large in defense conversion, and all communities engaged in redevelopment find themselves in precarious positions after losing jobs, residents, and revenue. Communities also risk service cuts when redevelopment projects do not generate anticipated eco-nomic growth and extra revenue. Engaging master developers can finance redevelopment without squeezing already-struggling schools and other local services, but this strategy risks concentrating the benefits of redevelopment in relatively few hands. The city serving as master developer, as in Alameda, and including community benefit agreements in financing deals are two ways to distribute redevelopment benefits more broadly, protect community services, and maintain fiscal health. Yet community benefits might not make it into development or redevelopment deals without an active civil society and institutional mechanisms to hold policy makers and private-sector partners to account.

Cities and public officials must have incentives to look beyond their immediate financial bottom line and negotiate for community benefits, no matter what form that accountability takes. For example, cities that demonstrate political control over their assets can also extract concessions in financing, improve city debt ratings, and sustain services. Thus, city officials can strengthen their own positions as they govern redevelopment processes directly, where they are more accountable to the public. Again, strong governance is critical for achieving accountability in all communities, not just those converting military bases.

The Future of BRAC

The Pentagon called for additional BRAC rounds every year from 2012 to 2016. These calls grew louder in 2016 and were accompanied by threats to empty bases of troops, stop budgeting for maintenance, and close bases by default if a new round of closures were not approved for 2019. However, a new round has not been approved as this book goes to press. It is not clear when another round of closures will occur, but more domestic bases will close at some point. Credibly promising support for these defense communities will be necessary for garnering congressional support for another BRAC round. More importantly, supporting these communities through the closure, conveyance, and conversion process is critical for their viability and for their residents' well-being. Ensuring that new BRAC legislation includes the transfer of more federal resources through the Office of Economic Adjustment and nonmilitary agencies across the federal government will go far to assist defense communities in conversion efforts. Understanding more about how communities across the country use federal resources and how their use could be improved is another desirable step toward converting closed bases in the public interest.

Exploring redevelopment inputs, processes, and outcomes for international bases is also important. International bases operate within different political, social, and economic contexts. Their closure and subsequent conversion experiences also occur under these distinctive circumstances. Broadening the analytic lens would help to explore similarities and differences between conversion on American bases overseas as well as on non-American bases around the world. That way, a clearer picture of how different national contexts influence redevelopment outcomes would come into focus. This research would also provide more contextualized policy recommendations for all communities facing redevelopment challenges, not just those in the United States.

Final Thoughts

A clear view of defense conversion shows *how* military redevelopment occurs, *where* it takes place, *why* it takes certain forms and scale, *who* benefits, and *what* this knowledge means for policy makers and practitioners. This research also holds practical implications for communities pursuing development and redevelopment. Defense conversion depends on governance. A wide variety of public, private, and nonprofit entities contribute to the conversion process and do so across many different scales. The realities of converting a former military base into a sustainable, redeveloped site require communities to understand and structure the relationships among governments, firms, workers, and private citizens. The information in this book therefore has the potential to change how revitalization occurs by harnessing macro- and micro-level analysis to influence investment decisions and redevelopment policy at the local, regional, and federal levels. In turn, scholars and policy makers can identify problems and solutions in redevelopment, generate policy recommendations across the country, and ultimately convert closed bases in the public interest.

Appendix

VARIABLES AND DESCRIPTIONS FOR QUANTITATIVE MODELS

Dependent Variables

Job Creation

The data set includes a measure of jobs created through the redevelopment process relative to jobs lost based on a survey from the U.S. defense communities and other public documents from former defense communities. A per capita measure of jobs created in the redevelopment process based on the size of the local population supplements the first variable. It should be noted that jobs created rarely approach jobs lost for the bases in the data set. The mean number of jobs created over jobs lost is 0.19, and the standard deviation is 0.16. The mean number of jobs created relative to the size of the local population is 0.08 per local resident, and the standard deviation is 0.09.

Revenue Generation

Measuring revenue can provide a broader view of how conversion can refill public coffers and provide the opportunity to retain or extend public services. Revenue generation may therefore be a precursor to extending the benefits of conversion to a broad population of stakeholders and thus represents a superior measure of redevelopment success than jobs alone. The measure of local revenue comes from the U.S. Department of Commerce's annual survey of cities and counties (2016). The measure takes two forms: 2015 revenue as a percentage of revenue in the year before the base closure announcement and 2015 per capita revenue, both in constant 2010 dollars. The percentage of 2015 revenue relative to revenue prior to base closure is 0.68, and the standard deviation is 0.21. Mean revenue among former defense communities is $1.28 per resident, and the standard deviation is 0.73.

Municipal Bond Rating

Municipal bond ratings over the course of the redevelopment process are also important for fiscal health because they reflect the risk associated with lending money to an affected city and the subsequent cost of borrowing money to finance redevelopment, capital improvement projects, and service delivery. Information on municipal bond ratings comes from Standard and Poor's (2016) on an annual basis and estimates the likelihood of cities holding AA ratings or better over time. The median bond rating in the data set is A–. The models use the median bond rating across different entities in cases where multiple cities or counties fund redevelopment collaboratively.

Percentage of Land Transferred

The percentage of the base that is transferred at a certain time is also a key indicator for how the redevelopment process is progressing because land must pass from the military to another entity before conversion can occur. Conveying land does not mean that it will be redeveloped in a way that represents the highest and best use of the former site or redeveloped at all. Yet transferred land does mean that conversion projects have advanced beyond the planning stage or will advance in the future. The Association of Defense Communities collects this data for former bases through 2013 (Association of Defense Communities 2013). The mean percentage of transferred land is 0.67 (67%), and the standard deviation is 0.14. The data set also includes a dichotomous measure of the site's former military function. Bases receive a score of 1 if they featured a weapons plant, weapons depot, or testing facility and a score of 0 if they did not.

Low-Income Housing

The relative presence of low-income housing on a base is another way to determine the extent to which defense conversion benefits a specific, vulnerable population. Twenty-four percent of former bases feature at least some low-income housing as part of their conversion (U.S. Department of Housing and Urban Development 2018).

Environmental Remediation

The Association of Defense Communities estimates these costs as of 2013 through a survey of former defense communities. The total mean cost for remediation on former bases is $88 million, with a standard deviation of $25 million. This information underlies a measure of per capita remediation cost, which we transform using its logarithm to ensure normality. The mean per capita, logged score is 3.25, with a standard deviation of 0.62. Overall, 36 percent of former defense communities completed their environmental remediation by 2013.

Equitable Conversion Benefits

The data set records the projects that are physically present on each former military site, such as a private shipyard, a public park, a commercial shopping center, a nonprofit organization's headquarters, and private housing. Then we categorize these projects as one of the following land uses: residential, commercial, industrial, institutional, recreational, and airport. This approach fosters a general understanding of the ways that communities use former military land. This information also offers a valuable point of departure for evaluating smaller categories or project-specific endeavors such as parks or museums on former military sites.

Information on land use following defense conversion leads us to construct an index of the breadth of beneficiaries that conversion serves. The index is scaled from 1 to 5, which reflects the breadth of land-use categories described above (residential, commercial, industrial, institutional, recreational, and airport). A score of 1 describes narrow conversion, where only one type of land use appears on the former base. These types of projects may be very important to the city-region in terms of jobs and revenue, such as with a large industrial park. However, they do not serve a broad group of stakeholders directly and do not foster sustainable, equitable redevelopment. Similarly, a score of 2 often reflects complementary projects that can serve as the foundation for economic clustering. For example, an industrial park and a port facility foster market access for manufactured goods and additional commercial traffic for the port. These uses might be sensible from a reuse perspective because they attract jobs and revenue to the city-region. Nevertheless, they do not create the sense of place and community that a score of 4 or 5 reflects.

The mean defense conversion score in the data set is 2.41, and the standard deviation is 1.13.

Independent Variables

Government Funding Partnerships

The federal government is a funding partner in 71 percent of cases, whereas local governments provide direct funding in only 35 percent of former sites (this does not include other ways that local governments support projects such as through off-budgeting techniques, land transfers, infrastructure services, fast permitting and development services, and capital support). State governments provide at least some of the funding in 45 percent of cases. This information serves as the foundation for an indicator of funding collaboration at scale, with communities pursuing conversion with local funds alone receiving scores of 1, with local and state funding scored as 2, and with local, state, and federal funding scored as 3.

Number of Funding Entities across Public, Private, and Nonprofit Sectors

The mean number of partners is 4.72, and the standard deviation is 2.88. Projects attracting multiple nonprofit funders may be different from those attracting multiple private firms and are likely to serve different stakeholders. For instance, multiple private-sector partners may reflect the possibility for high profits, whereas a greater number of nonprofit partners may reflect attempts to meet communities' noncommercial needs. We evaluate this prospect by coding the number of nonprofit, private, and public redevelopment funders as separate variables and use them in the statistical models that we present in table A.3.

Redevelopment Funding and Staffing

We use information on redevelopment authority websites and Association of Defense Communities data to capture variation across communities in redevelopment funding and staffing. The mean per capita funding level is $5.31, with a standard deviation of $2.80. The mean staffing level is 11.2 employees, with a standard deviation of 6.3. However, it is often unclear what redevelopment authorities ultimately spend or what their permanent staff might be in any given year. We therefore divide former base communities by terciles into low, medium, and high staffing levels based on the available information we collect in this area and whether communities fall into the bottom third, middle third, or top third of spending and staffing relative to other former defense communities.

Environmental Remediation

The Association of Defense Communities estimates these costs as of 2013 through a survey of former defense communities. The total mean cost for remediation on former bases is $88 million, with a standard deviation of $25 million. This information underlies a measure of per capita remediation cost, which we transform using its logarithm to ensure nor-mality. The mean per capita, logged score is 3.25, with a standard devi-ation of 0.62.

Former Military Use

The database includes a parallel measure based on the former military function of the site. The database includes a dummy variable for air bases and shipyards (coded 1) relative to other former bases (coded 0) to account for these "easy" conversion opportunities to better explain con-version outcomes. These data come from the authors' coding.

Location Relative to Metropolitan Statistical Areas

The data set includes information on whether the former base is in a county containing at least part of a U.S. Census Bureau Metropolitan Sta-tistical Area (MSA) or bordering on an MSA (U.S. Census Bureau 2016b). This information then translates to a dummy variable, where scores of 0 indicate a location outside of an MSA and scores of 1 reflect a location within or bordering on an MSA. This allows us to assess whether 66 per-cent of closed bases are in counties within or bordering on an MSA.

Early vs. Late BRAC Rounds

The BRAC round in which bases close may also reflect time's influence on redevelopment success. It is entirely possible that the DoD selected cer-tain bases for early closure because of their high redevelopment potential (82% of the bases in the data set closed before 1995). Somewhat surpris-ingly, the bases that closed in the most recent BRAC round have com-pleted just as much of their environmental cleanup as bases that closed earlier, on average. Overall, 36 percent of former defense communities completed their environmental remediation by 2013.

Physical Size of the Base

The mean size of the former bases in our data set is 6.4 square miles, with a standard deviation of 2.9.

Geographic Region of the Country

Communities in one part of the country, such as the West, may pursue systematically different land-use strategies in military base redevelopment than communities in another part, such as the Northeast. Geographically speaking, bases closed since 1988 are overwhelmingly situated in the West and the South (38% and 31%, respectively).

Local GDP per Capita

Mean per capita GDP is $34,615, and the standard deviation is 5,396. Models use a transformed version of this indicator (log base 10) to ensure normality. The data come from the U.S. Department of Commerce, 2017.

TABLE A.1 Multinomial logit model of land use in U.S. military base redevelopment, 1991–2010

Independent variables	Odds ratio for leveraged projects	Odds ratio for replacement communities
Federal funding	1.058 (0.483)	1.435** (0.518)
State funding	1.035 (0.399)	1.147** (0.530)
Local funding	1.016 (0.628)	0.992 (0.531)
Number of public/private/ nonprofit collaborators	1.037* (0.275)	1.072* (0.466)
Environmental hazards	0.594** (0.385)	0.278** (0.249)
Per capita gross local product (by county, logged)	1.203** (0.176)	1.511** (0.208)
Late BRAC round	1.036 (0.562)	1.045 (0.348)
County with MSA	0.915 (0.328)	0.961 (0.530)
Size of the base (square miles, logged)	1.016 (0.288)	1.027 (0.302)
West	0.868 (0.432)	0.920 (0.569)

(*Continued*)

TABLE A.1 (Continued)

Independent variables	Odds ratio for leveraged projects	Odds ratio for replacement communities
Midwest	0.895	0.963
	(0.318)	(0.294)
Northeast	1.029	1.044
	(0.326)	(0.479)
Constant	−0.483	−0.322
	(0.297)	(0.264)
Log likelihood	84.34	
Wald $X^2(3)$	25.67	
Number of bases	122	
Pseudo R^2	0.503	

Notes: Isolated project redevelopment is the baseline category. Using regional dummy variables, the South is the omitted category.

Standard errors in parentheses are robust to heteroskedasticity. $^*p < .05$; $^{**}p < .01$; $^{***}p < .001$.

TABLE A.2 Multinomial logit model of land use in U.S. military base redevelopment, 1991–2010

Independent variables	Odds ratio for leveraged projects	Odds ratio for replacement communities
Federal funding	1.041	1.366***
	(0.352)	(0.410)
State funding	1.025	1.103*
	(0.336)	(0.474)
Local funding	1.024	1.001
	(0.619)	(0.573)
Number of public/private/ nonprofit collaborators	1.020 (0.579)	1.053* (0.402)
Environmental hazards	0.928*	0.307**
	(0.516)	(0.310)
Per capita gross local income (by county, logged)	1.415** (0.363)	1.523** (0.570)
Late BRAC round	1.022	1.013
	(0.581)	(0.497)
County with MSA	1.009	1.014
	(0.521)	(0.593)
Size of the base (square miles, logged)	1.030 (0.324)	1.007 (0.418)

Independent variables	Odds ratio for leveraged projects	Odds ratio for replacement communities
Constant	−0.329 (1.378)	−0.318 (1.493)
Log likelihood	80.36	
Wald $X^2(3)$	25.48	
Number of bases	122	
Pseudo R^2	0.494	

Notes: Isolated project redevelopment is the baseline category, using county-level per capita income instead of citywide GDP.

Standard errors in parentheses are robust to heteroskedasticity. *p < .05; **p < .01; ***p < .001.

TABLE A.3 Multinomial logit model of land use in U.S. military base redevelopment, 1991–2010

Independent variables	Odds ratio for leveraged projects	Odds ratio for replacement communities
Number of nonprofit funders	1.039 (0.522)	1.026* (0.415)
Number of private funders	1.045 (0.490)	1.031* (0.412)
Number of public funders	1.023 (0.576)	1.028* (0.386)
Environmental hazards	0.742* (0.616)	0.370** (0.213)
Per capita gross local income (county, logged)	1.418** (0.347)	1.533** (0.382)
Late BRAC round	1.016 (0.438)	1.013 (0.491)
MSA within county	0.994 (0.489)	1.011 (0.569)
Size of the base (square miles, logged)	1.004 (0.301)	1.015 (0.418)
Constant	−0.333 (1.497)	−0.306 (1.458)
Log likelihood	79.45	
Wald $X^2(3)$	26.90	
Number of bases	122	
Pseudo R^2	0.455	

Notes: Isolated project redevelopment is the baseline category, using the number of nonprofits, private firms, and public entities funding redevelopment as primary independent variables. We exclude the federal and state funding dummy variables from this model because they are multi-collinear with the number of public funders variable, with Variance Inflation Factors of 7.1 and 6.3.

Standard errors in parentheses are robust to heteroskedasticity. *p < .05; **p < .01; ***p < .001.

TABLE A.4 Ordinary least squares model of local revenue in former military communities, through 2015

Independent variables	Dependent variables		
	Per capita revenue	2015 revenue as a percentage of pre-closure revenue	City bond rating
Collaborative governance*local GDP	0.53** (0.07)	0.30** (0.05)	0.34** (0.02)
Funding across scales	0.25* (0.10)	0.06* (0.03)	0.14* (0.06)
Number of public/private/ nonprofit collaborators	0.04 (0.03)	0.03 (0.02)	0.06 (0.05)
Funding for redevelopment authority (per capita, logged)	0.11** (0.03)	0.05* (0.02)	0.08* (0.04)
Former airbase or shipyard	0.12 (0.07)	0.10* (0.04)	0.04* (0.02)
Environmental remediation costs (per capita logged)	−0.16** (0.01)	−0.13** (0.02)	−0.21* (0.09)
Per capita gross local product (by county, logged)	0.17* (0.08)	0.11* (0.04)	0.22* (0.10)
Late BRAC round	0.07 (0.07)	0.14 (0.12)	−0.16 (0.13)
MSA within county	0.35** (0.13)	0.27* (0.12)	0.14** (0.03)
Size of the base (sq. miles, logged)	0.11 (0.14)	0.08 (0.05)	−0.08 (0.08)
Constant	0.55 (0.32)	0.37** (0.11)	0.40* (0.19)
Number of bases	122	122	122
R^2	0.75	0.66	0.58

Note: Standard errors in parentheses are robust. *$p < .05$; **$p < .01$

TABLE A.5 List of U.S. bases closed since 1988 under BRAC

Installation	City	State
Mather AFB	Sacramento	CA
Moffett NAS	Mountain View	CA
Deseret Chemical Depot	Tooele	UT

Installation	City	State
Umatilla Chemical Depot	Hermiston	OR
Naval Weapons Station Seal Beach Detachment Concord	Concord	CA
Riverbank Army Ammunition Plant	Modesto	CA
Marine Corps Air Station Tustin	Irvine	CA
Hunters Point Annex	San Francisco	CA
Fort Wingate	Gallup	NM
Onizuka Air Force Station	Sunnyvale	CA
NWEF Albuquerque	Albuquerque	NM
Fort Baker	Sausalito	CA
Naval Hospital Oakland, aka Oak Knoll Naval Hospital	Oakland	CA
Castle AFB	Merced	CA
Naval Station Long Beach	Long Beach	CA
Sacramento Army Depot	Sacramento	CA
Naval Shipyard, Long Beach	Long Beach	CA
Camp Bonneville	Camas	WA
Defense Distribution Depot Ogden	Ogden	UT
Fort Douglas	Salt Lake City	UT
Naval Training Center San Diego	San Diego	CA
Kapalama Military Reservation Phase III	Honolulu	HI
Naval Station Puget Sound (Sand Point)	Seattle	WA
Hamilton Air Force Base	Novato	CA
Navajo Depot	Coconino	AZ
Presidio of San Francisco	San Francisco	CA
Norton AFB	San Bernardino	CA
George AFB	Victorville	CA
Fort Ord	Seaside	CA
Lowry AFB	Denver	CO
Williams AFB	Mesa	AZ

(*Continued*)

Installation	City	State
Naval Supply Center Oakland, Oakland Naval Supply Center	Oakland	CA
Marine Corps Air Station El Toro	Irvine	CA
Tooele Army Depot	Tooele	UT
Naval Air Station Alameda	Alameda	CA
Naval Aviation Depot Alameda	Alameda	CA
Naval Air Station Barbers Point	Kapolei	HI
Naval Station Treasure Island	San Francisco	CA
Mare Island Naval Shipyard	Vallejo	CA
Fitzsimons Army Medical Center	Denver	CO
Adak NAF	Adak	AK
Fort Missoula	Missoula	MT
McClellan AFB (Sacramento ALC)	North Highlands	CA
North Highlands Air Guard Station	North Highlands	CA
Ontario IAP Air Guard Station	Ontario	CA
Branch US Disciplinary Barracks	San Francisco	CA
Kulis Air Guard Station	Anchorage	AK
Vancouver Barracks	Vancouver	WA
Naval Air Station Atlanta	Fair Oaks	GA
Naval Station Lake Charles	Lake Charles	LA
Reese AFB	Lubbock	TX
Brooks AFB	San Antonio	TX
Fort Pickett	Blackstone	VA
Fort Gillem	Forest Park	GA
Fort McPherson	Atlanta	GA
Naval Station Pascagoula	Pascagoula	MS
Carswell AFB	Fort Worth	TX

Installation	City	State
Chase Field NAS	Beeville	TX
Coosa River Annex	Anniston	AL
Cameron Station	Alexandria	VA
Lone Star Army Ammunition Plant	Hooks	TX
Cecil Field NAS	Jacksonville	FL
Homestead ARB	Homestead	FL
Alabama Ammunition Plant	Childersburg	AL
Naval Station Galveston	Galveston	TX
Nike Site, Aberdeen Proving Ground	Aberdeen	MD
Fort Holabird	Baltimore	MD
New Orleans Military Ocean Terminal	New Orleans	LA
Myrtle Beach AFB	Myrtle Beach	SC
Naval Training Center Orlando	Orlando	FL
Fort Chaffee	Fort Smith	AR
Fort McClellan	Anniston	AL
England AFB	Alexandria	LA
Bergstrom AFB	Austin	TX
Eaker AFB	Blytheville	AR
Naval Station Charleston	Charleston	SC
Charleston Naval Shipyard	North Charleston	SC
Naval Hospital Orlando	Orlando	FL
Vint Hill Farms Station	Cedar Run	VA
Naval Air Station Dallas	Grand Prairie	TX
Naval Station Mobile	Theodore	AL
Defense Distribution Depot Memphis	Memphis	TN
Fort Ritchie	Cascade	MD
FISC Charleston	North Charleston	SC
Fort Monroe	Hampton	VA
Naval Station Ingleside	Ingleside	TX

(*Continued*)

TABLE A.5 (Continued)

Installation	City	State
Mississippi Army Ammunition Plant	John C. Stennis Space Center	MS
Fort Indiantown Gap	Fort Indiantown Gap	PA
Fort Monmouth	Oceanport	NJ
Roslyn Air Guard Station	East Hills	NY
Naval Air Station Willow Grove	Willow Grove	PA
Fort Dix	New Hanover Township	NJ
South Weymouth NAS	South Weymouth	MA
Naval Hospital Philadelphia	Philadelphia	PA
Camp Pedricktown	Pedricktown	NJ
Stratford Army Engine Plant	Stratford	CT
Pease AFB	Portsmouth	NH
Naval Station New York (Brooklyn)	New York	NY
Naval Station Philadelphia	Philadelphia	PA
Philadelphia Naval Complex (Naval Shipyard)	Philadelphia	PA
Fort Devens	Devens	MA
Loring AFB	Limestone	ME
Naval Station Staten Island (Stapleton Homeport)	New York	NY
Griffiss Air Force Base	Rome	NY
Fort Totten	New York	NY
Military Ocean Terminal Bayonne	Bayonne	NJ
Seneca AD	Romulus	NY
Camp Kilmer	Highland Park	NJ
NAWC-AD Open Water Test Facility Oreland	Oreland	PA
Fort Sheridan	Fort Sheridan	IL
Savanna Army Depot Activity	Hanover	IL
Richards-Gebaur ARS	Kansas City	MO
Kansas Army Ammunition Plant	Parsons	KS
Jefferson Proving Ground	Madison	IN

Installation	City	State
Chanute AFB	Rantoul	IL
Fort Benjamin Harrison	Lawrence	IN
Wurtsmith AFB	Oscoda	MI
Newark AFB	Heath	OH
O'Hare IAP ARS	Des Plaines	IL
Naval Air Station Glenview	Glenview	IL
Naval Air Facility Detroit	Grosse Ile	MI
K. I. Sawyer AFB	Marquette Township	MI
Newport Chemical Depot	Clinton	IN
W. K. Kellogg Airport Air Guard Station	Battle Creek	MI
Gen. Mitchell International Airport ARS	Milwaukee	WI
Naval Air Facility Midway		Midway Islands
Brunswick Naval Air Station	Brunswick	ME
Kelly AFB	San Antonio	TX
Pueblo Army Ammunition Depot	Pueblo	CO
Galena AFB	Galena	AK
Ship Repair Facility, Guam		GU

NOTES

Introduction

1. The appendix includes a list of all base closures with key features.

2. Other well-known cases include Brooklyn's Navy Yard on the East River and Philadelphia's Navy Yard on the Delaware River.

3. We use the term *community* because of its conceptual relationship to those places: the book emphasizes the people that live in and around former military bases; their shared attitudes, interests, and goals; and how redevelopment impacts their lives. These people remake places as they jointly redevelop closed bases and rebuild communities. We therefore refer to these areas near shuttered bases as former defense communities.

4. The data set does not cover the entire range of closed DoD installations because most of these facilities are single-use, small facilities. Instead, it includes the 122 full bases that have closed since 1989.

5. Of course, there are some differences across the sites: the nearby populations vary in size and density, but the metropolitan statistical areas (MSAs) are broadly similar because Fort Ord is part of the greater San Jose-Sunnyvale-Santa Clara MSA. Fort Ord also represents a much larger physical parcel than the other two bases.

6. The three California cases closed under similar state-level circumstances as almost one-quarter of the national bases shuttered under BRAC, in the sense that approximately 122 large facilities closed nationally.

7. On Fort Ord, 15,000 to 17,000 acres are reserved for conservation areas under the purview of the U.S. Bureau of Land Management, 1,000 acres for coastal conservation are

under the jurisdiction of the California Department of Parks and Recreation, and 2,692 acres are designated as recreational land.

1. BRAC and Federal Public Policy

1. Precisely when the next round of base closures will occur is impossible to say, but the Pentagon has formally requested closure rounds each year from 2012 to 2016. Congress has not complied with these requests, and the 2017 defense budget includes funds for feasibility studies of unilateral closures if Congress will not authorize a new BRAC round.

2. Local redevelopment refers to entities serving as community contact points relating to closure and realignment: these entities are tasked with preparing and implementing redevelopment plans under BRAC legislation. California created a parallel system of community redevelopment agencies (CRAs) that also frequently served as the LRA on former bases until the state of California dissolved all CRAs in 2011.

3. FUDS are closed installations preceding BRAC rounds, primarily from the world wars.

4. Military gains in war-fighting capabilities through base closure cost savings may occur only in the very long term. The high costs of environmental remediation in the most recent rounds of base closures suggest that the Department of Defense may not be enjoying projected cost savings in the short or medium terms.

2. National Trends in Military Redevelopment

1. The release of this database, "Salvaging Community," will coincide with the printing of this book.

2. The appendix contains a full description of all variables and their sources. The data for this book come from public records such as government budgets and government documents on project updates to evaluate the hypotheses above.

3. We do not assess the strength of these partnerships or how they change over time because of very limited data availability. Instead, we record the source of conversion funding, by sector, as a count of the total number of funding entities across public, private, and nonprofit sectors.

4. Mean per capita GDP is $34,615, and the standard deviation is 5,396. Models use a transformed version of this indicator (log base 10) to ensure normality.

5. The database includes a dummy variable for air bases and shipyards (coded 1) relative to other former bases (coded 0) to account for these "easy" conversion opportunities to better explain conversion outcomes.

6. The models explicitly account for potential selection bias in base closures: the potential differences in bases selected for closures in early and late BRAC rounds motivate the inclusion of a dummy variable indicating whether bases closed in the early rounds (1988–1995, coded "0"), or the most recent round (2005, coded "1"). Eighty-three percent of bases were part of the early rounds of base closures (1988–1995).

7. The data set includes information about whether the former base is in a county containing at least part of an MSA or bordering on an MSA (U.S. Census Bureau 2016b).

8. The mean size of the former bases is 6.4 square miles with a standard deviation of 2.9.

9. Many of the variables in the data set do change over time, but the information necessary to measure most of the independent and dependent variables as they change for each former defense community is not available in any given year.

10. The mean number of jobs created over jobs lost is 0.19, and the standard deviation is 0.16. The mean number of jobs created relative to the size of the local population is 0.08 per local resident, and the standard deviation is 0.09.

11. The measure of local revenue comes from the U.S. Department of Commerce's annual survey of cities and counties (2016). The measure takes two forms: 2015 revenue as a percentage of revenue in the year before the base closure announcement and 2015 per capita revenue, both in constant 2010 dollars. The percentage of 2015 revenue relative to revenue prior to base closure is 0.68, and the standard deviation is 0.21. Mean revenue among former defense communities is $1.28 per resident, and the standard deviation is 0.73.

12. Information on municipal bond ratings comes from Standard and Poor's (2016) on an annual basis and estimates the likelihood of cities holding AA ratings or better over time. The median bond rating in the data set is A–. The models use the median bond rating across different entities in cases where multiple cities or counties fund redevelopment collaboratively.

13. The Association of Defense Communities collects this data for former bases through 2013 (Association of Defense Communities 2013). The mean percentage of transferred land is 0.67 (67%), and the standard deviation is 0.14. The data set also includes a dichotomous measure of the site's former military function. Bases receive a score of 1 if they featured a weapons plant, weapons depot, or testing facility and a score of 0 if they did not. The above measures are highly positively correlated and are therefore not used in the same defense conversion models. Models using the dichotomous measure of former military function appear in the appendix.

14. The Association of Defense Communities collects data on these outcomes though 2013. Many of the bases from early BRAC rounds have a remediation head start of at least a decade over those that closed in 2005 (82% of the bases in the data set closed before 1995). Somewhat surprisingly, the bases that closed in the most recent BRAC round have completed just as much of their environmental cleanup as bases that closed earlier, on average. Overall, 36% of former defense communities completed their environmental remediation by 2013.

15. Airfields on former bases are frequently converted to airports. Airports benefit a broad array of stakeholders but are almost always the only type of land use featured on bases that have them because of the noise pollution, air pollution, and safety concerns associated with situating residential or commercial areas near airports. They do not accord with the concept of equitable, sustainable redevelopment in a community setting and therefore receive a score of 1 on the conversion index, just as an industrial park would.

16. The mean defense conversion score in the data set is 2.41, and the standard deviation is 1.13.

17. Better-staffed redevelopment authorities are also connected to these outcomes.

18. Models using interaction terms show how collaborative governance coupled with strong economic conditions are associated with the *highest* levels of redevelopment performance across former defense communities. These models are available in Table A4 of the appendix.

3. Planning for Transformation

1. "Save Our NTC" lost three of these suits and agreed to a $100,000 settlement in the fourth. However, this does not mean that the group's complaints lack salience.

2. Douglas DeHaan, personal interview with the authors, March 25, 2013.

4. Collaborative Governance

1. For regime theory, see Stone 1989 and Hoxworth and Clayton-Thomas, 1993. For growth machines, see Molotch 1976, Logan and Molotch 2007, and Molotch 1993. For the ways that neoliberal development has limited local services, hindered human development, and undermined vulnerable populations' prospects, see Imbroscio 2012, Tasan-Kok

and Baeten 2011, Leitner et al. 2007a, and Kirkpatrick and Smith 2011. For analysis surrounding the urban-rural divide, see Galston and Baehler 1995, Ilbery 2014, Clawson 2013, and Rakodi 2014.

2. This share grew since the passage of Proposition 13, which put strict limits on municipal ability to tax residents (California Board of Equalization 2009).

3. This reflects Allen and Cochrane's (2007, 1162) concept of political assemblages whose "provisional mix of cross-cutting institutional agencies, partnerships, businesses and interest groupings" address redevelopment challenges at scale.

5. The Pursuit of Integration

1. For example, Save Our NTC in San Diego, the Sierra Club on Fort Ord, and developers as well as residents in Alameda.

REFERENCES

Adams, Carolyn. 2007. "Urban Governance and the Control of Infrastructure." *Public Works Management Policy* 11, no. 3: 164–76.

Agnew, John. 2016a. "Spatializing Politics." *Territory, Politics, Governance* 4, no. 3: 265–68.

Agnew, John. 2016b. "Understandings of the Changing Nature of Space and the Future of Global Governance." *Geography Research Forum* 20: 1–13.

Alameda Point. 2011. *Alameda Point Reuse Plan*. Alameda, CA: Alameda Point.

Alameda Point. 2013. *History of Redevelopment on Alameda Point*. https://alamedaca. gov/alameda-point/site-development.

Allen, John, and Allan Cochrane. 2007. "Beyond the Territorial Fix: Regional Assemblages, Politics and Power." *Regional Studies* 41, no. 9: 1161–75.

Almazan, Krista. 2014. "Fort Ord 2.0." *KQED News*, December 12. https://ww2.kqed. org/news/2014/11/28/fort-ord-revitalizing-an-old-base.

Althubaity, Amer, and Andy Jonas. 1998. "Suburban Entrepreneurialism: Redevelopment Regimes and Coordinating Metropolitan Development in Southern California." In *Entrepreneurial City: Geographies of Politics, Regime and Representation*, edited by Tim Hall and Phil Hubbard, 102–35. Chichester, UK: Wiley.

Altshuler, Alan, and David E. Luberoff. 2003. *Mega-projects: The Changing Politics of Urban Public Investment*. Washington, DC: Brookings Institution Press.

Amin, Ash, and Steven Graham. 1997. "The Ordinary City." *Transactions of the Institute of British Geographers* 22, no. 4: 411–29.

Amin, Ash, and Nigel Thrift. 2002. *Cities: Reimagining the Urban.* Cambridge: Polity.

Andersson, Linda, Johan Lundberg, and Magnus Sjöström. 2007. "Regional Effects of Military Base Closures: The Case of Sweden." *Defence and Peace Economics* 18, no. 1: 87–97.

Ansell, Chris, and Allison Gash. 2008. "Collaborative Governance in Theory and Practice." *Journal of Public Administration Research and Theory* 18, no. 4: 543–71.

Armey, Dick, and Barry Goldwater. 1987. "Close the Obsolete Military Bases." *Washington Post*, May 7.

Ashley, Amanda Johnson. 2015. "Beyond the Aesthetic: The Historical Pursuit of Local Arts Economic Development." *Journal of Planning History* 14, no. 1: 38–61.

Ashley, Amanda Johnson, and Michael Touchton. 2016. "Reconceiving Military Base Redevelopment: Land Use on Mothballed US Bases." *Urban Affairs Review* 52, no. 3: 391–420.

Ashton, Phillip. 2009. "An Appetite for Yield: The Anatomy of the Subprime Mortgage Crisis." *Environment and Planning* 41 (A): 1420–41.

Association of Defense Communities. 2013. *State of Base Redevelopment Report.* Washington, DC: Association of Defense Communities.

Associated Press. 2016. "TIF Financing Subsidizes Wealthy Chicago Developers." October 11.

Bagaeen, Samer Ghaleb. 2006. "Redeveloping Former Military Sites: Competitiveness, Urban Sustainability and Public Participation." *Cities* 23, no. 5: 339–52.

Baker, Tom, Ian R. Cook, Eugene McCann, Cristina Temenos, and Kevin Ward. 2016. "Policies on the Move: The Transatlantic Travels of Tax Increment Financing." *Annals of the American Association of Geographers* 106, no. 2: 459–69.

Barthel, Diane. 1996. "Getting in Touch with History: The Role of Historic Preservation in Shaping Collective Memories." *Qualitative Sociology* 19, no. 3: 345–64.

Beaulier, Scott A., Joshua C. Hall, and Allen K. Lynch. 2011. "The Impact of Political Factors on Military Base Closures." *Journal of Economic Policy Reform* 14, no. 4: 333–42.

Behrens, Kristian, Gilles Duranton, and Frederic Robert-Nicoud. 2014. "Productive Cities: Sorting, Selection, and Agglomeration." *Journal of Political Economy* 122, no. 3: 507–53.

Bennett, Kelly. 2011. "Tax Bill Ordeal Makes NTC's Arts Vision Pricier." *Voice of San Diego*, March 2.

Benton-Short, Lisa. 1998. *The Presidio: From Army Post to National Park.* Boston: Northeastern University Press.

Bill, Bobby. 2014. *Presidio of San Francisco: Post Closure.* Bloomington, IN: Authorhouse.

Blount, Casey, Wendy Ip, Ikuo Nakano, and Elaine Ng. 2014. "Redevelopment Agencies in California: History, Benefits, Excesses, and Closure." U.S. Department of Housing and Urban Development Working Paper No. Emad-2014–01.

Brandt, Timothy. 2015. Personal interview, May 28.

California Board of Equalization. 2009. *Report on Community Redevelopment Agencies.* Sacramento: State of California.

California Little Hoover Commission. 2000. *Special Use Districts.* Sacramento: State of California.

California Military Base Reuse Task Force. 1994. *Report of the California Military Base Reuse Task Force to Governor Pete Wilson: A Strategic Response to Base Reuse Opportunities.* Sacramento: State of California.

California State Board of Equalization. 2007. *Annual Report.* Sacramento: State of California.

California State Controller. 2009. *Community Redevelopment Agencies Annual Report, Fiscal Year 2007–2008.* Sacramento: State of California.

California State Controller. 2016. *Government Data and Accountability.* Sacramento: State of California.

California State Senate, Local Government Committee. 2009. *Report on Community Redevelopment Agencies.* Sacramento: State of California.

California State Treasurer. 2016a. *Debt Issuer by Type.* Sacramento: State of California.

California State Treasurer. 2016b. *Special Districts.* Sacramento: State of California.

Charest, Linda. 2014. Personal interview, April 6.

Charles, Camille Z. 2006. *Won't You Be My Neighbor: Race, Class, and Residence in Los Angeles.* New York: Russell Sage Foundation.

City of Alameda. 2009. *Alameda Point Development Initiative: Election Report Executive Summary.* Alameda, CA: City of Alameda.

City of Alameda. 2011. *Alameda Point Development Initiative Update.* Alameda, CA: City of Alameda.

City of Monterey. 2016. *Blue Silicon Valley.* Monterey, CA: City of Monterey.

City of San Diego. 1994. *Redevelopment for Naval Training Center San Diego.* San Diego: City of San Diego.

City of San Diego. 1998. *Naval Training Center San Diego Reuse Plan.* San Diego: City of San Diego.

Clark, Gordon L., and Kevin O'Connor. 1997. "The Informational Content of Financial Products and the Spatial Structure of the Global Finance Industry." *Spaces of Globalization:* 89–114.

Clawson, Marion. 2013. *Suburban Land Conversion in the United States: An Economic and Governmental Process.* Abingdon, UK: Routledge.

Clinton, William J. 1993a. "Remarks Announcing the Defense Conversion Plan." Press conference, July 2. http://www.Presidency.Ucsb.Edu/Ws/Index.Php?Pid=46793.

Clinton, William J. 1993b. "Remarks to the Community in Alameda, California." Presidential speech, August 13.

Collier, David, Henry E. Brady, and Jason Seawright. 2004. "Sources of Leverage in Causal Inference: Toward an Alternative View of Methodology." In *Rethinking Social Inquiry: Diverse Tools, Shared Standards,* edited by Henry Brady and David Collier, 229–66. Lanham, MD: Rowman and Littlefield.

Congressional Quarterly. 1965. *Congress 1965—the Year in Review.* Washington, DC: Government Printing Office.

Congressional Quarterly. 1987. *Congress 1987—the Year in Review.* Washington, DC: Government Printing Office.

Congressional Record 17762. 1988. Washington, DC: Government Printing Office.

Congressional Record. 2014. Senate Resolution 132. Washington, DC: Government Printing Office.

Corwin, Miles. 1991. "Impending Closure of Fort Ord Draws Numerous Pet Projects." *La Times,* August 25.

Cowan, Tadlock. 2012. *Military Base Closures: Socioeconomic Impacts.* Washington, DC: U.S. Government Printing Office.

Cox, Kevin R. 2010. "Institutional Geographies and Local Economic Development: Policies and Politics." In *Handbook of Local and Regional Development,* edited by Andy Pike, Andres Rodríguez-Pose, and John Tomaney. Abingdon, UK: Routledge.

Cox, Kevin R. 2013. "Territory, Scale, and Why Capitalism Matters." *Territory, Politics, Governance* 1, no. 1: 46–61.

Dalton, Gordon J., and Tony Lewis. 2011. "Metrics for Measuring Job Creation by Renewable Energy Technologies, Using Ireland as a Case Study." *Renewable and Sustainable Energy Reviews* 15, no. 4: 2123–33.

Dardia, Michael. 1998. *Subsidizing Redevelopment in California.* San Francisco: Public Policy Institute of California.

Davidson, Mark, and Kevin Ward. 2014. "'Picking Up the Pieces': Austerity Urbanism, California and Fiscal Crisis." *Cambridge Journal of Regions, Economy and Society* 7, no. 1: 81–97.

Davis, Jeffrey, Jessica Hayes-Conroy, and Victoria Jones. 2007. "Military Pollution and Natural Purity: Seeing Nature and Knowing Contamination in Vieques, Puerto Rico." *Geojournal* 69, no. 3: 165–79.

Davis, Steven J., Jason Faberman, and John Haltiwanger. 2006. "The Flow Approach to Labor Markets: New Data Sources and Micro–Macro Links." *Journal of Economic Perspectives* 20, no. 3: 3–26.

Davis, Susan. 2007. "Crown Beach: Pristine or Polluted?" *Alameda,* August 28.

Defense Manpower Data Center. 2016. *U.S. Military Personnel.* Washington, DC: Department of Defense.

DeFilippis, James, and Susan Saegert. 2013. *The Community Development Reader.* Abingdon, UK: Routledge.

Dell, Robert. 1998. "Optimizing Army Base Realignment and Closure." *Interfaces* 6 (1998): 1–18.

De Rosa, Simona, and Luca Salvati. 2016. "Beyond a 'Side Street Story'? Naples from Spontaneous Centrality to Entropic Polycentricism, towards a 'Crisis City.'" *Cities* 51: 74–83.

Dreier, Peter, John Mollenkopf, and Todd Swanstrom. 2004. *Place Matters: Metropolitics for the Twenty-First Century.* Lawrence, KS: University Press of Kansas.

Dumenil, Gerard, and Dominique Levy. 2004. *Capital Resurgent: Roots of the Neoliberal Revolution.* Cambridge, MA: Harvard University Press.

East Bay Times. 2015. "How Google Turned Alameda into a Mad Science Laboratory," June 16.

Elliott, Kim. 2014. Personal interview, April 4.

Erie, Steven P. 2004. *Globalizing LA: Trade, Infrastructure, and Regional Development.* Palo Alto, CA: Stanford University Press.

Erie, Steven, Vladimir Kogan, and Scott Mackenzie. 2011. *Paradise Plundered: Fiscal Crisis and Governance Failures in San Diego.* Palo Alto, CA: Stanford University Press.

European Union. 1999. *Committee on Spatial Development Report.* Brussels: European Union.

Fainstein, Susan. 2001. *The City Builders: Property Development in New York and London, 1980–2000.* Lawrence, KS: University Press of Kansas.

Farr, Sam. 2015. Personal interview, March 28.

Ferreira, Joao, Susana Garrido, and Mario Raposo. 2012. "Specialization of Regional Clusters and Innovative Behavior: A Case Study." *Competitiveness Review* 22, no. 2: 147–69.

Fields, Desiree. 2015. "Contesting the Financialization of Urban Space: Community Organizations and the Struggle to Preserve Affordable Rental Housing in New York City." *Journal of Urban Affairs* 37, no. 2: 144–65.

Fischel, William A. 2001. "Homevoters, Municipal Corporate Governance, and the Benefit View of the Property Tax." *National Tax Journal:* 157–73.

Fitzgerald, Joan, and Nancey Green Leigh. 2002. *Economic Revitalization: Cases and Strategies for City and Suburb.* Thousand Oaks, CA: Sage.

Fort Ord Redevelopment Act. 1994. Senate Bill 899, Senate of California. Sacramento: State of California.

Fort Ord Reuse Authority. 2013. *Fort Ord Reuse Plan.* Monterey, CA: Fort Ord Reuse Authority.

Freedman, Michael, and Tim Ransdell. 2005. "California Institute Special Report: California's Past Base Closure Experiences and the 2005 BRAC Round." *California Institute for Federal Policy Research.*

Fulton, William, Ross Pendall, Mai Nguyen, and Alicia Harrison. 2001. *Who Sprawls Most? How Growth Patterns Differ across the US.* Washington, DC: Brookings Institution Center on Urban and Metropolitan Policy.

Galston, William A., and Karen Baehler. 1995. *Rural Development in the United States: Connecting Theory, Practice, and Possibilities.* Covelo, CA: Island Press.

Garey, Jennifer. 2013. Personal interview, March 23.

George, Alexander L., and Andrew Bennett. 2005. *Case Studies and Theory Development in the Social Sciences.* Cambridge, MA: MIT Press.

Gilmore, Gerry. 2005. "Fitzsimons' Closure Attracts Investment, High-Tech Jobs." *American Forces Press,* July 5.

Glaeser, Edward. 2011. *Triumph of the City.* New York: Penguin.

Goodavage, Maria. 1991. "Base Closing Battle Underway; Fort Ord Future Is Bleak." *USA Today,* April 15.

Gotham, Kevin F., and Miriam Greenberg. 2014. *Crisis Cities: Disaster and Redevelopment in New York and New Orleans.* New York: Oxford University Press.

Graham, Stephen, and Simon Marvin. 2001. *Splintering Urbanism: Networked Infrastructures, Technological Mobilities and the Urban Condition.* Abingdon, UK: Routledge.

Greenbaum, Robert T. 2004. "Siting It Right: Do States Target Economic Distress When Designating Enterprise Zones?" *Economic Development Quarterly* 18, no. 1: 67–80.

Greenbaum, Robert T., and Daniele Bondonio. 2004. "Losing Focus: A Comparative Evaluation of Spatially Targeted Economic Revitalization Programmes in the US and the EU." *Regional Studies* 38, no. 3: 319–34.

Hall, Peter. 2000. "Creative Cities and Economic Development." *Urban Studies* 37, no. 4: 639–49.

Hansen, Kenneth. 2004. *The Greening of Pentagon Brownfields: Using Environmental Discourse to Redevelop Former Military Bases*. Lanham, MD: Lexington.

Hanson, Victor. 1994. "Fight over Low-Income Housing on BRAC Sites." *Washington Times*, September 9.

Harvey, David. 2003. *The New Imperialism*. New York: Oxford University Press.

Harvey, David. 2007. *A Brief History of Neoliberalism*. New York: Oxford University Press.

Hegarty, Peter. 2012. "Planning Board Reviews Strategy for Alameda Point." *Oakland Tribune*, November 29.

Hegarty, Peter. 2013. "City Begins Process of Creating a Draft EIR for Alameda Point." *Oakland Tribune*, January 31.

Hess, Ron. 2001. *The Closing and Reuse of Philadelphia Naval Shipyard*. Santa Monica, CA: Rand.

Hill, Catherine, Sabina Deitrick, and Ann Markusen. 1991. "Converting the Military Industrial Economy: The Experience at Six Facilities." *Journal of Planning Education and Research* 11, no. 1: 9–36.

Hitchcock, David. 2006. "Tax Increment Bond Criteria and Rating Trends." *Council of Development Finance Agencies* 1 (2006): 1–15.

Hoch, Charles. 1984. "Doing Good and Being Right: The Pragmatic Connection in Planning Theory." *Journal of the American Planning Association* 50, no. 3: 335–45.

Hooker, Mark, and Michael Knetter. 2001. "Measuring the Economic Effects of Military Base Closures." *Economic Inquiry* 39, no. 4: 583–98.

Houlemard, Michael. 2013. Personal interview, March 23.

Hoxworth, Dan H., and John Clayton-Thomas. 1993. "Economic Development Decision-Making in a Fragmented Polity: Convention Center Expansion in Kansas City." *Journal of Urban Affairs* 15, no. 3: 275–92.

Hultquist, Andy, and Tricia Petras. 2012. "An Examination of the Local Economic Impacts of Military Base Closures." *Economic Development Quarterly* 26, no. 2: 151–61.

Hutchison, Kay Bailey, and Michael O'Hanlon. 2013. *Saving Defense Dollars: From Base Realignment and Closure to Overhead Realignment and Closure*. Washington, DC: Brookings Institution.

Ilbery, Brian. 2014. *The Geography of Rural Change*. Abingdon, UK: Routledge.

Imbroscio, David. 2012. "Beyond Mobility: The Limits of Liberal Urban Policy." *Journal of Urban Affairs* 34, no. 1: 1–20.

Indovina, Francesco. 2016. "New Urban Forms: The Distinctive Character of the European Metropolis." *Cities in the 21st Century* 60: 35–61.

Institute for Taxation and Economic Policy. 2015. *Who Pays? A Distributional Analysis of the Tax System in All 50 States.* Washington, DC: Institute for Economic Policy.

Iselin, Steven. 2014. Personal interview, April 5.

Jackson, Matthew. 2008. *Social and Economic Networks,* vol. 3. Princeton, NJ: Princeton University Press.

Jacobs, Jane. 1969. *The Economy of Cities.* London: Penguin.

Johnson, Chip. 2015. "Naval Air Station Alameda Development Finally Set to Take Off." *Sf Gate,* June 30.

Jonas, Andy, and Kevin Ward. 2007. "Introduction to a Debate on City-Regions: New Geographies of Governance, Democracy and Social Reproduction." *International Journal of Urban and Regional Research* 31, no. 1: 169–78.

Jones, Carolyn. 2011. "Navy Turns Alameda Air Station Over to City." *Sf Gate,* September 30.

Jones, Carolyn. 2013. "Naval Air Station Land Handed to Alameda." *Sf Gate,* June 24.

Kane, Kevin, and Rachel Weber. 2015. "Municipal Investment and Property Value Appreciation in Chicago's Tax Increment Financing Districts." *Journal of Planning Education and Research* 36, no. 2: 167–81.

Keefer, Phillip, and David Stasavage. 2003. "The Limits of Delegation: Veto Players, Central Bank Independence, and the Credibility of Monetary Policy." *American Political Science Review* 97, no. 3: 407–23.

Keyser Marston Associates. 2012. *Alameda Point Reuse Report.* Alameda, CA: City of Alameda.

Kirby, Andrew. 1992. *The Pentagon and the Cities.* Newbury Park, CA: Sage.

Kirkpatrick, Lowen, and Michael Peter Smith. 2011. "The Infrastructural Limits to Growth: Rethinking the Urban Growth Machine in Times of Fiscal Crisis." *International Journal of Urban and Regional Research* 35, no. 3: 477–503.

Kosla, Nicholas. 2010. *Over a Decade of Failure: Why Military Base Reuse at the Naval Air Station, Alameda (Alameda Point) Has Been Unsuccessful.* Sacramento: California State University, Sacramento.

Kotin, Allan, and Richard Peiser. 1997. "Public-Private Joint Ventures for High Volume Retailers: Who Benefits?" *Urban Studies* 34, no. 12: 1971–86.

Lawrence, Martin, and Geofrey Stapledon. 2008. *Infrastructure Funds: Creative Use of Corporate Structure and Law—but in Whose Interests?* Research Paper No. 314, School of Law, University of Melbourne, Australia.

Leigland, James. 1995. "Public Infrastructure and Special Purpose Governments: Who Pays and How?" In *Building The Public City: The Politics, Governance and Finance of Public Infrastructure,* edited by David Perry, 138–68. Thousand Oaks, CA: Sage.

Leitner, Helga, James Peck, and Eric Sheppard, eds. 2007a. *Contesting Neoliberalism: Urban Frontiers.* New York: Guilford.

Leitner, Helga, James Peck, and Eric Sheppard. 2007b. "Squaring Up to Neoliberalism." In *Contesting Neoliberalism: Urban Frontiers,* edited by Helga Leitner, James Peck, and Eric Sheppard, 311–327. New York: Guilford.

Levi-Faur, David. 2012. *The Oxford Handbook of Governance.* New York: Oxford University Press.

Lewis, Michael. 1997. "Fort Ord Reuse Plan and Environmental Report." *Planning* 63, no. 4: 10–12.

Leyshon, Andrew, and Nigel Thrift. 2007. "The Capitalization of Almost Everything: The Future of Finance and Capitalism." *Theory, Culture & Society* 24, nos. 7–8: 97–115.

Lieberman, Evan. 2005. "Nested Analysis as a Mixed-Method Strategy for Comparative Research." *American Political Science Review* 99, no. 3: 435–52.

Logan, John R., and Harvey Molotch. 2007. *Urban Fortunes: The Political Economy of Place*. Berkeley, CA: University of California Press.

Logan, John R., Wenquan Zhang, and Richard Alba. 2002. "Immigrant Enclaves and Ethnic Communities in New York and Los Angeles." *American Sociological Review*: 299–322.

Long, Norton E. 2010. "Planning and Politics in Urban Development." *Journal of the American Institute of Planners* 25, no. 4: 167–69.

Luckey, David S., and Kevin P. Schultz. 2001. *Defining and Coping with Wicked Problems: The Case of Fort Ord Building Removal*. Monterey, CA: Naval Postgraduate School.

Lynch, John. 1970. *Local Economic Development after Military Base Closures: Conversion of Industry from a Military to Civilian Economy*. New York: Praeger.

Mahoney, James. 2010. "After KKV: The New Methodology of Qualitative Research." *World Politics* 62, no. 1: 120–47.

Markusen, Ann. 1992. "Dismantling the Cold War Economy." *World Policy Journal* 9, no. 3: 389–99.

Markusen, Ann. 1996. "Sticky Places in Slippery Space: A Typology of Industrial Districts." *Economic Geography* 72, no. 3: 293–313.

Markusen, Ann, Peter Hall, Scott Campbell, and Sabina Deitrick. 1991. *The Rise of the Gunbelt: The Military Remapping of Industrial America*. New York: Oxford University Press.

Martin, Isaac William. 2008. *The Permanent Tax Revolt: How the Property Tax Transformed American Politics*. Palo Alto, CA: Stanford University Press.

Matson, Melinda. 2014. Personal interview, April 3.

Mayer, Kenneth. 1999. "Limits of Delegation: The Rise and Fall of BRAC." *Regulation* 22: 32–45.

McCabe, Barbara Coyle. 2000. "Special-District Formation among the States." *State and Local Government Review* 32, no. 2: 121–31.

McCann, Eugene J. 2003. "Framing Space and Time in the City: Urban Policy and the Politics of Spatial and Temporal Scale." *Journal of Urban Affairs* 25, no. 2: 159–78.

McDermid, Riley. 2016. "Google Snags Lease, Will Bring 150 New Jobs to Alameda." *San Francisco Business Times*, January 7.

McDonald, Judy. 2014. Personal interview, March 24.

Mizany, Kimia, and April Manatt. 2002. *What's So Special about Special Districts? A Citizen's Guide to Special Districts in California*. Sacramento: California State Legislature, Senate Local Government Committee.

Molnar, Philip. 2013. "Fort Ord Access Alliance Gets Enough Signatures for Ballot." *Monterey Herald*, June 14.

Molotch, Harvey. 1976. "The City as a Growth Machine: Toward a Political Economy of Place." *American Journal of Sociology* 82, no. 2: 309–32.

Molotch, Harvey. 1993. "The Political Economy of Growth Machines." *Journal of Urban Affairs* 15, no. 1: 29–53.

Monroe, Bryant. 2014. Personal interview, April 7.

Morgan, Neil. 2006. "San Diego's Potemkin Villages." *Voices of San Diego*, September 29.

Moss, Timothy, and Simon Marvin. 2016. *Urban Infrastructure in Transition: Networks, Buildings and Plans*. New York: Routledge.

Municipal Officials for Redevelopment Reform (MORR). 2002. *Redevelopment, the Unknown Government*. Washington, DC: Coalition for Redevelopment Reform.

Munitz, Barry. 2013. Personal interview, March 8.

Musterd, Sako, and Wim Ostendorf. 2013. *Urban Segregation and the Welfare State: Inequality and Exclusion in Western Cities*. New York: Routledge.

National Coalition for the Homeless. 2009. *Homeless Veterans*. Washington, DC: National Coalition for the Homeless.

Newburn, David A., and Peter Berck. 2006. "Modeling Suburban and Rural—Residential Development beyond the Urban Fringe." *Land Economics* 82, no. 4: 481–99.

Niu, Kuei-Hsien, Grant Miles, Seung Bach, and Kenichiro Chinen. 2012. "Trust, Learning and a Firm's Involvement in Industrial Clusters: A Conceptual Framework." *Competitiveness Review* 22, no. 2: 133–46.

Obama, Barack. 2012. Radio interview, *Wavy Hampton Roads*, August 7.

O'Brien, Patrick. 2014. Personal interview, April 3.

O'Mara, Margaret Pugh. 2015. *Cities of Knowledge: Cold War Science and the Search for the Next Silicon Valley*. Princeton, NJ: Princeton University Press.

Ostovary, Fariba, and Janet Dapprich. 2011. "Challenges and Opportunities of Operation Enduring Freedom/Operation Iraqi Freedom Veterans with Disabilities Transitioning into Learning and Workplace Environments." *New Directions for Adult and Continuing Education* 132: 63–73.

O'Toole, Randal. 2011. "Crony Capitalism and Social Engineering: The Case against Tax-Increment Financing." *Cato Institute Policy Analysis* 676: 1–13.

Ott, Jennifer. 2013. Personal interview, March 26.

Pagano, Michael A., and David Perry. 2008. "Financing Infrastructure in the 21st Century City." *Public Works Management & Policy* 13, no. 1: 22–38.

Page, Sasha, William Ankner, Cheryl Jones, and Robert Fetterman. 2008. "The Risks and Rewards of Private Equity in Infrastructure." *Public Works Management and Policy* 13, no. 2: 100–13.

Paloyo, Alfredo. R., Colin Vance, and Mathias Vorell. 2010. "The Regional Economic Effects of Military Base Realignments and Closures in Germany." *Defense and Peace Economics* 21, nos. 5–6: 567–79.

Pastor, Manuel, and Chris Benner. 2008. "Been Down So Long: Weak-Market Cities and Regional Equity." In *Retooling for Growth: Building A 21st Century Economy in America's Older Industrial Cities*, edited by Richard Mcgahey and Jennifer Vey, 89–118. New York: Columbia University Press.

Patton, Gary. 2013. Personal interview, March 24.

Perry, David. 1994. *Building the Public City: The Politics, Governance and Finance of Public Infrastructure.* Thousand Oaks, CA: Sage.

Pierre, Jon. 2011. *The Politics of Urban Governance.* New York: Palgrave Macmillan.

Piven, Frances Fox, and Roger Friedland. 1984. "Public Choice and Private Power: A Theory of Fiscal Crisis." *Public Service Provision and Urban Development:* 390–420.

Point Loma Association. 2016. *Point Loma Awards.* San Diego: Point Loma Association.

Poppert, Patrick, and Henry Herzog, Jr. 2003. "Force Reduction, Base Closure, and the Indirect Effects of Military Installations on Local Employment Growth." *Journal of Regional Science* 43, no. 3: 459–71.

Porter, Michael E. 1990. *The Competitive Advantage of Nations.* New York: Free Press.

Porter, Michael E. 2008. *On Competition.* Boston: Harvard Business School Publishing.

Raffesberger, Wayne. 2013. "Liberty Station Is a San Diego Success Story." *San Diego Union Tribune,* July 27.

Rakodi, Carole. 2014. *Urban Livelihoods: A People-Centred Approach to Reducing Poverty.* New York: Routledge.

Reifsnyder, James, and Barry Holman. 2005. *Military Base Closures: Updated Status of Prior Base Realignments and Closures.* Washington, DC: Government Accounting Office.

Roux, Whitney. 2014. Personal interview, March 25.

Ruiz, Sebastian. 2011. "NTC Foundation Seeks to Ease Tax Burden on Liberty Station Tenants." *Sd News,* April 19.

Saegert, Susan, Desiree Fields, and Kimberly Libman. 2009. "Deflating the Dream: Radical Risk and the Neoliberalization of Homeownership." *Journal of Urban Affairs* 31, no. 3: 297–317.

Saegert, Susan, Desiree Fields, and Kimberly Libman. 2011. "Mortgage Foreclosure and Health Disparities: Serial Displacement as Asset Extraction in African American Populations." *Journal of Urban Health* 88, no. 3: 390–402.

Sagalyn, Lynne. 1990. "Explaining the Improbable: Local Redevelopment in the Wake of Federal Cutbacks." *Journal of the American Planning Association* 56, no. 4: 429–41.

Sagalyn, Lynne. 1997. "Negotiating Public Benefits: The Bargaining Calculus of Public-Private Development." *Urban Studies* 34, no. 12: 1955–70.

Sagalyn, Lynne. 2007. "Public/Private Development: Lessons from History, Research, and Practice." *Journal of the American Planning Association* 73, no. 1: 7–22.

Sasson, Amir, and Torgor Reve. 2015. "Complementing Clusters: A Competitiveness Rationale for Infrastructure Investments." *Competitiveness Review* 25, no. 3: 242–57.

Save Our NTC. 1995. *Save Our NTC Mission Statement.* San Diego: Save Our NTC.

Save Our NTC. 2003. *Liberty Station Land Giveaway.* San Diego: Save Our NTC.

Savitch, Harold V., and Paul Kantor. 2002. *Cities in the International Marketplace: The Political Economy of Urban Development in North America and Western Europe.* Princeton, NJ: Princeton University Press.

Sbragia, Alberta M. 1983. *The Municipal Money Chase: The Politics of Local Government Finance.* Boulder, CO: Westview.

Scarborough, Rowan. 2012. "Congress Won't Let Panetta Close Bases." *Washington Times,* June 20.

Scott, Allen J. 2011. "Emerging Cities of the Third Wave." *City* 15, nos. 3–4: 289–321.

Sega, Roberto. 2015. "Productive Ecologies: Redefining the Centrality and Marginality of the City-Territory." In *Conference Proceedings of the Horizontal Metropolis: A Radical Project*, 331–39.

Shaw, Frederick. 2004. *Locating Air Force Base Sites: History's Legacy*. Washington, DC: U.S. Air Force.

Showley, Roger. 2011. "Liberty Station Honored with International Award." *San Diego Tribune*, May 26.

Sölvell, Örjan, Göran Lindqvist, and Christian Ketels. 2003. *The Cluster Initiative Greenbook*. Stockholm: Ivory Tower.

Sorenson, David S. 1998. *Shutting Down the Cold War: The Politics of Military Base Closure*. New York: Palgrave Macmillan.

South, Scott. J., Kyle Crowder, and Erick Chavez. 2005. "Migration and Spatial Assimilation among US Latinos: Classical versus Segmented Trajectories." *Demography* 42, no. 3: 497–521.

Standard and Poor's. 2016. *Municipal Bond Ratings*. New York: Standard and Poor's.

Stanley, Lois. 2002. *Community Asset Building in Rural Development: An Analysis of Military-Base Redevelopment in Rural Host Communities*. Cambridge, MA: Department of Urban Studies and Planning at the Massachusetts Institute of Technology.

Stead, Dominic. 2014. "The Rise of Territorial Governance in European Policy." *European Planning Studies* 22, no. 7: 1368–83.

Stern, Julie D. 2006. *Urban Land Institute: Award Winning Projects*. Washington, DC: Urban Land Institute.

Stone, Clarence. 1989. *Regime Politics: Governing Atlanta, 1946–1988*. Lawrence, KS: University Press of Kansas.

Tasan-Kok, Tuna, and Guy Baeten. 2011. *Contradictions of Neoliberal Planning: Cities, Policies, and Politics*. New York: Springer.

Ter-Minassian, Teresa, and Jon Craig. 1997. "Control of Subnational Government Borrowing." *Fiscal Federalism in Theory and Practice*: 156–72.

Theobald, David M. 2001. "Land-Use Dynamics beyond the American Urban Fringe." *Geographical Review* 91, no. 3: 544–64.

Torfing, Jacob. 2012. *Interactive Governance: Advancing the Paradigm*. New York: Oxford University Press.

Touchton, Michael. 2016. "The Benefits of Balance: Credibility, the Rule of Law, and Investment in Latin America." *Latin American Research Review* 51, no. 2: 195–216.

United Nations Development Programme. 2014. *Democratic Governance*. New York: United Nations.

United States Census Bureau. 2016a. *Employment*. Washington, DC: Government Printing Office.

United States Census Bureau. 2016b. *Quarterly Summary of State and Local Tax Revenue*. Washington, DC: Government Printing Office.

United States Department of Commerce. 2016. *Economic Indicators*. Washington, DC: Department of Commerce.

United States Department of Commerce. 2017. *GDP by Metropolitan Area*. Washington, DC: Government Printing Office.

United States Department of Defense. 1998. *Base Closure and Realignment Report.* Washington, DC: U.S. Department of Defense.

United States Department of Defense. 1999. *Economic Renewal: Community Reuse of Former Military Bases.* Working paper 042199. Washington, DC: U.S. Department of Defense.

United States Department of Defense. 2005. *Base Closure and Realignment Report.* Washington, DC: U.S. Department of Defense.

United States Department of Defense. 2006. "Revitalizing Base Closure Communities and Addressing Impacts of Realignment." *Federal Register* 71: 14–26.

United States Department of Defense. 2010. *Base Structure Report.* Washington, DC: U.S. Department of Defense

United States Department of Defense. 2015. *DoD Announces European Infrastructure Consolidation.* Washington, DC: U.S. Department of Defense.

United States Department of Defense. 2016a. *DoD Office of Small Business Programs.* Washington, DC: U.S. Department of Defense.

United States Department of Defense. 2016b. *Legacy Resource Management Program.* Washington, DC: U.S. Department of Defense.

United States Department of Defense. 2016c. *National Defense Authorization Act 2017.* Washington, DC: U.S. Department of Defense.

United States Department of Housing and Urban Development. 2018. *Housing on Former Military Bases.* Washington, DC: Government Printing Office.

United States Environmental Protection Agency. 2006. *Turning Bases into Great Places: New Life for Closed Military Facilities.* Washington, DC: United States Environmental Protection Agency.

United States Environmental Protection Agency 2008. *MOU Governing Environmental Restoration on BRAC Sites.* Washington, DC: United States Environmental Protection Agency.

United States Environmental Protection Agency. 2013. *Defense Infrastructure: Communities Need Additional Guidance and Information to Improve Their Ability to Adjust to DoD Installation Closure and Growth.* Washington, DC: United States Government Accountability Office.

United States Environmental Protection Agency 2015. *Turning Bases into Great Places,* vol. 2. Washington, DC: United States Environmental Protection Agency.

United States Federal News Service. 2007. *Audit of San Diego NTC Redevelopment.* Washington, DC: U.S. Federal News Service.

United States General Accounting Office. 1997. *Military Bases: Lessons Learned from Prior Base Closure Rounds.* Washington, DC: U.S. General Accounting Office.

United States General Accounting Office. 1998. *Military Bases: Status of Prior Base Realignment Closure Rounds.* Washington, DC: U.S. General Accounting Office.

United States General Accounting Office. 2002a. "Environmental Contamination: Corps Needs to Reassess Its Determinations That Many Former Defense Sites Do Not Need Cleanup." GAO-02–658.

United States General Accounting Office. 2002b. *Military Base Closures: Progress from Completing Actions from Prior Realignments and Closures.* Washington, DC: U.S. General Accounting Office.

United States Government Accountability Office. 2007a. *Military Base Closures. Management Strategy Needed to Mitigate Challenges and Improve Communication to Help Ensure Timely Implementation of Air National Guard Recommendations.* Washington, DC: United States Government Accountability Office.

United States Government Accountability Office. 2007b. *Military Base Closures. Opportunities Exist to Improve Environmental Cleanup Cost Reporting and to Expedite Transfer of Unneeded Property.* Washington, DC: United States Government Accountability Office.

United States Government Accountability Office. 2010. *Defense Infrastructure Opportunities Exist to Improve the Navy's Basing Decision Process and DoD Oversight. Report to Congressional Committees.* Washington, DC: Government Accountability Office.

United States Office of Economic Adjustment. 2015. *Fiscal Year 2016 Budget Estimates.* Washington, DC: United States Department of Defense.

United States Office of Management and Budget. 2015. *Budget of the United States Government Fiscal Year 2016.* Washington, DC: Government Printing Office.

United States Office of Management and Budget. 2016. *Budget of the United States Government Fiscal Year 2017.* Washington, DC: Government Printing Office.

Urban Land Institute. 2009. *Development Case Studies: The Navy Yard.* Washington, DC: Urban Land Institute.

Vargas, Juan. 2012. California State Bill 314 an Act to Amend Section 214 of the Revenue and Taxation Code, Relating to Taxation, to Take Effect Immediately, Tax Levy. Sacramento, State of California.

Ward, Kevin, and Andy Jonas. 2004. "Competitive City-Regionalism as a Politics of Space: A Critical Reinterpretation of the New Regionalism." *Environment and Planning* 36, no. 12: 2119–39.

Weber, Rachel. 2002. "Extracting Value from the City: Neoliberalism and Urban Development." *Antipode* 34, no. 3: 519–40.

Weber, Rachel. 2010. "Selling City Futures: The Financialization of Urban Redevelopment Policy." *Economic Geography* 86, no. 3: 251–74.

Weber, Rachel, and Sara O'Neill-Kohl. 2013. "The Historical Roots of Tax Increment Financing, or How Real Estate Consultants Kept Urban Renewal Alive." *Economic Development Quarterly* 27, no. 3: 193–207.

Williamson, Thad, David Imbroscio, and Gar Alperovitz. 2002. *Making a Place for Community: Local Democracy in a Global Era.* New York: Psychology Press.

Wilson, William. 2012. *The Truly Disadvantaged: The Inner City, the Underclass, and Public Policy.* Chicago: University of Chicago Press.

Yin, Robert K. 2013. *Case Study Research: Design and Methods.* Thousand Oaks, CA: Sage.

Zemke, Ron, Claire Raines, and Bob Filipczak. 1999. *Generations at Work: Managing the Clash of Veterans, Boomers, Xers, and Nexters in Your Workplace.* New York: Amacom.

Zettinig, Peter, and Zsuzsanna Vincze. 2012. "How Clusters Evolve." *Competitiveness Review* 22, no. 2: 110–32.

Ziter, Alan. 2014. Personal interview, April 3.

INDEX

CPSIA information can be obtained
at www.ICGtesting.com
Printed in the USA
FSHW020132020619
58603FS